BLAISE PASCAL

Modern Critical Views

Henry Adams
Edward Albee
A. R. Ammons
Matthew Arnold
John Ashbery
W. H. Auden
Jane Austen
James Baldwin
Charles Baudelaire
Samuel Beckett
Saul Bellow
The Bible
Elizabeth Bishop
William Blake
Jorge Luis Borges
Elizabeth Bowen
Bertolt Brecht
The Brontës
Robert Browning
Anthony Burgess
George Gordon, Lord
  Byron
Thomas Carlyle
Lewis Carroll
Willa Cather
Cervantes
Geoffrey Chaucer
Kate Chopin
Samuel Taylor Coleridge
Joseph Conrad
Contemporary Poets
Hart Crane
Stephen Crane
Dante
Charles Dickens
Emily Dickinson
John Donne & the Seven-
  teenth-Century Meta-
  physical Poets
Elizabethan Dramatists
Theodore Dreiser
John Dryden
George Eliot
T. S. Eliot
Ralph Ellison
Ralph Waldo Emerson
William Faulkner
Henry Fielding
F. Scott Fitzgerald
Gustave Flaubert
E. M. Forster
Sigmund Freud
Robert Frost

Robert Graves
Graham Greene
Thomas Hardy
Nathaniel Hawthorne
William Hazlitt
Seamus Heaney
Ernest Hemingway
Geoffrey Hill
Friedrich Hölderlin
Homer
Gerard Manley Hopkins
William Dean Howells
Zora Neale Hurston
Henry James
Samuel Johnson and
  James Boswell
Ben Jonson
James Joyce
Franz Kafka
John Keats
Rudyard Kipling
D. H. Lawrence
John Le Carré
Ursula K. Le Guin
Doris Lessing
Sinclair Lewis
Robert Lowell
Norman Mailer
Bernard Malamud
Thomas Mann
Christopher Marlowe
Carson McCullers
Herman Melville
James Merrill
Arthur Miller
John Milton
Eugenio Montale
Marianne Moore
Iris Murdoch
Vladimir Nabokov
Joyce Carol Oates
Sean O'Casey
Flannery O'Connor
Eugene O'Neill
George Orwell
Cynthia Ozick
Walter Pater
Walker Percy
Harold Pinter
Plato
Edgar Allan Poe
Poets of Sensibility & the
  Sublime

Alexander Pope
Katherine Ann Porter
Ezra Pound
Pre-Raphaelite Poets
Marcel Proust
Thomas Pynchon
Arthur Rimbaud
Theodore Roethke
Philip Roth
John Ruskin
J. D. Salinger
Gershom Scholem
William Shakespeare
  (3 vols.)
  Histories & Poems
  Comedies
  Tragedies
George Bernard Shaw
Mary Wollstonecraft
  Shelley
Percy Bysshe Shelley
Edmund Spenser
Gertrude Stein
John Steinbeck
Laurence Sterne
Wallace Stevens
Tom Stoppard
Jonathan Swift
Alfred, Lord Tennyson
William Makepeace
  Thackeray
Henry David Thoreau
Leo Tolstoi
Anthony Trollope
Mark Twain
John Updike
Gore Vidal
Virgil
Robert Penn Warren
Evelyn Waugh
Eudora Welty
Nathanael West
Edith Wharton
Walt Whitman
Oscar Wilde
Tennessee Williams
William Carlos Williams
Thomas Wolfe
Virginia Woolf
William Wordsworth
Richard Wright
William Butler Yeats

These and other titles in preparation

Modern Critical Views

BLAISE PASCAL

Edited and with an introduction by
Harold Bloom
Sterling Professor of the Humanities
Yale University

CHELSEA HOUSE PUBLISHERS
New York ◇ Philadelphia

Printed and bound in the United States of America

10 9 8 7 6 5 4 3 2 1

∞ The paper used in this publication meets the minimum
requirements of the American National Standard for
Permanence of Paper for Printed Library Materials,
Z39.48–1984.

Library of Congress Cataloging-in-Publication Data
Blaise Pascal/edited and with an introduction by Harold Bloom.
        p.   cm. — (Modern critical views)
    Bibliography: p.
    Includes index.
    ISBN 1-555-46373-8
    1. Pascal, Blaise, 1623-1662.   I. Bloom,
Harold.   II. Series.
B1903.B44   1988   87-18344
230′.2′0924—dc19   CIP

Contents

Editor's Note

This book brings together a representative selection of the most illuminating modern criticism of Blaise Pascal—philosopher, scientist, mathematician, controversialist, aphorist, and Christian religious writer. The critical essays are reprinted here in the chronological order of their original publication. I am grateful to James Swenson for his assistance in editing this volume.

My introduction meditates upon Pascal's influence-anxieties in relation to Montaigne, and charts the swerve away from Montaigne in the *Pensées*. Monsignor Ronald A. Knox begins the chronological sequence with his discussion of the relation between Pascal and his fellow Jansenists.

The triumph of evil in Pascal's thought, as shown by his association of political power with original sin, is the subject of the essay by Erich Auerbach, distinguished scholar of European mimesis. A defense of Pascal as an improviser, Stendhalian and Mozartean, is made by Jean-Jacques Demorest against the accusations of sophistry by Voltaire and Valéry.

Lucien Goldmann centers upon the Pascalian "wager" that God exists, and that the paradoxical and incomprehensible Christian religion is the only answer to the paradoxical and incomprehensible nature of human existence. Pascal's grand formulation of the three Orders—Flesh, Spirit, Charity—is analyzed by Martin Price as "a brilliant rhetorical device for making us see false orders replacing true."

Jean Mesnard expounds Pascal's vision of the mystery of Revelation, while Jan Miel gives an exegesis of the Augustinian basis of Pascal's theology. The *Provincial Letters* are read by Philip Lewis as a work that communicates truth and establishes a context for dialogue precisely "through the lack of dialogue."

Paul de Man, the great theoretician of reading, examines Pascal's *Réflexions* in order to uncover the Pascalian theory of rhetoric, or "allegory of persuasion." At the other extreme of Pascal's intellectual career, Robert J.

Nelson expounds the *Memorial* in which Pascal recorded his mystical conversion.

The discourse of power in Pascal is depicted by Louis Marin, after which Sara E. Melzer concludes this volume by finding in Pascal's theory of metaphor the mirror that reflects the double aspect of language in Pascal, rhetoric as Fall and rhetoric as Redemption.

Introduction

Pascal never loses his capacity to offend as well as to edify. Contrast his very different effects upon Paul Valéry and T. S. Eliot. Here is Valéry:

> I hate to see a man using artifice to turn others against their lot, when they are in it in spite of themselves and are doing what they can to make the best of it; to see a man trying to persuade others that they must expect the worst, must always keep in mind the most intolerable notion of their predicament, and be alert to whatever is most unbearable in it—which is precisely the notion of suffering and risk, and anxiety about the risk—using the notion of eternity as an almighty weapon, and developing it by the artifice of repetition.

This is to accuse Pascal of being an obscurantist rhetorician, rather resembling the T. S. Eliot of the religious prose writings. Here is Eliot on Pascal:

> But I can think of no Christian writer, not Newman even, more to be commended than Pascal to those who doubt, but who have the mind to conceive, and the sensibility to feel, the disorder, the futility, the meaninglessness, the mystery of life and suffering, and who can only find peace through a satisfaction of the whole being.

I suspect that Valéry and Eliot are saying much the same thing, the difference being the rival perspectives towards Pascal of a secular intellectual and a Christian polemicist. Pascal essentially is a polemicist, rather than a religious or meditative writer. The *Pensées* ultimately are not less tendentious than the *Provincial Letters*. A Christian polemicist in our time ought to find his true antagonist in Freud, but nearly all do not; they either evade Freud, or self-defeatingly seek to appropriate him. Pascal's Freud was Montaigne,

1

who could not be evaded or appropriated, and who scarcely can be refuted. But Pascal's case of influence-anxiety, in regard to Montaigne, was hopelessly overwhelming. Eliot, putting the best case for Pascal, insisted that Montaigne simply had the power to embody a universal skepticism, in which Pascal necessarily shared, though only to a limited degree. Doubtless Eliot attributed to Montaigne one of the essayist's plethora of authentic powers, but a secretly shared (and overcome) skepticism hardly can account for the full scandal of Montaigne's influence upon Pascal. Tables of parallel passages demonstrate an indebtedness so great, extending to figuration, examples, syntax, actual repetition of phrases, that Pascal would be convicted of plagiarism in any American school or university, with their rather literal notions of what constitutes plagiarism. The frequent effect in reading Pascal is that he begins to seem an involuntary parody of his precursor. This is particularly unfortunate whenever Pascal overtly denounces Montaigne, since sometimes we hear the pious son castigating the unbelieving father in the father's inescapable accents.

It has been surmised that Pascal jotted down his *Pensées* with his copy of Montaigne's *Essays* always lying open before him. Whether this was literally true or not, we may say that Montaigne was for Pascal quite simply a presence never to be put by. Eliot speaks of Montaigne's readers as being "thoroughly infected" by him, and certainly Pascal must have known inwardly the anguish of contamination. What are we to do with Pensée 358, one example out of many:

> Man is neither angel nor brute, and the unfortunate thing is that
> he who would act the angel acts the brute.

That would have been admirable, had it not been lifted from the best essay ever written, Montaigne's "Of Experience," where it is expressed with rather more force and insight:

> They want to get out of themselves and escape from the man.
> That is madness: instead of changing into angels, they change
> into beasts; instead of raising themselves, they lower themselves.

It is an ancient commonplace, but Montaigne plays variations upon his sources, since his sense of self is his own. What is distressing is that Pascal does not evade or revise Montaigne but simply repeats him, presumably unaware of his bondage to his skeptical precursor. Since Pascal's mode is polemic, and Montaigne's is rumination and speculation, the rhetorical edge is different; Pascal emphasizes moral action, while Montaigne centers upon moral being. Yet the reader is made uncomfortable, not because Pascal has appropriated Montaigne but because Pascal has manifested a paucity of invention. Voltaire and Valéry would seem to be confirmed. Pascal writes as a pragmatic enemy of Montaigne, and this necessarily makes Pascal, as Valéry said, into an enemy of humankind. We are in a difficult situation enough, without being castigated by Pascal merely for being what we have to be. Do we still need Pascal? We read Montaigne as we read Shakespeare and Freud. How can we read Pascal?

Nietzsche insisted upon finding in Pascal an antithetical precursor, and shrewdly located Pascal's major error in the famous "wager":

> He supposes that he proves Christianity to be true because it is necessary. This presupposes that a good and truthful providence exists which ordains that everything necessary shall be true. But there can be necessary errors!

Later Nietzsche observed: "One should never forgive Christianity for having destroyed such men as Pascal." Yet Nietzsche also remarked, in a letter to Georg Brandes, that he almost loved Pascal for having been "the only *logical* Christian." The true link between the two was in their greatness as moral psychologists, a distinction they share with Montaigne and with Kierkegaard, and in another mode with Swift. Pascal's strong swerve away from Montaigne, which transcends his guilt of obligation to a naturalistic and skeptical master, is manifested in the development of a new kind of religious irony. Montaigne urges relativism because we are opaque to ideas of order other than our own, but this is precisely Pascal's motivation for our necessary surrender to God's will. Since God is hidden, according to Pascal, our condition is not less than tragic. A hidden God is doubly an incoherence for us; intolerable if he exists, and equally intolerable if he does not. We are thus reduced to an ironic quietism, in which we are best off doing nothing in regard to worldly realities. We reject the order of society so thoroughly that pragmatically we can accept it totally.

The extraordinary ironies of the *Provincial Letters* are founded upon this Pascalian stance, that allows him to chastise the Jesuits for worldliness while defending society against them:

> What will you do with someone who talks like that, and how will you attack me, since neither my words nor my writings afford any pretext for your accusation of heresy and I find protection against your threats in my own obscurity? You feel the blows of an unseen hand revealing your aberrations for all to see. You try in vain to attack me in the persons of those whom you believe to

be my allies. I am not afraid of you either on behalf of myself or
of anyone else, as I am attached to no community and no individual whatsoever. All the credit you may enjoy is of no avail as
far as I am concerned. I hope for nothing from the world; I fear
nothing from it, I desire nothing of it; by God's grace I need no
one's wealth or authority. Thus, Father, I entirely escape your
clutches. You cannot get hold of me however you try. You may
well touch Port-Royal, but not me. Some have indeed been
evicted from the Sorbonne, but that does not evict me from where
I am. You may well prepare acts of violence against priests and
doctors, but not against me who am without such titles. You have
perhaps never had to deal with anyone so far out of your range
and so well fitted to attack your errors, by being free, without
commitments, without allegiance, without ties, without connex-
ions, without interests; sufficiently acquainted with your precepts
and determined to drive them as far as I may believe myself
obliged by God to do, without any human consideration being
able to halt or check my pursuit.

Implicit in this superbly polemical paragraph is the unassailable rhetorical position of the ironic quietist, beyond this world yet its only true
defender. One calls this "unassailable" in Pascal's stance, because his rhetoric
and psychology are so intimately related to his cosmology, and the three
indeed are one. We have fallen into figuration, psychic division, and the
eternal silence of the infinite spaces, and all these ought to terrify us equally.
Sara Melzer usefully emphasizes Pascal's difference from negative theology,
to which I would add Gnosticism, as the most negative of all theologies.
God's otherness, the Pascalian version of which is hiddenness, has nothing
in common with the alien God of the Gnostics and the hermeticists. For
Pascal, the hiddenness leads to the wager of faith, rather than to a negation
of all tropes, terms for order, and scientific postulates.

If this is error, it is at least one of the necessary errors, psychologically
speaking. Pascal never found his way out of the shadow of Montaigne, not
I think because Montaigne spoke also for Pascal's own skepticism, but because
Montaigne was too authentic a self and too strong a writer to need wagers
of any kind. A paragraph like this, from the *Apology for Raymond Sebond*, must
have been a permanent reproach to Pascal:

Furthermore, it is here in us, and not elsewhere, that the powers
and actions of the soul should be considered. All the rest of its
perfections are vain and useless to it; it is for its present state that

all its immortal life is to be paid and rewarded, and for man's life that it is solely accountable. It would be an injustice to have cut short its resources and powers; to have disarmed it, and to pass judgment and a sentence of infinite and perpetual duration upon it, for the time of its captivity and imprisonment, its weakness and illness, the time when it was forced and constrained; and to stop at the consideration of so short a time, perhaps one or two hours, or at worst a century, which is no more in proportion to infinity than an instant; in order, from this moment of interval, to decide and dispose definitively of its whole existence. It would be an inequitable disproportion to receive eternal compensation in consequence of so short a life.

Against this, Pascal's eloquence and psychic intensity must fall short, even in the most notorious of the *Pensées:*

205

When I consider the short duration of my life, swallowed up in the eternity before and after, the little space which I fill, and even can see, engulfed in the infinite immensity of spaces of which I am ignorant, and which know me not, I am frightened, and am astonished at being here rather than there; for there is no reason why here rather than there, why now rather than then. Who has put me here? By whose order and direction have this place and time been allotted to me? *Memoria hospitis unius diei prætereuntis.*

206

The eternal silence of these infinite spaces frightens me.

"It is here in us, and not elsewhere, that the powers and actions of the soul should be considered." Montaigne remains in our mind, Pascal in our heart. Freud, the Montaigne of our era, reminded us that the voice of reason was not loud but would not rest until it gained a hearing. Montaigne's voice is never-resting, while Pascal's voice is restless. As Montaigne's involuntary and perpetual ephebe, Pascal always knew which voice was stronger.

RONALD A. KNOX

Pascal and Jansenism

Admiring Pascal as a genius, edified by Pascal as a Christian, we forget
to pity Pascal as an invalid. Yet an invalid he undoubtedly was; Madame
Périer, in her sketch of his life, tells us that the illness which overshadowed
his last four years was only "a redoubling of the great disorders he was
subject to from the time of his youth." He was constitutionally bilious, and
in consequence somewhat atrabilious by temperament. The satirist of the
Provincial Letters was a man, I think, who was hard put to it all his life to
restrain his fidgets. "The extraordinary vivacity of his temper," says Madame
Périer, "made him sometimes so impatient that it was difficult to please him";
the "spark of the lion" which Sainte-Beuve notes in his attitude was partly
native to him. He was predisposed to take the jaundiced view; his lovableness,
we may add, is by that all the more remarkable. A little time before his
conversion, it seems (I mean his complete conversion in 1654), this jaundiced
outlook had begun to colour his whole mind. "Although" (writes Sister
Euphemia) "for more than a year he has had a great contempt for the world,
and an almost intolerable disgust for all the people in it—a state of mind
which might well carry him to great excesses, with the heated temperament
(*humeur bouillante*) he has, he nevertheless displays a moderation over it which
gives me quite high hopes of him." Observe that she appears to regard his
discontent with the world as something belonging, in itself, to nature; it is
in the *moderating* of these transports that the promise of grace is to be seen.
He might have tears of joy at his conversion, but he did not emerge into
that serenity which would enable him to say, with Mother Julian, "All thing

From *Enthusiasm: A Chapter in the History of Religion.* © 1950 by A. P. Watt Ltd.

shall be well, and all manner of thing shall be well." He had the markings of an embittered atheist; grace caught him and turned him into a Christian pessimist.

Hence the characteristic note of the *Pensées*. Bremond hardly exaggerates when he describes Pascal as *obsessed* by the idea of original sin. "La foi chrétienne ne va principalement qu'à établir ces deux choses, la corruption de la nature et la rédemption de Jésus Christ." This is the foundation of his edifice, and he will not let us leave out of sight for a moment the depravity of man or the misery which is its punishment and counterpart. (It was easier for him than for us to treat sin and suffering as obverse and reverse of the same medal, because, like Port Royal generally, he accepted Descartes's notion that animals are automata, without feeling.) "It is equally dangerous for man to know God without knowing his own misery, and to know his own misery without knowing the Redeemer." "There is nothing in the world which does not betray either man's misery, or God's mercy, or man's impotence without God, or man's power with God's help." Original sin is the only key which fits the whole puzzle of existence. And so he leads up to the terrific twenty-fifth Thought, on the Feebleness of Man, and twenty-sixth Thought, on the Misery of Man. For Sainte-Beuve the *Pensées* are consciously, or almost consciously, an answer to Montaigne. It may be so, but I do not think Pascal needed Montaigne to give him any depressing information about human existence. He could read it himself, all too clearly, in his own sickly body, and his restless mind, impatient of that clogging companionship.

I am not suggesting that it was Pascal who taught the Jansenists to be gloomy; they had the art of it long before his time. But I think he helped fix in them that mood of despair which took it for granted that nearly everybody was damned. St. Cyran (a neuropath, if Bremond is right) certainly had it, especially about the rich. And I think Prunel is right in suggesting that there is a humanness, a lightness of touch about Mother Angélique while she is still under Zamet's direction which she loses afterwards. Of all the Jansenist tricks none is more clearly un-Catholic than the readiness with which they assume their neighbour's damnation. St. Cyran, for example, giving the *petites écoles* a lesson on Virgil, "ce grand auteur qui s'était damné, disait-el, en faisant de si beaux vers, parce qu'il ne les faisait pas pour Dieu." How infinitely more gracious was the legend, current in an earlier Christendom, of St. Paul reaching Naples, and weeping over Virgil's tomb:

> Quem te (inquit) reddidissem,
> Si te vivum invenissem,
>   Poetarum maxime!

What is least forgivable in the Jansenists is that seeing the world as a *massa damnationis*, rushing on to its ruin, they could find no other remedy for its unhappiness but to make war on the Jesuits.

Thus obstinately ultrasupernatural in its approach to morals, has Jansenism a corresponding attitude towards the intellect? We have seen [elsewhere] that some enthusiastic movements—that of the Lollards, for example—are characterized by a distrust of human learning, and of human reasoning, as something "carnal" for which the children of light have no further use. The intuition which comes from the direct *afflatus* of the Holy Spirit shall replace, for them, all their natural powers of discernment or of speculation. It must be freely confessed that the sectaries who use this language with most confidence are not, as a rule, men remarkable in any case for intellectual gifts; there is a suggestion of sour grapes about the Lollard protest against the learned clearks of their day. And the Jansenists, evidently, were in a different position; Port-Royal quite certainly had brains, and knew how to use them. Learning was encouraged there, and not only learning but reasoning; the Logic written for and taught in its *petites écoles* was famous. Only in two directions does it express hesitation. The love of learning for its own sake, "curiosity" as they call it, is censured as likely to puff up the soul with pride. And "reasoning" about the faith is sometimes alluded to with disapproval; thus St. Cyran observed of St. Thomas, "Nul saint n'a tant raisonné sur les choses de Dieu"; and the *Augustinus* itself contrasts the method of the schoolmen unfavourably with that of the Fathers. If it be objected that St. Augustine never stopped arguing, and that his Jansenist followers were more than worthy of him in this respect, we shall be told that Truth is sometimes compelled to meet subtlety with subtlety, but that this is no excuse for *recherches trop curieuses* and a *trop grand désir de savoir*. Such sentiments, however, reflect little more than the Jansenist grudge against St. Thomas, who had substituted Aristotle for St. Augustine as the *maestro di color che sanno*. Port-Royal distrusts the human reason as an appetite, but not as an instrument.

It may be questioned, however, whether Pascal does not go farther. His supernaturalism was more far-reaching than that of his colleagues; Arnauld and Nicole had to tone it down when they bowdlerized the *Pensées*. And the apologetic method of the *Pensées*, even as we have them, is highly characteristic. Pascal recognizes the classical proofs of God's existence and admits the force of them, but he dislikes them. You may almost say that if he had been in a position to do it he would have hushed them up. He *wanted* our fallen nature, left without grace, to be as weak and miserable as possible;

"l'homme n'est donc qu'un sujet plein d'*erreurs* ineffaçables sans la grâce";
his picture of man's misery remained incomplete, lopsided, if you could
think of man unredeemed as possessing any skylight, even, that gave on the
supernatural. A purely speculative knowledge of God, such as the Five Proofs
offer to us, is (in Pascal's view) worse than no knowledge at all; it is *nuisible*.
The only saving knowledge of God is that which approaches him with and
through the knowledge of our own misery, so that we are looking for him
as our Redeemer. Speculative knowledge, instead of bringing us to our knees,
puffs us up with pride, and we are worse off than the atheist. Deism, he
says, and atheism are two things which the Christian religion equally abhors.
Even a cursory reading of the *Pensées* makes it clear that it was written against
the former, rather than the latter; and its criticisms, as against the deist,
obviously have weight. But how could Pascal be so certain that a proof of
God's existence by way of natural philosophy could not be at least the remote
preparation for a true conversion of the heart to God? Evidently because he
believed that such conversion must be a *simultaneous* discovery of God's
existence and our Redemption. The Fall, instead of being a doctrine revealed
to us as part of a general revelation, must be an axiom grasped intuitively
in the experience of conversion. You must not take two bites of the apple.

The fact is that his thought approximates to Marcionism. The figure of
the Redeemer so fills the canvas, as to obscure all thought of God in his
eternal attributes. "Pascal," says Bremond, "exalte le médiateur, mais il
cache, il exile Dieu." So Joubert complained that the Jansenists "ôtent au
Père pour donner au Fils." This habit of Christocentricity does not desert
Pascal even when he is writing as a prophet new-inspired. In his *Mémorial*,
those burning lines which he wrote, as if stupefied with some drug, after
his conversion on the 23rd of November 1654—even in his *Mémorial* he is
sufficiently master of his own thoughts to repudiate, carefully, the imputation
of Deism. "Dieu d'Abraham, Dieu d'Isaac, Dieu de Jacob"; and, having got
so far, he must needs add "non des philosophes et savants." It is as if two
Gods existed, and he, Pascal, were determined that his petition should go
to the right address; lest there should still be any doubt, he goes on "Dieu
de Jésus Christ." This last phrase, so foreign to the vocabulary of the Church,
is wrung out of him by the necessity of explaining to himself, even at such
a moment, that he writes as Pascal the Christian, not as Pascal the geometer.
All things have been made new.

I have described St. Cyran as an illuminist; can we trace, in the movement which owes it origin to him, and cousinship to those enthusiastic sects
which claim for every Christian a kind of prophetic endowment, an inner
light which lends certainty to his beliefs? It recalls the rigorism of the Do-

natist; does it recall, equally, the ecstasies of the Montanist? It is interesting to observe that in early days those who knew St. Cyran expected something of the kind. In a letter which records his arrest, Jean Louis de Balzac writes: "On a peur, à mon avis, que l'Abbé voulût faire secte et qu'il pût devenir hérésiarque. Je ne parle pas de ces hérésies charnelles et débauchées, comme celle de Luther et de Calvin, mais de ces hérésies spirituelles et sévères comme celles d'Origène et de Montanus." The writer is hard, perhaps, on the morals of the Reformers, but how admirably he seizes the point which I have tried to illustrate [elsewhere], in discussing the Reformation, that Luther's movement never achieved its proper destiny as a spiritual movement, remained "carnal" in the sense given to that word by the vocabulary of enthusiasm! The mention of Origen is perhaps inappropriate; there was no Father whom the Jansenists so much detested, because of his views on grace. But Montanus is in point; there is a kinship between him and St. Cyran. But did the followers of St. Cyran tread the path which Balzac had marked out for them? Were they, in any sense, illuminists?

Those theologies which lay great stress on the corruption of human nature, and the difficulty of salvation, are apt to make up for it by offering to the elect *sensible experiences* of God's favour. It may be the complete inner conviction of the Calvinist that he is bound for heaven; it may be the warm consciousness of the Wesleyan that his sins are, here and now, forgiven: in either case, there is the feeling that things can never be the same again, a threshold has been crossed, nature has been supernaturalized. So it is with the more modern enthusiast who tells you that "his life has been changed"; with that moment of decision to look back upon, he finds (at least for a time) that virtues or abstinences which hitherto meant laborious effort now "come easy to him." Instead of resolving to conquer his temptations, he believes that he will conquer his temptations, and does. Pascal's experience seems to have been something of this kind. The word "certitude," occurring in the *Mémorial*, definitely points to this, and Bremond's treatment of the subject seems to establish beyond doubt that Pascal expected and came to believe that he had been granted a sign from heaven. Whether it was a full assurance of his ultimate salvation, as Bremond seems to assume, is more doubtful; there is an obvious parallel to be drawn between his experience and Wesley's. It is clear that from that moment onwards the severe discipline which he imposed on his life ceased to be a matter of uphill struggle, *seemed* at any rate to be made easy for him. This can be inferred from the curious document written by him on a loose sheet of paper, and preserved for us by Madame Périer, towards the end of the *Life*. He gives a list of his own moral qualities, startlingly reminiscent of the Pharisee's thanksgiving in the temple, and then adds: "I bless my Redeemer every day of my life for having engrafted (these sentiments) in me; from one who was a man full of weakness, misery, concupiscence, pride and ambition, he has made me a man exempt from all these evils, by the power of his grace, to which only it is owing; in myself, I find nothing but misery and horror." The language of a perfectionist could hardly go further.

I am not sure, however, that Bremond is justified when he seems to suggest that the Jansenists, at least in the earlier part of their history, identified the sweetness which sometimes comes to us in prayer with grace itself, with that *sancta delectatio* which, as we have seen, tips the scale in the moral conflict, in the Augustinian view. The language of Port-Royal does, occasionally, suggest this interpretation. Thus, the *Fréquente Communion* tells us that an act of contrition is valueless when we do not *feel*, in making it, detachment from the world and joy in the expectation of eternal happiness; we are only making *actes imaginaires de contrition*. Arnauld even falls foul of Père Sesmaisons for telling his penitent that we ought to communicate "lors même que l'on ressent peu de dévotion." But elsewhere he distinguishes between the want of zeal which should, and the want of sensible devotion which should not, keep us away from Communion. I suppose, then, that in the two earlier passages he is thinking, not of any quasi-mystical experience, but of a fixed attitude of the will.

But, while it is not clear that the Jansenist expected, as a matter of course, to find *positive* feelings of sweetness or consolation about the practice of his religion, it is clear that "dryness" in prayer was sometimes read by the Jansenist as a sign that grace had been withdrawn from him. "Il vaut donc mieux sans doute s'en tenir à la spiritualité des Pères, et prendre les sécheresses pour une absence de grâce, et par conséquent pour un état où l'amour est moins fort." This pestilent doctrine arises from a gross misunderstanding of spiritual authors like Thomas à Kempis, who are apt to use the word *gratia* to describe sensible devotion. In 3.54 of the *Imitation*, for example, the word *gratia* is used in its proper sense, of that quality, unseen, unfelt, inhering in the soul after the manner of an accident, whose motions cannot be distinguished from those of mere nature, except by a man of great spiritual enlightenment. But in 3.7 the author is talking of something quite different, which he defines in the first sentence as *devotionis gratia*, and refers to afterwards as *gratia* for short.

I do not feel convinced, then, that for Port-Royal grace was something *foncièrement délectable*; I would rather say that Port-Royal shook its head over you if it heard you found prayer tedious. But this is not to say that the illuminism of St. Cyran died suddenly with St. Cyran. There was, evidently, a channel of mystical tradition among his followers, which soon dried up. The name principally connected with it is that of M. Barcos, his nephew; a priest whose influence on the councils of Port-Royal seems to have been tentative and intermittent. He was, perhaps, too much of a genuine solitary to have much relish for the perpetual atmosphere of controversy which reigned there; it is possible that he was, in more ways than one, inconveniently wedded to his uncle's ideas, at a time when Arnauld, Nicole and the rest were anxious to interpret those ideas in their own sense. For Barcos contemplation was something to be preferred to meditation, if only because it owes less to human effort; our nature, hopelessly corrupted by the fall, must contribute as little as possible to the machinery of our prayer. It is unquestionable, too, that the Jesuits, as being committed to the tradition of St. Ignatius, were the official exponents of formal meditation; and this alone was enough to condemn it in Jansenist eyes. Meanwhile, the *attraction* which contemplative prayer has for the mystic, seeming to claim him and beckon him to itself instead of having to be cultivated by his own assiduity, could easily be identified with that *victrix delectatio*, that overmastering pleasure, which was, for the Augustinian, the hallmark of grace.

The disappearance, or rather deliberate choking, of this stream of mystical tradition was due to a curious accident. It arose from the conversion and what followed the conversion of that rather *opéra-bouffe* figure, the Sieur de Desmarets. A dramatist at the height of his fame, he was converted from worldliness to ways of piety. This was in itself bad enough, for he was not converted by Port-Royal or according to the formula of Port-Royal. He retired into no wilderness, but began writing works of devotion. It was an age when, it must be confessed, the religious world was rather too fond of methods by which the secret of interior prayer might be learnt in sixteen lessons; "ce fut alors une pluie de moyens courts"; and Desmarets produced his *Delights of the Spirit*, a book of unexceptionable piety, but hardly to be expected from one whose interest in religion was of such recent growth; it aroused the suspicion of charlatanism. Then, as if that were not enough, he produced a violent attack on the Jansenists, in which he repeated many of the most improbable charges which malice had invented against their orthodoxy. The Peace of the Church happening about this time, Nicole was on the look out for somebody to write against, without mention of the word "grace." His pragmatical mind had already been disturbed by finding a tendency towards mysticism in his own party. He sat down and wrote *Les Visionnaires*, an elaborate but fundamentally stupid attack on contemplative prayer generally, which Bremond has dignified by a long exposure of its fallacies. This had the effect of creating an anti-mystical prejudice among

the defenders of Port-Royal, which was hardened by their subsequent controversy with the Quietists. Contemplation, instead of being a stick to beat
the *Exercises* with, became suspect as a Jesuit trick, calculated to distract the
mind of fallen man from the all-important business of working out his own
salvation in fear and trembling.

With all the wisdom of the first six centuries for its oracle, Port-Royal
did not need, as other separatist movements have needed, an inner light for
its guidance, inner convictions of sinfulness and of redemption. On another
side, it was strangely open to invasions of the supernatural. Signs and wonders were to accompany the mission of the apostles, and few enthusiatic
sects have been proof against the craving for signs and wonders, as an
evidence of true mission. Port-Royal should have been above this; it had
never forsaken the communion of the Catholic Church, and inherited, in
common with the rest of Christendom, a chain of continuous life which
bound it, visibly, to the apostolic age. Pascal, in an almost latitudinarian
vein, protests that there is no need of miracles now, as there was in the first
ages of the Church, to be proof of her divine origin. But, at a crisis in Port-
Royal's history, an event happened which gave a new and dangerous direction
to Jansenist thought. In 1656, just when the persecution which ultimately
took place in 1661 was on the point of starting, Pascal's niece, a daughter
of Madame Périer, was cured suddenly of an obstinate eye trouble, when
she had been touched in the church at Port-Royal by a relic, a Thorn
supposedly from the Crown of Thorns. The medical evidence was satisfactory, the *réclame* of the fact enormous; at the instance of Cardinal de Retz,
then in exile, permission was given for a Te Deum. Anne of Austria, it is
said, was profoundly impressed by the story, and the persecution was held
off for another five years.

It would not be in place here to consider the genuineness of the miracle,
or its theological implications; both have been widely canvassed. The effect
was, as Sainte-Beuve points out, that Port-Royal accepted the miracle not
as proof that the relic was a true relic, but as a proof that Port-Royal was
right and the Jesuits were wrong. From that time onwards the normal Catholic belief in ecclesiastical miracles was reinforced by a confidence that, when
need arose, Almighty God could be trusted to perform *Jansenist* miracles.
Eighty others, in the years that followed, were attributed to the same relic.
Once whetted, the appetite grew. When M. de Pontchâteau died, in 1690,
his coffin had to be taken away forcibly from the church, where a crowd of
relic-hunters had already torn his shroud to pieces. Thus arose among the
Jansenists that mood of "looking for a sign from heaven," which was destined

to produce such extraordinary fruits, forty years later, in the convulsions of St. Médard.

That later Jansenism belongs to a different age, and a different world, from the Jansenism which took its cue and its colour from Port-Royal. St. Médard will deserve our study, in a later chapter, among the influences which determined the eighteenth-century attitude towards enthusiasm. Meanwhile, what epitaph is to be written on Port-Royal itself? Pathetically enough, it was always to the verdict of posterity that the Jansenists appealed, when they were not appealing to the verdict of antiquity. "La postérité saurait toute chose," said D'Andilly, and Nicole confidently assumes that in fifty years' time all these disputes will be thought quite trifling; the good name of Port-Royal will be vindicated, since time, in the seventeenth century as much as in the fourth, would be the real test of orthodoxy. That was the origin of the Jansenists' prodigious literary activity; the *relations*, the *mémoires*, the collections of *pièces justificatives*, the obituaries, the biographies. It was for this that they edited, so painstakingly and in such jealous spirit, their necrology. They believed the Catholic Church would come to see that they had been right, and would treasure these memorials of the few souls who stood firm, in the bad days when the world groaned to find itself Molinist.

Instead of that, their notions about grace have passed into the textbooks, in the next paragraph after Pelagius; their rigorism no longer finds support, their attitude about Holy Communion died out under Pius X; their pet aversion, devotion to the Sacred Heart, has spread through the world and become imbedded in the liturgy. *Exoriare aliquis*, quotes Sainte-Beuve, *nostris ex ossibus ultor*—but the champions they have found in later times, men of study who have delighted to quarry among their inexhaustible archives, have not been of their camp, nor of their mentality. Evangelicals, like Frances Martin, hail them as choice souls who aimed at the purifying of religion, but have to admit that they insisted, beyond the wont of Catholics, upon absolute submission to the advice of a director. High Churchmen, like Lord St. Cyres, fraternize with them over their devotion to the first six centuries, only to find them turning Ultramontane when it suits their policy. Liberal thinkers, with a taste for dabbling in spirituality, like Saint-Beuve, acclaim them as the antagonists of a relaxed morality, yet trace in them a rapid declension from the high ideals of their founder. What is admired in them chiefly is their pagan virtues; the fortitude of Arnauld reminds the scholar of Horace's *praeter atrocem animum Catonis*—the pagan virtues of men and women who held the virtues of the pagans to be sin! If the three authors I have mentioned had applied for a night's lodging together at Port-Royal,

Mother Angélique would perhaps have allowed Frances Martin the bread and cider of the lackeys, but only after explaining that she did so out of pure charity; Lord St. Cyres would have been soundly rated by Arnauld for his Protestant insincerity; and I doubt if Pascal would have accorded an interview to Sainte-Beuve.

Meanwhile, what legacy did they bequeath to the Church of which they remained, so obstinately, members? French religion in the eighteenth century is overlaid, for the most part, with a joyless moralism that has lost the fire and the fervour of the old Port-Royal; the country that had once been so rich in saints and mystics was now condemned to dissipate its energies in controversy. The sharp distinction drawn between nature and supernature disheartened the libertine, and lost for the Church her hold over the consciences of sinners. The doctrine of the *Fréquente Communion* held its unlovely sway; just when it first appeared, St. Vincent of Paul complained that hundreds among the parishioners of St. Sulpice had given up the practice of monthly Communion; and the generations which followed were content with Communion once a year. Meanwhile, the constant echoes of controversy between the two parties in the Church weakened her influence, and left her ill-prepared to face the crisis of the Revolution. Such was the harvest which St. Cyran reaped from his effort to reform Christendom.

The enthusiast wants to see results; he is not content to let the wheat and the tares grow side by side until the harvest. It must be made possible somehow, even in this world, to draw a line between the sheep and the goats. Thus a little group of devout souls isolates itself from the rest of society, to form a nucleus for the New Jerusalem; and in doing so it loses touch with the currents of thought that flow outside, grows partisan in its attitude, sterile of new ideas. Jansenism was not (except in Holland) a severed limb of the Church, like Donatism before it; but it was like a limb which has been tied up with a tourniquet, so that the blood no longer courses freely in it. For that reason its splendid energies declined, its ardours paled, its literary achievement dwindled into insignificance. We may yet need, in the centuries which lie before us, a tightening-up of discipline, a general return to more exacting standards, a recovery of our origins. But if such a movement owes anything to Jansenism, it will owe nothing more than those lessons of greater prudence which the Church, with her long memory, derives from the record of failure in the past.

ERICH AUERBACH

On the Political Theory of Pascal

Fragment 298 of Pascal's *Pensées* is a vigorous attempt to show the weakness of human justice. It runs as follows in the Brunschvicg edition:

> Il est juste que ce qui est juste soit suivi: il est nécessaire que ce qui est le plus fort soit suivi. La justice sans la force est impuissante; la force sans la justice est tyrannique. La justice sans force est contredite, parce qu'il y a toujours des méchants; la force sans la justice est accusée. Il faut donc mettre ensemble la justice et la force; et pour cela faire que ce qui est juste soit fort ou que ce qui est fort soit juste.
>
> La justice est sujette à dispute, la force est très reconnaissable et sans dispute. Ainsi on n'a pu donner la force à la justice, parce que la force a contredit la justice et a dit que c'était elle que était juste. Et ainsi, ne pouvant faire que ce qui est juste fût fort, on a fait que ce qui est fort fût juste.

A stylistic analysis of the propositions making up this fragment is not difficult; their structure becomes immediately apparent if they are arranged as follows:

> It is right that what is just should be obeyed:
> It is necessary that what is strongest should be obeyed.

From *Scenes from the Drama of European Literature*. © 1959 by Meridian Books, Inc.

Justice without might is helpless:
Might without justice is tyrannical.

Justice without might is challenged, because there are
    always offenders;
Might without justice is impugned.

We must then combine justice and to this end make
what is just strong,
or what is strong just.

Justice is subject to dispute,
Might is easily recognizable and is not disputed.

So
We cannot give might to justice,
because might has challenged justice and has said, it
    is I who am just

and thus
being unable to make what is just strong,
we have made what is strong just.

When the fragment is disposed in this way, it becomes evident that
Pascal has developed his thought by a play of antithetical propositions arranged in symmetrical pairs (isocola). There are six of these. The first three
describe the situation. This situation gives rise to a problem that can be
solved in two different ways: the fourth pair states the alternative in the
form of a syllogism: it was necessary to do either A or B; A was impossible;
therefore B was done. The second premise (A was impossible) is strongly
emphasized; the reason why A was impossible is given in the fifth pair of
isocola, which is not quite symmetrical since the second part is longer and
more definite. The second premise appears twice in the final couplet (which
closes the syllogism and the whole fragment). The conclusion is presented
in two phases: *ainsi . . .* and *et ainsi*. The first phase (*ainsi . . .*) is a dramatic
development of the second premise (note the accent on *elle*); and the second
(*et ainsi*), in a tone of bitter satisfaction, supplies the conclusion.

This brief analysis shows a characteristic feature of Pascal's style: its
unique fusion of logic, rhetoric, and passion. At first sight he seems merely
to be applying a logical method, but the rhetorical clash of concepts in
similarly constructed, conflicting propositions introduces a dramatic tension;
and when at the end Might emerges from the battle of the concepts, raising

its head and lifting up its voice (*et a dit que c'était elle* . . .), its triumph seems to stand before us as a concrete reality.

Effective as this parallelism may be, a critical modern reader, not too familiar with Pascal, may be inclined to suspicion and find an element of sophistry in it. Is not Pascal, he may ask, using the word *juste* in entirely different senses, as if they were identical? In the beginning *juste* signifies genuine, natural, absolute right; but later on, when it falls into the hands of might, it means established, positive right. What is contingent on might is therefore not really right, but only passes as such. But plausible as this may seem to a modern reader, such reasoning does not reflect Pascal's attitude. As we shall soon see, he believed that on this earth might represents not only actual positive right, but legitimate right as well. In order to understand Pascal's thought as he intended it, we must ask how it came into being. For homogeneous and with all its stylistic artifice simple as it may seem to us, it is made up of very diverse influences and experiences.

From Montaigne Pascal derived, sometimes to the letter, the idea that the dominant factor in the laws is not reason or even the natural agreement of all men, but merely custom. But custom is contingent on time and place and is always changing. What is permitted and even praised in one country or period, is regarded as a crime in another; even absurd, arbitrary, and obviously unjust institutions are sanctioned by custom. Nevertheless, custom and the law based on it must be obeyed, not because the law is just but because it is in force, since there is no hope of finding a better one and the disorder involved in any change is a definite evil—which it is not worthwhile foisting on oneself and others, since the new custom would be no better or [more] reasonable than the old one. Pascal took all this from Montaigne, but in taking it over he changed the tone a little, shifted the accents, and ended up with something entirely different. To Montaigne the wavering of custom was no ground for horror or despair; his free, supple, tolerant mind moved courageously, one might almost say comfortably, amid the uncertainties of life; he felt no need of a fixed and absolute order, and I even doubt whether he would have been happy in one. But Pascal did feel the need of such an order and strove for it with a violent passion. He demanded the determinate, the enduring and absolute; he could not abide fluctuations and compromises, which he identified with evil.

Aside from difference in temperament, the change in the times may have contributed to this difference of outlook. Montaigne had lived in a period of political and religious struggles; he had witnessed the clash of untrammeled historical forces; he had seen customs change, and entertained the hope that these transformations and struggles, though he did not approve

of them, would result in a stable compromise, which if not good might at
least be moderate and tolerable. Pascal, on the other hand, lived in a period
of almost complete absolutism, in which one established power, the mon-
archy, was beginning to wield almost unlimited and clearly arbitrary authority. Still, I believe it was Pascal's character more than the historical
circumstances that led him to take a more critical view of custom than
Montaigne, to put it down as an evil pure and simple, and gradually replace
it by another and entirely different concept: the concept of might. Actually
one can read the same idea into Montaigne, for he says that we should obey
the law, not because it is just but because it is valid, because it is in force.
But according to Montaigne it has force and validity only because it is based
on custom. Pascal is inclined to deprive custom of its autonomy, considering
it as a function of force, established solely by force. In Pascal we find a
problem that Montaigne never treated, the relation between custom and
might. Custom without might he calls *grimace*; he finds a decided satisfaction
in collecting examples where *grimace* is compelled to cede to might, and in
general reducing custom to mere *imagination* or *opinion*. He was not interested
in the historical basis of customs, for which Montaigne had conceived a
beautiful image—*elles grossissent et s'anoblissent en roulant comme nos fleuves* ("like
our rivers, they take on breadth and nobility as they flow")—to Pascal's
mind they originated in an arbitrary act of power, the caprice of the legislators. Might could repeat this arbitrary act at any time, radically changing
the custom. Montaigne never speaks expressly of might; but it is clear from
the general nature of his ideas that for him it could only have been the
executant of custom. In his view, two sets of customs, both having force
behind them, may perfectly well come into conflict; one may destroy the
other; but naked force, unsupported by custom, depending solely on the
whim of the powerful, has no place in the *Essais*. Pascal, on the other hand,
speaks of the pure power which creates custom and law as it pleases—indeed,
as we shall see later on, he says with a kind of bitter triumph that this is as
it should be, because there is no other justice than that which is in the hands
of might. What, he asks, would become of us, should we try to settle
differences according to merit and justice? No solution would be possible.
Who takes precedence, you or I? You have four footmen, I have one: the
situation is plain, one has only to count.

Here we come to a second set of ideas that helped to mold Pascal's view
of justice: the ideas of Port-Royal on the fundamental corruption of human
nature. Actually Montaigne also says that we have lost our nature and that
only art and custom remain—but he nevertheless puts his faith in human
nature, or if you will, in a human nature that history has transformed into

custom. He trusted in custom as he trusted in nature, because he was at home in the flow of historical life, and gladly let himself be caught up in it, as the swimmer in water or the drinker in wine. But Pascal accepted the extreme Augustinianism of the "gentlemen of Port-Royal," according to which the world is fundamentally and necessarily evil, in diametric opposition to the kingdom of God; one must decide whether to follow the one or the other.

Here I shall not attempt to discuss the ideas of Port-Royal from a philosophical or historical point of view; this has been done exhaustively in the rich literature of the last century, from Sainte-Beuve to Laporte. Up to Pascal's time, in any case, they did not include a political theory, but at most certain notions about the attitude that a Christian should take toward the world: on the one hand, he should detach himself from the world, on the other, submit to it—the detachment being taken in an inward, the submission in an outward sense. Anyone who can free himself outwardly as well, that is, enter a cloister, should do so. Here as in all things a Christian should follow God's will more than his own, and he is much more likely to ascertain God's will through the circumstances of life than through the essentially unstable movements of his soul. Where a high and responsible social position or family considerations forbid outward retirement from the world, the believer should remain at the post to which God's will has assigned him. Even within the world, you can detach yourself from it by turning your heart away from it, by taking no part in its pleasures and lusts, but participating rather in its cares and sufferings, since suffering is our strongest bond with Christ. As for the submission, it consists in recognizing the institutions, particularly the political and social institutions, of this world, in obeying the secular powers and serving them in accordance with your position; for although the world has succumbed to concupiscence and is therefore evil, a Christian has no right to condemn it, much less oppose it by worldly means, since he himself is in the same state of sin, and the evil of this world is the just punishment and penance that God has appointed to fallen man. The injustice of this world corresponds then to the true justice of God, which we must gladly suffer; where God permits true justice to prevail, he is moved to do so not by justice but by mercy. In rejecting criticism of the world's institutions, this line of thought seems to preclude political theory. Evil as it may be, the world was established by God; a Christian can only submit. Indeed, Port-Royal did not occupy itself with political theory and in all probability Pascal himself would not have done so, if outward events had not brought the political problem home to him.

These events were the incidents in the conflict between Port-Royal and

the Jesuits. If it is a Christian's duty to submit to the world, it is surely—
and far more so—his duty to obey the Church. The Church is the community
of the faithful, established by God; its mission is to teach, to administer the
sacraments indispensable to all who seek salvation. To stand outside the
Church, to break away from it of their own free will like the Protestants—
for the Jansenists this was unthinkable. But if corruption prevails within the
Church, if the powers of evil beguile and ensnare the heads of the Church,
the bishops and the pope, and make willing tools of them; if thereupon the
Church, on the strength of its authority and the obedience imposed on the
faithful, constrains the few to whom God has granted true knowledge to
condemn openly and solemnly what they regard as the very essence of faith;
if moreover the Church, supported by the secular power and itself acting as
a secular power, sets out to destroy right by might, the consequence will be
a situation without issue, a disastrous crisis. Such was the situation of Port-
Royal in the years of Pascal's closest association with it. He directly experienced most of this crisis, and inevitably it impressed him as the triumph
of evil within the Church itself. In those years the problem of justice and
might became real for him; this was the period of the *Pensées* and other short
pieces containing his political theory. Now Montaigne's conception of right
as mere custom combined with the radical Augustinian view of the world
as a realm of evil; the result was the picture described above of custom as
an emanation of might, pure caprice of the Devil.

    Pascal was always inclined to carry things to extremes. In his last years,
during the crisis of Port-Royal, he gave this inclination free rein in the belief,
supported by ecstatic visions and a miracle, that he was doing the will of
God. Among the extreme ideas of this period, there are three, closely related
to one another, which constitute what I call his political theory: his hatred
of human nature (and hence of his own); his condemnation of existing law
as purely arbitrary and evil; his belief that this was the only justice which
could lay claim to legitimacy.

    His hatred of human nature derived from radical Augustinianism. In
his famous distinction between *uti* and *frui*, Augustine taught that we should
not love the creatures for their own sake, but for the sake of the Creator;
that they are entitled to an *amor transitorius* and not an *amor mansorius*; that
it is not permissible to love one's own person for itself, so setting it before
God, and that this had been Adam's sin. He taught that God is the only
enduring object of our love, that all things worthy to be loved are united in
Him; that created things are worthy of love only insofar as they reflect His
essence. This is a universal Christian doctrine, widely held even before
Christianity. In Port-Royal, particularly with Pascal in his last years, it

underwent a shift of accent which gave it a peculiar sharpness of radicalism. Toward the end of his life, Pascal is said to have shown those closest to him a certain coldness, to have rebuffed their affection for him on the ground that love among human beings was a theft from God. On a number of occasions he said quite emphatically that love for the creature must inevitably lead to disillusionment and despair. For the object of such love and the qualities for which we love it are transitory. To him this thought was intolerable; he was horrified at the idea that the treasure to which our heart clings should dwindle from moment to moment, that it might be torn away from us irrevocably at any time. For him what is perishable, what must return to nothingness, is nothing: heaven and earth, friends and relatives, our own mind and body; only God is enduring, invariable, immutable; only God is worthy to be loved. Man's frailty and mutability are primarily a consequence of original sin, of Adam's excessive self-love, the grotesque and wicked error which has come down to his posterity and represents what is most hateful in us. Despite his obvious imperfection and mortality, each man invariably regards himself as the center of the universe, loves nothing so much as himself, judges everything on the basis of himself: clearly a hideous error deserving of hatred. And in this connection the word "hatred" takes on a violence of tone peculiar to Pascal.

The word is used in this sense by other Christian authors; it occurs even in the Gospels, in certain fundamental passages in St. Luke and St. John. But I do not believe that this hatred had ever so completely dominated the whole picture of man's love for God. Pascal's famous words about the hateful self are not his most drastic expression of this idea. He said that one should love only God and hate only oneself; that the Christian religion teaches self-hatred; that self-hatred is the true and unique virtue. There are also moderate formulations, but the radical ones set the tone of the *Pensées*. Obviously this self-hatred does not refer to Pascal's fortuitous self, but to the self of every man, since all men share the same transience and the same abominable self-love. Hatred of himself and men was by no means natural to Pascal; he was capable of passionate, even jealous attachments, and he had difficulty in combating a high esteem for his own person, the *orgueil* to which, from an earthly point of view, he was more entitled than most men. His religious radicalism triumphed only by violence over his natural disposition, which itself to be sure contained a good measure of violence. Self-hatred and hatred of mankind, even in the radical form they assumed with Pascal, can be justified by Christian dogma and tradition. But where as in Pascal this motif is emphasized, isolated from other Christian ideas, it threatens to come into direct conflict with Christian ethics. The injunction to "love thy neighbor as thyself," presupposes a love of oneself; without it *one would hate one's neighbor as oneself*. Moreover, such extreme conceptions imply a certain coolness toward creation as a whole; not only man but all created nature is rendered unworthy of our love by its transience. Nature aroused curiosity, admiration, and terror in this great physicist, but no love. Few religious, mystic, or idealistic writers have been further from the thought that divine truth and beauty are reflected in the phenomena of this world. And this no doubt accounts for his emphatic rejection of all attempts to prove the existence of God by the manifestations of nature.

The second idea, the condemnation of earthly law as arbitrary and evil, is closely related to the first, for apart from all experience it follows logically from the corruption of human nature. Our law and our politics—here "politics" is taken in the widest sense, comprising all our dealings in this world— can only be evil, and so they are, as experience confirms. Neither reason nor justice prevails, but chance and violence. Pascal was descended from the *robe*, or bourgeois officialdom; he was a man of the highest intelligence and discernment. Though the most honorable positions were open to him and his class, he was barred from all political freedom, from all activity involving political reponsibility. In the epoch of total absolutism the population of all classes had become a mere object and had ceased to be in any respect a subject of politics. His class had just lost the last vestiges of its political independence in the struggles of the Fronde. Still, it seems unlikely that any dissatisfaction arising from these circumstances contributed to his political views. Pascal held aloof from any participation in the Fronde, though involvement would have been quite in keeping with his family traditions. Yet its seems inconceivable that a man of his social and intellectual stature would have held (and acted on) such political opinions at any other time. His certainty that all political institutions are based on delusion, chance, and violence is expressed in his characteristically cutting, paradoxical manner, which sometimes, it seems to me, echoes motives other than Christian. Though intended to support radically Christian conclusions, his critique is open to much broader interpretation. In *Trois Discours sur la condition des grands*, he proves to a *grand seigneur* that his prestige and power are not based on any natural and authentic right, but solely on the will of the legislators— a different whim, a different *tour d'imagination* on their part, and he would be poor and powerless. True, his position, like all existing institutions recognized by positive law, is legitimate; but it brings him only outward deference and obedience (for it is foolish and base to withhold obedience from existing institutions), and no inward respect. Even if according to the standards of this world he uses his power honestly and benevolently—which is his duty—it is always a power opposed to the kingdom of God; for God, who dispenses the goods of love, is the King of Charity; whereas he, who administers and distributes the goods of this world is a king of concupiscence. Even if he governs this kingdom honestly, but does strive to do more, he will be eternally damned, though indeed as a gentleman: *Si vous en demeurez-là, vous ne laisserez pas de vous perdre, mais au moins vous vous perderez un honnête homme*. The kingdom of grace and salvation begins far beyond all human *honnêteté*.

These same ideas recur in the *Pensées*, where the absurdity and fortui-tousness of human institutions are described in a way that would be highly revolutionary if not for the Augustinian setting. To give an example, killing is the worst of crimes according to all divine and human law; but if my neighbor, whom I ought to love, lives across the river where another prince rules, and if he happens to be at war with my prince, then I am entitled to kill him, in fact it becomes my duty. He lives on the other side of the river. This is the basis, the only basis of my right to kill him. The whole era of absolutism, the whole era of cabinet wars which the peoples had to endure but otherwise took no part in, is embodied in these words. And it is inter-esting to observe that such ideas (which were widespread though no one else formulated them so sharply) were perfectly compatible with complete and even hyperbolically expressesd loyalty toward the sovereign. Never has an epoch been more nominalistic.

In Pascal, of course, this whole line of thought is based on an extreme development of the idea of the corruption of this world. Through original sin and Christ's sacrifice, the world has become the perpetual murderer of Christ, man has lost his first nature, and any *opinion* or *imagination* can become his second. But what is actually done at any particular time is decided by the right of the stronger, by might. Real power is the only human phenom-enon for which Pascal shows a certain amount of respect and esteem, though it is often expressed with an insidious bitterness that seems to border on cynicism. He respects the law of the wicked, precisely because of its candid, unfalsified clarity; and in a number of passages he explains this sentiment in detail. It is not so vain to dress with elegance, he says; it shows that you have many hands working for you: the tailor, the embroiderer, the barber, the valet. What is revealed in this way is not something external, not a delusion, but genuine power; to dress well is to show your power. In their respect for power and its outward signs, the people show a sound instinct though their motives are mistaken: they believe that they must respect might because it is just, and that is a fallacy. Might should be respected not because it is just but for its own sake, because it exists. However, it is dangerous to enlighten the people about this mistake.

Here we approach Pascal's third idea, namely the legitimacy of right

based on might. But before going into it I must digress, for my assertion
that Pascal respected nothing on earth but power calls for qualification.
Actually he recognized another realm, situated between worldly power and
divine love: the realm of human thought, of the earthly intellect, which he
sometimes (in the second of the *Discours sur la condition des grands* and in
fragments 332, 460, and 793 [Brunschvicg] of the *Pensées*) contrasts with the
realm of power. He draws careful boundary lines between the three realms;
the realm of material power is infinitely remote from the realm of God, and
this distance symbolizes the infinitely more infinite distance separating the
realm of the human intellect from the supernatural realm of divine charity.
The greatness peculiar to each of these three realms is without value or
influence in the others: the mighty of this earth, the geniuses, and the saints,
have each their own domain, closed to any effective intervention by the
others. For Pascal man is a *roseau pensant*, a thinking reed; frailty is his misery,
thought his greatness. But this realm of the human mind does not fit in very
well with Pascal's political views; how, from the standpoint of practical
politics, can we conceive of thought and might as two distinct spheres im-
pervious to each other's influence? Either the human mind can triumph over
might or might can repress it. True, Pascal is thinking first and foremost of
such relatively unpolitical forms of human thought as mathematics and physics, but experience shows that even these can come into conflict with might,
and Pascal himself dealt with one such case, that of Galileo, in the eighteenth
letter of his *Provinciales*. It is not sufficient to maintain a theoretical separation
between the two realms and to brand any potential infringement of might
on mind as an unjustified tyranny that will be unable to repress the truth
in the long run, for this would justify revolution in the name of the mind,
which is exactly contrary to Pascal's intention. Logically he would have had
to abase science and thought to the same level as all other aspects of man;
he would have had to put down their activity and achievements as mere
opinion and delusion which, like everything else on earth, were dependent,
and rightly so, on might. To this he could not consent. That had been easier
for Montaigne.

However, where Pascal speaks of political matters, he does not mention
the human mind. Thus the inconsistency is not apparent and I can conclude
my digression here. In the political world as he represents it, might, that is
evil, rules exclusively—and by right. In elaborating this paradox—the third
of the ideas enumerated above—Pascal again goes much further than St.
Augustine or his friends of Port-Royal and involves himself much more
deeply than the latter in practical, earthly problems.

The moral code of the *honnête homme* prescribed submission to the prevailing political and social powers; to know one's proper place in the existing, established order, and take an attitude fully consonant with it: this was the ethical and aesthetic ideal which was then taking form and which Pascal's friend Méré contributed a good deal to molding. It derived from an old Christian idea which now assumed a new significance: it is the Christian's duty to endure this world and most particularly its injustice, for Christ voluntarily suffered injustice and every Christian should follow in his footsteps. Above all, the Christian should endure political authority, for Christ himself, throughout his life and particularly in the Passion, submitted to the state. Though committing the supreme injustice, this state power which put Christ to death was nonetheless just, for the divine order of salvation prescribed that it should (in conformance with the laws of the state, hence legally) carry out the sacrifice which, as expiation for Adam's sin, was just also in the eyes of God. Christ's sacrifice should be reenacted in every Christian; all those who are held worthy to suffer injustice, particularly at the hands of the state power, are by that same token held worthy to partake of Christ's sacrifice, and should rejoice. Our joy in the injustice we suffer should be limited only by charity. The only reason why we should not wholeheartedly wish injustice to befall us, is that this would be wishing someone to do us an injustice, and to wish our neighbor to commit an injustice is a grievous sin.

Although this doctrine, to which Port-Royal adhered in theory and still more in practice, relates to injustice in the world, it did not lead to political criticism: it taught men to endure whatever happens in the world; whether it be right or wrong. The question of whether what happens is sometimes or always wrong, or wrong only in particular cases, was not taken into consideration. To be sure Port-Royal followed St. Augustine in regarding the world in general as evil; but it did not ask, and certainly it did not apply the methods and standards of human reason to ascertaining, whether individual legislators and governments might not be moved by God's grace and mercy, so causing a certain amount of justice to prevail, frequently or occasionally, or whether this was never the case.

But on the basis of Montaigne, Méré, and his own experience, Pascal did undertake this inquiry. He combined the negative conclusions of Montaigne and Méré with extreme Augustinianism and thus, in accordance with his temperament, developed the Christian idea we have been discussing into a tragic paradox, both powerful and dangerous.

Through reason and experience Pascal infers that the institutions and the whole process of this world are based on chance and arbitrary power; that our whole earthly order is sheer folly. He believed he was serving the faith by demonstrating, forcefully and convincingly, that misery and injustice, violence and folly, are the foundations of our life; and then he goes on to say that a Christian, fully cognizant of these follies, should obey them, not because he respects folly, but because he respects the will of God who, in order to punish man and open the road of salvation to him while at the same time making it more arduous, has subjected him to these follies; because, accordingly, they are the just law, the only law we deserve. All this, I believe, is dogmatically unassailable; but certain points are overemphasized and (to speak in Christian terms) there is a presumptuous intrusion of rational insights; a faith driven to such extreme of paradox is almost bound to shift into the opposite of faith. In French the word *folie* means both foolishness and madness; thus I am not doing Pascal any great violence, I am exaggerating only slightly if I sum up his thought as follows: the political order of this world is madness and violence; a Christian must obey this madness and should not stir a finger to allay it; for the rule of madness and violence is God's will, it is the proper justice that we deserve; the triumph of madness and violence, the triumph of evil on earth is God's will. Surely few men would live under such a paradox and remain Christians; but Pascal adds, again irrefutably from the standpoint of dogma but again overstating the case, that the Christian religion is *la seule religion contre nature, contre le sens commun*. In the eighteenth century Voltaire and others took Pascal's ideas as a starting point for rationalistic polemics against Christianity.

One may incline to conclude from all this that a Christian adhering to these views—Pascal's or the more moderate version of Port-Royal—would not be able to fight for justice and truth. But this is not the case. Pascal himself fought: he is the author of the *Lettres provinciales*, one of the most important polemics in Christian—or for that matter, in all—literature. The Christian may fight, indeed he must fight as soon as he is convinced that he is fighting not for his own cause but for that of God. The Church itself fought in its beginnings, and even the Church triumphant must fight against its enemies without and within. But when can a Christian be sure that he is really fighting for the truth—when, in this earthly darkness, can he be certain that the grace of God is with him, that God has elected him as an instrument of His cause? *Incola sum in terra*, runs Pascal's favorite Psalm, the 118th, *non abscondas a me mandata tua*. In regard to the signs by which a Christian can ascertain that he is defending the cause of God and the frame of mind in which he should fight, Pascal has given us a document which, I believe, should be numbered among the great texts of Christian ethics. It is part of a letter, first published by Faugère; the date and addressee are unknown but the letter seems to have been written to a fellow member of

Port-Royal a year before Pascal's death, during the controversy over the signing of the formulary.

The letter begins with criticism of the behavior of some of Pascal's companions in struggle. They behave, he says, as though they were fighting for their own cause and not for that of God; they seem to forget that it is the same Providence which has revealed the truth to some and denied it to others; they seem to believe that the God they serve is not the God who permits obstables to stand in the way of the truth; and consequently they are dissatisfied, grumbling over the difficulties that beset them and the success of their adversaries. Such conduct, Pascal declares, is a product of self-will and self-conceit. For if we ardently desire something on the strength of our own will, we are angered by obstacles, because they are something outside us, something neither caused by us nor originating in us, which opposes us. But if it is really God who is acting through us, we experience no feelings that do not spring from the principle of our actions; we face no outside opposition; for the same God who inspires us permits others to oppose us; then it is not our spirit which combats another spirit outside us; no, it is one and the same spirit, namely, God, who produces good and permits evil. Awareness of this gives peace of soul, and such inner peace is the best sign that it is really God who is acting through us. For it is far more certain that God permits evil, even of the worst kind, than that he wishes to do good through us, vital as this may seem to us. It is always to be feared that what inspires us is not God but a secret egoism, and self-examination is far from reliable, but often a source of delusion. Far more trustworthy than the examination of our inner motives is the scrutiny of our outward conduct. The patient endurance of outward obstacles indicates a harmony in our soul between Him who inspires our will to fight and Him who permits opposition to our struggle, and since there can be no doubt that it is God who permits the opposition, we may be justified in humbly hoping that it is He who inspires our will to fight. Some men, however, act as though their mission were to bring about the triumph of truth, while in reality our mission is only to fight for it. The desire for victory is only too human and natural; if this natural desire is concealed beneath the desire to bring about the triumph of truth, it is easy to take the one for the other and to suppose that we are fighting for the glory of God whereas in reality we are striving for our own glory. Here again our conduct in the face of outward obstacles and the success of our adversary is the most reliable test. For provided we desire nothing but God's will, we must be just as content if the truth succumbs and remains hidden as if it conquers and is made manifest, for in the latter case it is God's mercy that triumphs and in the former his justice. And Pascal concludes the whole discussion with a reference to St. Augustine who, commenting on John 17:25 *(Pater juste, mundus te non cognovit)* declared the concealment of God to be an effect of His justice.

I should like to stress four main points in connection with this document. First of all, Pascal's distrust of his own inner movements is highly characteristic and distinguishes him from most other mystics. In his belief, self-examination is so unreliable, so likely to be falsified by self-love, that he urgently warns the believer not to trust in it alone. We have mentioned Pascal's belief that in deciding whether or not to enter a cloister, a man should not heed his inner voice alone if important external circumstances oppose the step. Here, in connection with a far more important and universal problem, he refuses to recognize a man's own feeling that he is right and doing good as in itself a valid criterion. Only a perfect peace of mind, based on humility and Christian patience, can prove that the good we think we are championing in our Christian actions really comes from God.

But what is the foundation of Christian patience and humility in such a situation? It is the insight that it is God, and not something extraneous, who permits the obstacles in the path of the good. We are opposed by nothing external, nothing capable of disturbing our peace of mind; God's will alone determines the course of the struggle, and since our will, if we really are fighting for the good, must accord with God's will, our soul must be filled with the peace, the patience, the harmony, which spring from the knowledge that it is the same God who produces good and permits evil.

Here I must caution the reader against a possible misunderstanding: there is nothing relativistic about this attitude, no suggestion of an understanding for the opposing standpoint. Pascal is not saying that "the adversary is right from his point of view," or even that one should try to understand him. He is not interested in the adversary and his cause, but solely in God, whose plan of salvation permits of obstacles in the way of His cause (the obstacles raised by a world that the fall of man has corrupted), so that God's cause on earth seems to be perpetually in a critical, even desperate situation. The few who champion it are by their nature as corrupt as their adversaries; only the grace of God has raised them above the corruption; the possession of grace itself is perpetually endangered and never secure.

A third important point is embodied in the proposition that our mission is to fight, not to win. For this involves the obligation to fight under any circumstances, regardless of the prospects. Such an obligation makes terrible demands, almost beyond the powers of human nature, on the combatant. But anyone who succeeds in adopting such an attitude is at least inwardly unconquerable, and even outworldly it will be hard to down him entirely in the long run. Experience shows that ordinary human bravery falters when the struggle seems hopeless—but the man who knows for certain that he must fight regardless of any prospect of success, is immune to despair or panic. And experience also shows that many of the greatest triumphs have been wrested from desperate situations—by men who refused to be defeated inwardly before they had been physically overpowered.

And the fourth, last point: even if, and most particularly if, the truth is defeated and remains hidden, justice is done; for God's justice resides precisely in His concealment of the truth; if He makes it known, it is out of compassion, grace, and love. This is a variant of the idea that we developed above: that to suffer injustice is the justice that befits men. From this it follows that before God no one on earth suffers injustice, or to put it still more sharply, that men can commit, but not suffer, injustice; for although the man who wrongs his neighbor is really doing wrong, the suffering neighbor is one corrupted by original sin, who deserves to suffer. This idea is definitely Christian in its essence and origin; yet the paradox that one can commit but not suffer injustice also has its place in a sphere of thought that is not strictly Christian, provided we interpret original sin as the inextricable fabric of heredity, historical situation, individual temperament, and the consequences of our own actions, in which we are everlastingly involved. Here it will be argued that in actual experience innumerable men suffer injustice every day. Of course it is impossible to prove the contrary; all that can be said is that strictly speaking each man can only decide in his own conscience whether the injustice that has been done him has really been undeserved. If he replies in the negative, this does not excuse, let alone justify, the man who has wronged him, for the transgressor is not authorized to subject his neighbor to an act whose legitimacy he is not competent to judge and the execution of which actually falls to him only by transference. Nor should the defensive position of the sufferer from injustice be weakened by our recognition of the legitimacy of the wrong he has incurred, for insofar as justice is meted out to him, it is by someone other than the transgressor.

The proposition that in the sense described a man can commit injustice but not suffer it, seems to me valuable as an ethical working hypothesis. At least in the initial phase, ethics can only be individual, that is, a question between me and my conscience. Anyone who succeeds in recognizing that whatever happens to him is just, regardless of how wrong others may have been in doing it, has, it seems to me, not only acquired a foundation for ethical thinking and his own ethical attitude, but has also found a new way of looking at everything that happens in the world. But it is no easy matter to make this insight a lasting basis for one's practical behavior.

Let us get back to our fragment. A study of the influences and planes of experience that entered into it was indispensable if we are to appreciate the classical clarity with which the thought is expressed. The expression is based on an opposition between two ideas which are assumed to be universally known and established—whereas the opposition itself shows them to be problematic. Might and justice are contrasted, but at first they are neither explained nor delimited. In the conflict between them, however, their true meaning is gradually brought out, and in the end it becomes clear that they are not opposites at all, but that one is merely a function of the other. When we hear that it is right to obey justice, that justice without might is powerless, that might without justice gives ground for complaint, that there are always wicked men who combat justice, we cannot but assume that Pascal recognizes the existence of an objective justice that is different from might, and at least for purposes of thought, independent of it. But when he goes on to say that justice is always subject to dispute, that might is undisputed and immediately recognizable, that there is no authority able or competent to arrive even at a theoretical decision in regard to a genuine objective justice, and that we are utterly at the mercy of the prevailing justice which is in the hands of might, then it becomes clear that the first premise dealt not with a really existing objective justice but with a mere word, an *imagination*. "It is right to obey justice." Yes, but is there a justice independent of might? Can we recognize it? No, we cannot. Are those who are oppressed by might without justice justified in complaining? Certainly not, for how do we know that they are in the right? Are the transgressors who challenge a justice without might objectively evil? Who can decide? *La justice est sujette à dispute . . .* And what about the might which challenges justice, claiming: I myself am justice. Is it in the wrong? Certainly not. For by what sign can we infallibly recognize justice if it does not predominate? Thus there is no justice other than that which is in the hands of might. Is might then "justice," is it good? Yes, it is justice, but it is not good, it is evil: our world is evil, but it is just that this should be so.

This last thought is not in our fragment, but must be supplied from other statements by Pascal, since it provides the key to the whole. The fragment then consists in a gradual clarification of the relations between the concepts of justice and might. At first they seem to conflict, but one of the two contestants—might—need only show itself, need only stand forth recognizable and indisputable, and justice will renounce its independent existence without a struggle, submit, and become the vassal of might; this is its proper place—with might, not against it.

Our investigation of the influences and planes of experience that produced Pascal's thought enables us not only to understand it more fully but also to appreciate the masterly way in which it is expressed. When an idea is accepted ready-made, because it is current coin, familiar to all—and this has been the lot of many ideas at the end of the nineteenth and the early part of the twentieth century—the expression usually becomes weak and inaccurate because the effort demanded by precise expression is held to be superfluous; an allusion, a catchword, a few familiar phrases suggesting a given trend of thought, seem to suffice; in such cases, a mere word about one of the ideas that are in the air suffices to induce a general understanding or at least a vague feeling of what the author wants to say. But an idea, which, as here in Pascal, is wrested from the writer's own experience by a spontaneous inner activity—such an idea is susceptible of a complete, appropriate expression that precludes the slightest misunderstanding, bars even the slightest displacement or evasion of its exact meaning, and yet permits of an understanding in varying degrees of depth. Sentences come into being which are at once so clear and so profound that a reader who himself aspires to express himself well, cannot withhold a feeling of admiration mingled with a certain envy.

The political ideas of Pascal, which we have outlined here, are in many respects related to those of other contemporary theorists. From the ruins of the political thinking of the Christian Middle Ages there developed two trends of thought, which appear in all sorts of combinations and mixtures. With one of these trends, the doctrine of natural law, Pascal has nothing in common. Nor, it goes without saying, is his thinking in any way related to the older, Catholic form of natural law developed by Thomism, for he did not recognize the idea of a law innate in all men, except perhaps in the Hobbesian form of a natural law that is simply the right of the stronger. But he is very close to the other trend, the empirical statecraft or *raison d'état* of absolutism, generally thought to have originated with Machiavelli. No doubt it had lost some of its spice and freshness since Machiavelli; the free elegance, compounded of Tuscan wit and humanistic boldness, had given way to juridical or pragmatico-political treatises, setting forth systems of politics which were usually methodic but often somewhat fantastic, based on ideas that one may approve or reject, but scarcely love or hate. Pascal's ideas are close to the theorists of *raison d'état*, particularly his contemporary Thomas Hobbes. Hobbes, too, regarded human nature as evil; to curb it, he too demanded a strong state, unimpeded by moral laws, and he demanded absolute obedience to this state, which alone can guarantee peace and prevent revolution. For Hobbes as for Pascal the laws of the state have no juridical basis other than its power; hence we owe them unconditional obedience but

no inward faith, just as we owe the state certain sacrifices but no heartfelt
devotion. Hobbes's construction is a pure police state, and as has often been
noted, this state with all its deployment of force is designed to safeguard the
freedom, or better still, the tranquillity of the individual. Pascal comes very
close to this, but since in his thinking negative concern for the tranquillity
of the individual is replaced by a positive preoccupation with man's immortal
soul, the same ideas take on an entirely different coloring. Like Hobbes he
stresses the necessity and legitimacy of a powerful state, but he is much
more profoundly aware that this "legitimacy" is evil. In Pascal we have not
so much a bargain between the state and the individual—in which the individual owes the state obedience and material sacrifices in return for peace
and security—as Christian submission to the evil of this world, regardless
of whether or not the evil offers the individual any counterpart. In Pascal,
too, the purpose or rather the natural function of power is to create and
preserve peace—in this connection he cites Luke 11:21; but even if the
individual gains nothing by this, even if he suffers perpetual oppression and
never gains peace, he must obey. Here Pascal disregards all the theorists of
the Renaissance and the Middle Ages and goes back to St. Augustine, whose
radicalism he even surpasses. St. Augustine had taught that all government
on earth, all power of man over man is a consequence of original sin; without
the injustice of the original sin, which had destroyed the natural peace and
equality among men, there would be no need for punishment, for the coun-
terinjustice of human power on earth. In the hope of future liberation the
Christian must patiently obey this power imposed upon him as a penance:
*donec transeat iniquitas, et evacuetur omnis principatus et potestas humana, et sit
Deus omnia in omnibus* (*De civitate Dei*, 19, 15, citing Ps. 56:2 and 1 Cor.
15:24). From this one can infer that the Christian owes obedience to power
even when it is evil, but not that earthly power must necessarily be evil.
We may conclude (for example, from the chapter on the *paterfamilias*) that
in St. Augustine's opinion a Christian state could perfectly well use its power
for good earthly ends, although the power of man over man, in itself as an
institution, is an evil made necessary by original sin. But Pascal, living in
the midst of Christian states, lumped the two orders of evil together. For
him power as an institution is an evil deriving from original sin, whence it
follows that no exercise of it can be anything but injustice and folly.

   In order to arrive at this extreme conclusion, Pascal needed the nominalistic and pessimistic ideas of the theorists of *raison d'état*; he combined
them with Augustinianism, so creating a system which despite its appearance
of radical Christianity, contained many secular elements and even the germs
of a revolutionary social criticism. Nearly all the theorists of *raison d'état* had

more or less radically—some approvingly, others disclosing an element of horror—taught that if the state were really to fulfill its ends, it could not adhere to moral laws; fraud and cunning, treason and violence, were permissible; the justice of the state went as far as its might and was based on it. Pascal accepted this much. But the theorists were interested in the state for its own sake; they took it as a value in itself. Like Machiavelli they delighted in its dynamic vitality, or like Hobbes they took a keen interest in the benefit that a properly constructed state can confer on man here and now. All this was totally indifferent to Pascal. For him the inner dynamic of the state did not exist, and if it had existed, he would have regarded it as fundamentally evil. He combined the doctrine of *raison d'état* with Augustinianism and so arrived at the paradox of might as a pure evil, which one must obey unquestioningly, without regard for any possible benefit, but also without devotion, or rather from devotion to God.

JEAN-JACQUES DEMOREST

Pascal's Sophistry and the Sin of Poesy

Is Pascal a sophist? Voltaire wanted to believe it, Valéry as well, and recent
critics have sought to establish the fact. This critical tradition, clearly Voltairian in origin yet romantic in its trappings, has proceeded artfully: extolling
the writer, berating the thinker. Divide to conquer. A Solomonlike justice
threatens to sever dialectic man in two. The author of the Wager is offered
a dire choice: half-survive as a brilliant stylist or perish as a dangerous,
beguiling impostor. In no case is a paradoxical answer tolerated.

We wonder. Is the apparent opposition between a man aloof from the
grasping love of his neighbor and a man bent on saving the same neighbor,
between the solitary figure and the apologist, between the cynic and the
enraptured hoper — is this intense dichotomy rooted in Pascal's personality
or is it a figment of our own imagination? Where does the contradiction lie?
In us? In Pascal? Or in both? Did Pascal, in fact, lack rigor and constancy?
Was he unfaithful to his doctrine? In short, did he betray his ideal or are
we *incapables d'épouser les contraires?* Who is the sophist?

In condemning Pascal, the Voltairian tradition, best illustrated today
by the Marxist Henri Lefebvre, has repeatedly scored three aspects of the
Pensées: the Wager, the *pensée de derrière*, and the famed "Le silence éternel
de ces espaces infinis m'effraie" (Pensée 428; all Pascal references cite the
Brunschvicg edition). The arguments bearing on the Wager are too hack-
neyed and too mathematical in nature to be of much interest here. The other

From *Studies in Seventeenth-Century French Literature Presented to Morris Bishop*, edited
by Jean-Jacques Demorest. © 1962 by Cornell University. Cornell University Press,
1962.

two, however, and particularly the *pensée de derrière*, rarely discussed, may bear further examination.

We are not so much dealing with the overt old quarrel between belief and disbelief in the present case as with a tangential quarrel over literary perfection. The problem can be put succinctly: Is poetry a sin? For strangely enough, Pascal is being accused of poetry, and those who would brand him as a sinner untrue to his tenets profess to be atheists. By implication it is suggested, and later asserted, that brilliant writing must somehow hide shallowness of content and sophistry of intent. The counts of the indictment, then, are rather subtle. Pascal's thought is not impugned directly. The first step consists in sparing no praise of the remarkable faculties of the stylist; the second step questions the motives of a man who writes too well. From there the problem of the impurity of perfection is raised, and finally it is deduced that so dazzling a prose masks the agony of a tortured and deceitful conscience. Did Spinoza or Descartes feel the urge to compose a rhapsodically beautiful prose? Surely something is amiss in a man of austere religious convictions who nurtures the cadence of imagery and studies painstakingly the art of persuasion. Lefebvre infers that had Pascal polished his style less the sincerity of his thought would be less doubtful and moribund Christianity would have gasped a little while longer—all told then, it is really fortunate that the artifacts of poetry hastened the decay of faith!

It is an easy matter to mock the champions of the Voltairian tradition. For one thing, they are from the outset at an ungraceful disadvantage, obliged to interpret a man whose very being is bound to a vision of the world which they can neither share nor comprehend. They remain at a distance and cannot penetrate his position enough to undermine him significantly. Still their accusation of sophistry carries weight, if only because it is accepted by many today—among others by Claudel and Simone Weil, who can scarcely be regarded as devotees of Ferney. In truth, our times may be dubbed the Pascalian Age, yet the impeachment of Pascal has rarely been as concentrated, imposing, and imaginative.

There is some indication that Paul Valéry's concise condemnation renewed and revived a Voltairian tradition that had suffered somewhat at the hands of hotheaded romanticists. Indeed, the basic argument employed by Valéry was novel and, given the character of the accuser, nothing short of sensational: art suspected, poetry decried. Pascal incriminated for an abuse of the very qualities that should have secured him the admiring amity of the creator of *Charmes*, a fellow amateur in science and geometry. It was unexpected. Possibly Pascal owes this dolorous honor to the peculiar intellectual development of a poet who was determined at that precise moment *not* to resolve his own dialectical make-up and to use this specific confrontation as a hygienic exercise in a newly devised critical attitude: criticism *ab absurdo*, or more exactly criticism predicated on alienation, criticism based on a stanchly assumed antipathy towards the object of inquiry. Pascal proved to be an ideal opponent.

In Valéry, on the other hand, the aggressive converter encountered the most deliberately prejudiced but the most challenging adversary he had met in more than a century. The clash was as short and as lucidly cruel as Valéry's essay. Despite its forceful reverberations, which we intend to review here, it is not clear that Pascal came out the worst. For one thing, our contemporaries reading Valéry's Pythagorean arraignment are likely to judge the poet's arguments on their purely objective merits and not on the efficacy of the interior catharsis enjoyed by Valéry. Egotism has a limited posthumous appeal; its survival value is at best uncertain.

Essentially the poet is accusing Pascal of attaining unholy rhetorical ends through poetry. Or to dramatize the situation, the charge is: Impure Poetry.

The brief essay devoted to this crimination, "Variation sur une 'pensée,' " is based entirely on "Le silence éternel. . . ." Perhaps we should consider it as an improvisation and no more censure Valéry for his excessive rendition of the original than we would dare cavil at Mozart for the fanciful liberties he takes with a theme of Haydn's. There is a difference though: Mozart is not openly criticizing Haydn. Furthermore, Valéry's *variation* has become in time the source of a great number of other aggravated variations.

The poet insists on two aspects: silence and fright. It does not even come to his mind that Pascal's *pensée* should be attributed to the unbeliever. The reason for this lack of perceptiveness is to be found in Valéry's unconscious adherence to the Voltairian tradition as elaborated and made theatrical by the romanticists. In reality, his debt to the romanticists is far greater than we first allowed.

The tone gives him away. For instance, speaking of Pascal's intelligence: "La contemplation ne manque jamais de la faire hurler à la mort. Elle me fait songer invinciblement à cet aboi insupportable qu'adressent les chiens à la lune." And even when he mocks the romanticists' propensity to depict a tragic, Hamletlike Pascal, Valéry's approach remains romantic. His purposeful exaggeration of Pascal's despair, solitude, and terror is patently romantic. In effect, Valéry is not writing a variation on a *pensée* of Pascal; he is merely composing a brilliant improvisation on a romantic theme.

Elsewhere in the essay his tie to Voltaire is evident, and it is in this renewal and intensification of the Voltairian tradition that Valéry's originality lies. The contention is that the *misanthrope sublime* was guilty of argumentative duplicity and rhetorical insincerity. Neither Valéry nor Voltaire fully grasp the tactical implications of writing an *Apology*; they choose to ignore the apologetical requisites of the genre and consider the *Pensées* as entirely personal reflections which Pascal somehow wishes to impose on humanity. They do not sense the strong contradiction of their own position, nor do they make any provision for the fact that the *Pensées* are an unfinished work. Valéry, nevertheless, leads the disputation to higher ground, to a poetic ground that Voltaire was not too well qualified to appreciate. He, for one, does not call Pascal a *fourbe*, finding it more telling to stigmatize the Jansenist as too much of a poet:

> Une phrase bien accordée exclut la renonciation totale. Une détresse qui écrit bien n'est pas si achevée qu'elle n'ait sauvé du naufrage quelque liberté de l'esprit. . . . Il y a aussi je ne sais quoi de trouble, et je ne sais quoi de facile, dans la spécialité que l'on se fait des motifs tragiques et des objets impressionnants. . . . Je ne suis pas à mon aise devant ce mélange de l'art avec la nature. Quand je vois l'écrivain reprendre et empirer la véritable sensation de l'homme, y ajouter des forces recherchées, et vouloir toutefois que l'on prenne son industrie pour son émotion, je trouve que cela est impur et ambigu. . . . Je vois trop la main de Pascal. D'ailleurs quand même les intention seraient pures, le seul souci d'écrire, et le soin que l'on y apporte one le même effet naturel qu'une arrière-pensée.

Finally, Valéry implies that Pascal's philosophy was static. The manner in which he dismisses the theme of the *recherche*, so central to an understanding of the *Pensées*, is rather disquieting:

> Pascal avait "trouvé," mais sans doute parce qu'il ne cherchait plus. La cessation de la recherche, et la forme de cette cessation, peuvent donner le sentiment de la trouvaille. Mais il n'a jamais eu de foi dans la recherche en tant qu'elle espère dans l'imprévu.

The next and concluding step in Valéry's demonstration brings out the real cause of irritation:

> Il a tiré de soi-même le *silence éternel* que ni les hommes véritablement religieux, ni les hommes véritablement profonds n'ont jamais observé dans l'univers. Il a exagéré affreusement, grossièrement, l'opposition de la connaissance et du salut.

It is Valéry the mathematician, the amateur scientist, who is hurt to the quick. It is the scientist who is accusing Pascal of poetry. A just retribution; after all, had not Pascal himself leveled the accusation of *Poet* with a measure of contempt?

Obviously, Valéry does not care to understand Pascal. And perhaps this misunderstanding is more revealing than would be permissive agreement—that is, so long as the calculated quality of Valéry's opposition is well delineated. Such is not the case, however, with those who have taken Valéry's thesis over and, in the name of Marxism, have prosecuted the criminal investigation of Pascal's sophistry. Henri Lefebvre, for one, in his exposition and general espousal of Valéry's view, fails to mention that Valéry deliberately founded his criticism of Pascal on a sort of systematic egotistic malevolence, the object of which was to exercise and sharpen the critical tools while carrying on intellectual calisthenics salutary to the critic (*Pascal*). As a matter of fact, in *Autres Rhumbs*, Valéry explains his method of purposeful antipathy:

> La haine habite l'adversaire, en développe les profondeurs, dissèque les plus délicates racines des desseins qu'il a dans le coeur. Nous le pénétrons mieux que nous-mêmes, et mieux qu'il ne fait soi-même. Il s'oublie et nous ne l'oublions pas. Car nous le percevons au moyen d'une blessure, et il n'est pas de sens plus cuisant, qui grandisse et précise plus fortement ce qui touche, qu'une partie blessée de l'être.

This profession of faith in cultural sadism is perhaps more eloquent than efficacious—at least as regards Pascal.

In the case of Henri Lefebvre, however, there is no attempt to elucidate the peculiar viewpoint of Valéry. The major counts of the indictment are taken over with added virulence and with only a few corrections:

> Alors le visionnaire s'épouvante. . . . Il a commencé par tuer, en pensée, l'homme; et voici que le ciel reflète impitoyablement le désert terrestre. . . . Pascal va se tirer d'affaire en prétendant que ce qu'on cherche, on l'a déjà trouvé. . . . Le cri solitaire se répand au loin dans l'espace désert qu'il ne peut remplir. Mais que nous sommes loin du sanglot balbutiant auquel parviendront les poètes avec Rimbaud, avec Lautréamont, et qu'ils auront bientôt transformé à nouveau en beau style, en littérature. Valéry, qui s'y connaissait en littérature a bien senti la grande froideur du style pascalien. . . . Oui, mais Valéry n'a pas su voir combien le cri

angoissé de Pascal—angoissé malgré la réussite brillante, trop
brillante, du style—révèle le conflit douloureux des deux mondes:
celui de la science, celui de la religion. . . . Pascal symbolise la
situation de son temps.

This brief passage is indicative of the durability of the romantico-Vol-
tairian tradition within the Marxist framework. It also illustrates a contemporary tendency to allege fascination for Pascal the stylist before being led,
through the vagaries of historical research, to the "amazing" discovery of his
sophistry. For our purpose here we propose to use Lefebvre's intelligent and
biased interpretation as a provocative means of arriving at some definition
of the modern incrimination of Pascal as a sophist.

The premise, grossly simplified, can be summarized as follows: Pascal
is a Jansenist; Jansenism gave French classicism its myths, poetry, prag-
matism, taste, and its concern for literary perfection; in fact Jansenism is,
seen from another angle, a major element of classical stylization, itself a
reflection of the bourgeoisie's bad conscience. Pascal, as much by syllogistic
inference within the terms of the argument as by observation of the real
facts, was the leading Jansenist writer; hence, the man called upon to express
and stylize his time, in other words to reduce, mummify, and lie superbly:

Il exprime l'humanité de son temps, et *propose* une image de
l'homme, image illusoire et provisoire qu'il *impose* à force d'art.

L'étonnant, le stupéfiant, c'est que l'on puisse une seconde
prendre ce caractère stylistique pour un signe de vérité; au lieu
de considérer aussitôt avec méfiance cette forme d'affirmation.

Le trait, la force, l'éclat des formules pascaliennes tiennent aussi
à leur déficience idéologique.

This last claim is undoubtedly harder to establish. What is adduced is
that philosophy too well rendered becomes mere literature and falsehood.
Lefebvre, if he deigned, would have no difficulty, however, in mustering
support for his claim. Albert Bayet goes nearly as far: "Ses raisonnements
ne valent point. Il le sait. Mais l'important n'est pas qu'ils vaillent, c'est qu'ils
touchent (*Les "Pensées" de Pascal*). The frenetical interpretation of a Victor
Delbet, too excessive to be analyzed here, goes far beyond that of either
Bayet or Lefebvre. The latter, more moderate, still leads us to consider
Pascal not as a thinker but as an unholy artificer, a littérateur; worse yet, a
Jesuit!

Si les *Provinciales*, comme les *Pensées*, ont subi un déplacement et sont devenues pour nous une oeuvre d'art, seules certaines conditions initiales ont permis ce déplacement. . . . Pascal introduit la littérature dans la théorie et la métaphysique. Grandeur et décadence. . . . Jésuitisme! Quelle distance entre la haute sincérité du Discours cartésien et les *Provinciales*.

In this manner literature and Jesuitism, casuistry and poetry, are closely associated. Nor does Pascal's wit enjoy the privilege of any redeeming grace; on the contrary, wit is a sign of Christian decadence: "Il a fixé l'attitude chrétienne théorique en l'installant dans l'absence de sérieux devant la divine tragédie à laquelle elle feint encore de croire." From pleasantry to hypocrisy, a flattering progress! And Pascal wends a crooked path that ends in sheer blackmail, stylistic blackmail: "Ce tissu de banalités médiévales, ces thèmes des fresques et des développements oratoires, reprennent une valeur à cause du style. Ici, style égale chantage." Finally exposed, it will henceforth be Pascal's dubious honor to go down in history as *le grand désenchanteur, spécialiste du chantage à l'éternité*.

There is no doubt, though, that the central issue is Pascal's sophistry and his heinous sin poetry. We do not intend to survey the rest of Lefebvre's views nor even to refute those that concern us when they slip, as they do occasionally, into heavy-handed buffoonery. But what, in general, can be said in Pascal's defense?

There is no effective parry to the accusation of perfection, but it is hoped that in time this trait of Pascal's will no longer be considered quite so infamous. The seventeenth century cherished a style of unnatural naturalness; we cherish one of natural unnaturalness. The conflict between order and disorder, between a neat and a slovenly nature is too arduous to resolve—all the more so that Pascal's style in the *Pensées* comes closer to reconciling the two manners than any other work we can think of.

Much can be alleged in defense of his "sophistry," nevertheless. In the first place, a certain degree of ambiguity unavoidably stems from Pascal's description of a "median man" with whose condition and situation he identifies himself totally: "C'est sortir de l'humanité que de sortir du milieu. La grandeur de l'âme humaine consiste à savoir s'y tenir" (378). Albeit he may risk equivocation in formulating the discourses that express man's ambivalent position, Pascal will not demur from his stubborn conviction that the ambiguity of man is real. It is in any case a measured risk, for his repeated declarations of hatred for equivocation are illumined by his acts. When Nicole and Arnauld propose a clever solution to the obligatory signing of the *for-mulaire*, wherein by the use of equivocal language a good Jansenist might soothe his conscience and blind Rome, Pascal strongly rejects the proposed wording as *une voie moyenne, qui est abominable devant Dieu, méprisable devant les hommes*. In his mind, the ambiguity of man's condition is no excuse for generalized sophistry and mediocrity; the *milieu* is less an inert point of rest than the active center of man's racking between the two infinites.

That incessant torture and joy of a man who partakes of two natures is expressed in motion by a contrapuntal style which even affects matters as supposedly abstract as force and justice:

> La justice sans la force est impuissante; la force sans la justice est tyrannique. La justice sans force est contredite, parce qu'il y a toujours des méchants; la force sans la justice est accusée. Il faut donc mettre ensemble la justice et la force; et pour cela faire que ce qui est juste soit fort, ou que ce qui est fort soit juste.
>
> La justice est sujette à dispute, la force est très reconnaissable et sans dispute. Ainsi on n'a pu donner la force à la justice, parce que la force contredit la justice et a dit que c'était elle qui était juste. Et ainsi ne pouvant faire que ce qui est juste fût fort, on a fait que ce qui est fort fût juste.

(298)

Admirable as the counterpoint may be, is it fair to assume that brilliance deters from thought; or worse, that it glitters over empty banalities? Does not in fact stylistic perfection sharpen our understanding and enliven the idea? To impose the view that philosophical truth and literary perfection are inexorably incompatible is more often than not outright guile. Beauty is not necessarily impure.

It must be recognized, however, that Pascal's utter command of style can create a galling impression of self-assurance—a circumstance all the more ironical inasmuch as one of the purposes of his seeking perfection was to arrive at a sort of primeval simplicity in which his presence would be completely sacrificed and the reader would enjoy the satisfaction of being in direct contact with the thought. This ideal, obviously not attained, implied a measure of adjustment and compromise—"L'art de persuader a un rapport nécessaire à la manière dont les hommes consentent à ce qu'on leur propose, et aux conditions des choses qu'on veut faire croire" (*Esprit géométrique*)—not, however, to the point of depravation: " 'Dites-nous des choses agréables et nous vous écouterons' disent les Juifs à Moïse; comme si l'agrément devait régler la créance" (*loc. cit.*); "Il faut de l'agréable et du réel; mais il faut que l'agréable soit lui-même pris du vrai" (25). It would be strange indeed if a writer so aware of the psychological rules of his art, a man so intransigently suspicious of his own motives, should fall into the pitfalls of designedly deceptive reasoning.

Of course one cannot deny the existence of such a danger, particularly when Pascal and his unbeliever are locked in a fraternal dialectic combat: "S'il se vante, je l'abaisse; s'il s'abaisse, je le vante; et le contredis toujours jusqu'à ce qu'il comprenne qu'il est un monstre incompréhensible" (420). One of the major problems in the study of the *Pensées* is to determine who exactly is speaking, Pascal or the interlocutor. And what sort of a man (or of men) is that unbelieving interlocutor? There cannot fail to be, in so "impure" a genre as an apologetic dialogue, a slight degree of composition, of "sophistry." One simply does not speak to others as one speaks to oneself. It is a sign of reality and of integrity if in such a dialogue concessions to the other person do seep in. Were these concessions absent, there would be strong reasons to cry out against the author's sophistry. As matters stand, the important and debatable problem is that of the interlocutor's general identity.

The major accusations of sophistry aimed at Pascal are founded on the tenuous contention that nearly everything in the *Pensées* represents the author's beliefs or *is* the author. Maurice de Gandillac, for example, accepts the interpretation of Valéry and Lefebvre: confronted with the silence of the universe, Pascal is expressing his own fright and not that of the unbeliever. To this we might reply that expressions of fright appear only in passages having an oral ring that single them out as elements of a future dialogue and probably as statements of the unbeliever. We make this last inference because *all* the expressions of fright occur in passages easily ascribable to the unbeliever, but only ascribable to Pascal at the price of considerable sleight of hand. Were that fearful awe really Pascal's, would it not be seen in his other works and in the numerous fragments of the *Pensées* where indubitably only he is present? Such is not the case. An accusation of sophistry based on *le silence éternel*, such as that of Valéry, loses its vigor when the texts are closely examined.

The real difficulty, the source of most misunderstandings that are not deliberate, lies in the incompleteness of the *Pensées*. It is so trite an observation, and yet. . . . If we take as an example a collective work written by specialists, such as the interesting printed text of the Royaumont colloquium, we are appalled by the irrelevance of the erudite commentaries. Eminent historians of ideology weave fascinating and esoteric explications around Pascal. They tie him to remote figures he never read and interpret him by comparison to philosophical currents nonexistent in France between 1650 and 1660. This subtle and learned obfuscation, which at times waxes caustic, stems from a common reluctance to remember two facts: Pascal is bent on converting an unbeliever, not on expounding a metaphysical system; and the *Pensées* are not a definitive work, only notes and summary reflections. We would like to go further and suggest that the *Pensées* should not even be read as an Apology, but only as tactical projects and sketches. The author of the *Pensées* was an ardent young general surveying the forces at his command, improvising on the field; he was not a venerable marshal spinning tales of conquest during the long glowing evenings in comfortable winter quarters. In the thick of battle, he even loses a distinct notion of his identity. He is not seeking personal glorification but victory over unbelief and indifference. Eventually carried away by the storming of the objective, he subordinates his own individuality to that of the unbeliever, increases and exaggerates the unbeliever's rapid consciousness of self. The depersonalization of the author is directly proportionate to the overpersonalization of the unbeliever. Battles are dusty or muddy; there are long moments of indecision and confusion. The reader can in good faith mistake the unbeliever's cry for Pascal's, but he has little ground for censuring that cry as "sophistry" or for describing the battle as "theatrical disorder."

There are certainly other, more solid, causes of the recent charges of "sophistry"—we shall not discuss those springing from political or religious biases. One possible cause, less farfetched than may first appear, is suggested vaguely by a sentence in Valéry's essay: "D'ailleurs, quand même les intentions seraient pures, le seul souci d'écrire, et le soin qu'on y apporte ont le même effet naturel qu'une arrière-pensée." In reality, Pascal would have agreed with Valéry, even allowing that his own intentions were not entirely pure (see Pensée 150). Furthermore, his definition of the *art de persuader* is, in a way, an avowed recognition of the role the *arrière-pensée* plays in a successful rhetoric. The theme, in truth, is dear to Pascal; more colorfully, he refers to the *pensée de derrière*. Noting the frequency with which it provokes sarcastic reproaches of "Jesuitry" and "duplicity" on the part of critics, we have come to wonder whether it is not at the heart of the image of a sophistic Pascal. In any event it is central to Pascal's thought and to his being—hence, we trust, worth studying.

The *pensée de derrière* takes on various aspects and in Pascal's earlier works goes under several names. We shall try to outline its inception and evolution. Speaking with praise of Montaigne to M. de Saci, Pascal says of the essayist:

> Il conclut . . . qu'on doit prendre le vrai et le bien sur la première apparence, sans les presser . . . il agit comme les autres hommes; et tout ce qu'ils font dans la sotte pensée qu'ils suivent le vrai bien, il le fait par un autre principe.
>
> (*Entretien avec M. de Saci*)

This superficial conceit and necessary deceit derive, in fact, from a recognition of man's unconscious deceit of self: "C'est une maladie naturelle à l'homme de croire qu'il possède la vérité directement . . . au lieu qu'en effet il ne connaît naturellement que le mensonge" (*Esprit géométrique*). Unable to share the credulity of the islanders who mistake him for their long-lost king, the castaway nevertheless acts as a king, knowing full well that he is not: "Il cachait cette dernière pensée, et il découvrait l'autre" (*Premier Discours sur la condition des grands*). And Pascal, addressing himself more directly yet to the young son of the duc de Luynes, the future duc de Chevreuse, admonishes him: "Vous devez avoir, comme cet homme dont nous avons parlé, une double pensée . . . une pensée plus cachée mais plus véritable" (*loc. cit.*). Here truth is concealed, no longer out of a type of arrogant indifference towards others, but on the contrary out of humility and wisdom. The seeking out of truth is based on a refusal of society's values and on a deliberate effort of introspection: "Nous haïssons la vérité, on nous la cache; nous voulons être flattés, on nous flatte: nous aimons à être trompés, on nous trompe" (100). And the end is accomplished when Pascal, or the unbeliever, finally states: "J'aurai aussi mes pensées de derrière la tête" (310).

What is the origin of the *pensée de derrière* in Pascal? What is its significance? We shall have to find our own answer; none of Pascal's sympathizers or accusers treat the subject directly. We might, nevertheless, apply a general statement of Lefebvre's to this specific case; it would probably be the sort of response our question would elicit from Pascal's detractors:

> Au XVIIᵉ, le malaise inexplicable, le déchirement secret, aboutirent à une nuance tout à fait particulière du tragique: un sentiment profond et discret, le sentiment d'une blessure secrète et inguérissable, la conscience d'une douleur un peu honteuse que "l'honnête homme" dissimulait sous la politesse, sous l'etiquette, sous le style.

There is a fascination about such a sweeping prejudice encompassing all of history. The weakness, of course, lies in any system's inability to provide for the exceptional personality. And are we sure that man's psyche is determined by social forces, rather than vice versa? We shall have to pursue cautiously our analysis of the *pensée de derrière*.

The very notion implies a certain secretiveness, more akin to humility or to muzzled pride, as we saw above, than to deceit. The beginning of the *Entretien avec M. de Saci* may offer a clue, Pascal is commending the view Epictetus holds of man: "Il veut qu'il soit humble, qu'il cache ses bonnes résolutions, surtout dans le commencement et qu'il les accomplisse en secret; rien ne les ruine davantage que de les produire." This secretiveness, indicative of a personality and perhaps of a philosophy, appears even in small matters: "Je me moque de ceux qui disent que le temps me dure à moi, et que j'en juge par fantaisie: ils ne savent pas que je juge par ma montre" (5).

The notion of a concealed truth and a universally respected falsehood may account for the inclination towards what Pascal's detractors dub sophistry: "Lorsqu'on ne sait pas la vérité d'une chose, il est bon qu'il y ait une erreur commune qui fixe l'esprit des hommes" (18). Pascal, though, was acutely aware of the danger and relied upon his own *esprit de finesse* to guide him: "Il faut de l'agréable et du réel; mais il faut que cet agréable soit lui-même pris du vrai" (25).

Cacher, recéler, serrer (in the sense of "set aside," "hide") recur frequently in his vocabulary, often in banal circumstances that are nevertheless revealing of the man: "Les choses qui nous tiennent le plus, comme de cacher son peu de bien, ce n'est souvent presque rien: c'est un néant que notre imagination grossit en montagne" (85). The constant in the vocabulary reminds us of Pascal's own secretive acts of charity and penance: the hidden *Mémorial* sewn in his doublet, the immediate assistance to the young girl near Saint-Sulpice, the working family taken into his lodgings, his love of poverty, the belt of spikes which he concealed under his shirt; and other acts which have remained unknown:

> Les belles actions cachées sont les plus estimables . . . mais enfin elles n'ont pas été tout à fait cachées, puisqu'elles ont été sues; et quoi qu'on ait fait ce qu'on a pu pour les cacher, ce peu par où elles ont paru gâte tout; car c'est là le plus beau, de les avoir voulu cacher.

(159)

This inclination towards withdrawal and a deepening inner experience played an obvious role in Pascal's religious life, and perhaps sprang from it. As a matter of fact, the *Instruction* by Singlin, which, it is related, determined Pascal's ultimate conversion, is constructed around the idea that Christian perfection should remain *inconnue et secrète aux hommes*. Moreover, this inner

deepening is characterized, logically enough, by a degree of indifferent do-
cility to the exterior world, social or political. In Pascal's view the advantages
abandoned are of little value compared to the priceless inner freedom of spirit
acquired—and in a sense the Wager is centered on this uneven barter. The
same process applies to faith itself, and the ultimate consequence is a new
and higher aspect of the *pensée de derrière:*

> Il faut que l'extérieur soit joint à l'intérieur pour obtenir de Dieu;
> c'est-à-dire que l'on se mette à genoux, prie des lèvres, etc. . . .
> Attendre de cet extérieur le secours est être superstitieux, ne
> vouloir pas le joindre à l'intérieur est être superbe.
>
> (250)

> Les autres religions, comme les païennes, sont plus populaires,
> car elles sont en extérieur; mais elles ne sont pas pour les gens
> habiles. Une religion purement intellectuelle serait plus propor-
> tionée aux habiles; mais elle ne servirait pas au peuple. La seule
> religion chrétienne est proportionnée à tous, étant mêlée d'extér-
> ieur et d'intérieur. Elle élève le peuple à l'intérieur, et abaisse les
> superbes à l'extérieur; et n'est pas parfaite sans les deux, car il
> faut que le peuple entende l'esprit de la lettre, et que les habiles
> soumettent leur esprit à la lettre.
>
> (251)

The gist of our interpretation is that the *pensée de derrière* is founded
more upon religious conviction than upon purely political expediency or
obscure class frustrations. In a perspective such as ours, then, the above
example of submissiveness to the letter, and by extension, to the state and
to the corrupt temporality of our physical being, is in essence a preliminary
act of faith, an introductory exercise in humility. In any case, it seems
undeniable that the *pensée de derrière* is closely linked to the conception of a
hidden God:

> Toutes choses couvrent quelque mystère; toutes choses sont des
> voiles qui couvrent Dieu. Les Chrétiens doivent le reconnaître
> en tout.
>
> (*Fourth letter to the Roannez*)

> L'Ecriture . . . dit au contraire que Dieu est un Dieu caché.
>
> (242)

> Au lieu de vous plaindre de ce que Dieu s'est caché, vous lui
> rendrez grâces de ce qu'il s'est tant découvert.
>
> (288)

Toute religion qui ne dit pas que Dieu est caché n'est pas véritable.

(585)

There is no scarcity of such examples; but the link between faith in a hidden God and the nearly religious necessity of practicing the *pensée de derrière* is better elucidated in fragment 337, where it is considered in the various stages leading to Christian perfection:

> *Raison des effets.*—Gradation. Le peuple honore les personnes de grande naissance. Les demi-habiles les méprisent, disant que la naissance n'est pas un avantage de la personne, mais du hasard. Les habiles les honorent, non par la pensée du peuple, mais par la pensée de derrière. Les dévots qui ont plus de zèle que de science les méprisent, malgré cette considération qui les fait honorer pas les habiles, parce qu'ils en jugent par une nouvelle lumière que la piété leur donne. Mais les chrétiens parfaits les honorent par une autre lumière supérieure.

Here, quite clearly, the *pensée de derrière* does not represent the light of charity, but the median *order* characteristic of the *habiles*. Hence it would belong to the order of reason and be only a mundane, intellectual reflection of the *lumière supérieure;* yet in many passages, Pascal, a believer, a man who aspires to the higher, spiritual perception, ascribes the *pensée de derrière* to himself. This slight ambiguity, perhaps exaggerated by our own commentary, derives naturally from the fact that man by his very condition, no matter how perfect, must partake of the two lower orders. In a way the *pensée de derrière* leads to the order of charity; it is a perspective in which the *contraires* coexist and it is cognizance of the contrasting forces. If it were purely rational it would be communicable, but in fact it scarcely is. It is both the secret of the *habile* and the treasure of the saint. After all, the power of thought is hidden within the frailty of the *roseau pensant*. At times the reader gathers the impression that the capacity to develop a *pensée de derrière* is truly a God-given privilege and that the hidden message it withholds is a view of the world seen in God's eyes or a nearly rational disclosure of divine judgment and grace. The terms used by the unbeliever during the dialogue of the Wager are rather revealing: "Mais encore n'y a-t-il point moyen de voir le dessous du jeu?—Oui, l'Ecriture, et le reste."

Undoubtedly the *pensée de derrière* is a faculty that contributes to isolation of the individual. Still it is not to be discarded: "Il faut avoir une pensée de derrière et juger de tout par là, en parlant cependant comme le peuple" (336). Duplicity? No, its practice is old and respected; Plato observed it: "Le plus

sage législateur disait que pour le bien des hommes, il faut souvent les piper"
(294). Pascal also speakes of Plato and Aristotle *acting as if* their political
treatises were solemn and serious things, whereas in fact they were writing
laws for a lunatic humanity (331). The cruelty of the perception afforded
by the *pensée de derrière* is so naked that Pascal could scarcely imagine exposing
and teaching it to all men; and one wonders at the rare qualities of the young
man to whom such verities were dealt:

> Mais si vous étiez duc sans être honnête homme, je vous ferais
> encore justice: car en vous rendant les devoirs extérieurs que
> l'ordre des hommes a attachés à votre naissance, je ne manquerais
> pas d'avoir pour vous le mépris intérieur que mériterait la bassesse
> de votre esprit.
>
> *(Second Discours sur la condition des grands)*

The question has an interesting scientific facet. In the course of a dialogue with a fictitious supporter of the theory of a finite universe, Pascal's
retort brings the point home: "Il ne faut pas dire qu'il y a ce qu'on ne voit
pas.—Il faut donc dire comme les autres, mais ne pas penser comme eux"
(266). Here the patience and prudence which Pascal demonstrated as a scientist are brought out succinctly. He defers breaking with public opinion
until he has at hand positive experimental evidence to back his intuition of
the existence of infinite matter, time, and space; and in the meantime he will
still recognize the validity of scientific laws of which he is no longer sure.
In effect, he illustrated this strict observance of a pragmatic form of the *pensée
de derrière* during the protracted experiments on vacuum and the weight of
air. By the same token we can, perhaps, attribute his contradictory opinion
of the Copernican system to the *pensée de derrière*, which appears once again
as an earnest scientific scruple and not as sophistry.

Thus the *pensée de derrière* informs the attitude of the savant, of the
political thinker, and of the Christian. In fact it is a sign of universality: "Les
gens universels ne sont appelés ni poètes, ni géomètres, etc. . . . mais ils
sont tout cela et juges de tous ceux-là. On ne les devine point" (34). Pascal
normally refers to these universal beings—here possessing an inner secret—
as *honnêtes hommes*. They at least sought belief and probably were believers.
We have reason to expect that the *honnête homme* will practice some form of
the *pensée de derrière la tête* in proportion to his faith. In truth, is not the *pensée
de derrière* simply an expression of Christian irony, with all of the wounded
detachment that it implies? Is it not the spontaneous reaction of a man of
wit who seems to view this world from elsewhere with a mixture of restive
compassion, amused irritation, and secretive conviction?

Every time one studies Pascal, more new issues are raised than questions solved. The most elusive problem remains not that of Pascal's improbable sophistry but of our own integrity as critics. Sympathy for an author is no substitute for intelligence; but, with regard to Valéry and Lefebvre, intelligence is not a very satisfactory substitute for sympathy either. Gide states that cultivated men read works they do not take to instinctively. Read, yes; but, criticize?

Most of the difficulties—injustices and tortured eulogies—arise from the incompletion of the *Pensées* and from the fact that Pascal, by temperament as an individual, by necessity as an apologist, is a brilliant improviser. He belongs to the race of Mozart and Napoleon, and perhaps of Stendhal. If he is anti-Cartesian it is precisely because he sensed that Cartesianism was capable of leading French thought to mad extremes. He is in many ways a reactionary, a man who reacts excessively to excess.

In the case of his supposed sophistry, time is the culprit or the savior. It has split him in two: the thinker, the stylist. Voltaire, Valéry, Lefebvre, are not entirely at fault. In some ways, instead of aggravating the cleavage, the latter have added a dimension to Pascal and have helped reintegrate him dialectically by renewing a dialogue between Voltaire and himself which is the richest and the longest of the *Dialogues des vivants*.

Time is the Solomon; we are but an awed and divided jury. Nevertheless, an ironic and definitive verdict of "Poète et non honnête homme" does not quite appear in the offing.

LUCIEN GOLDMANN

The Wager: The Christian Religion

A study of Pascal's view of man, of living beings, of the physical universe, of epistemology, ethics, aesthetics and life in society has revealed the permanence of the same basic concept underlying all his ideas: man is a paradoxical being, who is both great and small, and who is equally incapable both of achieving real values in this world and of giving up the quest for them. He is therefore led to place his hope only in religion, and in the existence of a personal and transcendent deity.

There is, however, one further question to be answered: however great and rewarding Pascal's final position may appear on the level of will and of faith, it stands out by its essential poverty when judged by the standards of scientific and philosophical thought, or by those of human achievement in this world.

If the world offers man only the possibility of achieving relative values it can offer a mind governed by the categories of "all or nothing" sufficient interest to justify the devotion of only a very small fraction of his thought and action. Indeed, any interest shown in the vanity of a world empty of God can be the sign only of the sin involved in compromising with the fallen state of the Evil One. The extreme Jansenism of Barcos's group carried this attitude to its logical conclusion by abandoning the world and considering that the ideas of virtue and solitude, of the Christian and of the hermit, were virtually synonymous. But—unlike Pascal—men such as Barcos, Singlin and even Hamon did not leave behind them an analysis of physical and biological

From *The Hidden God: A Study of the Tragic Vision in the* Pensées *of Pascal and the Tragedies of Racine*, translated by Philip Thody. © 1964 by Routledge & Kegan Paul Ltd.

reality, and did not write down their ideas on epistemology, ethics or the social life. If they do mention these subjects it is solely in order to condemn any interest in them, and to remind the Christian that he should devote his life to God and God alone.

How, then, can we explain the fact that Pascal, who shared the views of these men, should not only have indulged in scientific research between 1657 and 1662, writing papers on mathematics and setting up the world's first public transport service, but should also have given us, in the *Pensées*, a detailed and realistic analysis of the relationship between man and the world, and have actually written an apology for religion?

This is not only a problem which the historian encounters as he looks back over the relationship between Pascal and Jansenism. It was also something which was widely discussed by the "Disciples of Saint Augustine," and which deeply affected the different ideological positions that they adopted. Arnauld, Barcos and Pascal were all fully aware, when they took up their own particular attitude, both of what it implied and by what arguments it could be defended. It is therefore not possible to explain the difference between these three men by accidental factors such as temperament or education.

I have already mentioned the different attitudes adopted by Barcos and Pascal and the practical results which these had. While the former refuses the world completely and withdraws into solitude, the latter both refuses the world and at the same time remains in it. In my view, Pascal's attitude stems from the fact that he carries the idea of the hidden God—or, rather, of the God who hides Himself—to the extreme point where he sees God as preventing man from discovering not only His will but also His existence. It is precisely because, for man in his fallen state, the existence of God has become a hope and a certainty of the heart—that is to say, an uncertain and paradoxical certainty—that man can no longer find a sure and certain refuge by simply withdrawing from the world. It is in the world, or at least in the presence of the world, that man must now express both his rejection of any relative values and his quest for values that shall be authentic and transcendent. It is because man in his fallen state no longer sees the existence of God as a pure and simple certainty that Pascal was both able and compelled to work out a theory of the world and of earthly, biological and social reality. And it is because man, in order to be man, cannot in any way accept an inadequate and relative world that this theory could attain so high a degree of realism, and one as free from any taint of worldly compromise or illusion. It is precisely because Pascal both rejected the world and lived in it, because he combined living in it, refusing it and analysing it, that his work attained the highest philosophical and scientific level that a thinker of his time could achieve.

Pascal finds everything in the world inadequate and sees no rest for man as long as he remains in this life. He also, however, denies that man can find a certain and non-paradoxical proof of God's existence and that he can turn away from the world to seek refuge in solitude and eternity. It is this dual attitude which must be explained and understood if we are to have any coherent account of his life and work.

It is the fact that no salvation can be found in an absolutely certain religious faith and in a complete rejection of this world that explains the importance and central position of fragment 233, generally known as the argument of the wager. If in fact—as I shall try to show later—the idea of a wager is also at the heart of the Hegelian and Marxist positions it is also completely at odds with the views adopted by most Christian thinkers both before and after Pascal, for whom such an argument is merely a useful *ad hominem* approach in apologetics. Such thinkers always see the existence of God, and, very often the will of God, as revealed to man in an absolutely convincing manner. They may base their arguments on reason or intuition, but they always reject the idea of risk or paradox in religious faith. This habit has led most Pascalian scholars to put forward an interpretation of the wager which I cannot accept. One does not, they say, wager on the existence of something of which one has certain knowledge. Moreover, they continue, Pascal was a Christian, and was therefore certain of God's existence; he could therefore not have attributed any importance to the argument of the wager in so far as he himself was concerned. Once this syllogism is accepted, the only question to be discussed is whether the wager argument was intended to appeal to a free thinker of the Méré type, whether it was merely a "stylistic exaggeration" or whether it marked a stage in the development of Pascal's own ideas or a step in the logical development of his argument.

The great objection to each of these interpretations is, in my view, the fact that they set out, either implicitly or explicitly, not from the actual text of fragment 233, but from a preconceived idea of faith and Christianity. None of the scholars who have put forward these different views seems, in my opinion, to consider the possibilty that his conception of Christianity fails to take into account an authentic form of the Christian faith, and one which happens to be that of Pascal.

What I propose to do is adopt the opposite approach. I shall study the actual text of the fragment in order to try to discover to what extent it justifies a view of Pascal as a man who makes the wager himself, and who therefore, unlike other Christian thinkers, links together the two ideas of wagering and believing. I shall study the place of the wager argument in the *Pensées* as a whole, in the ideology of the "Friends of Port-Royal" and finally in the history of philosophy.

Once we accept the idea that Pascal really believed what he wrote down, and decide to reject any interpretation based upon "stylistic exaggeration," the evidence of the text seems decisive. There are two passages in particular that in my view are quite unambiguous. In the first Pascal is replying to the objection put foward by a man who is already intellectually convinced (and who is made to say, in an imaginary dialogue, "That is obvious") but who says that he cannot bring himself to believe:

> You wish to attain faith, but do not know how to go about it; you want to cure yourself of your unbelief, and you ask for the remedy: *learn from those who have been tied as you are now tied, and who now wager all they have*, for they know the way that you would follow and have been cured of a sickness for which you seek a cure.
>
> (233, Brunschvicg ed.; my italics)

This phrase "learn from those who now wager all they have" seems quite decisive. It is Pascal himself who is speaking and who, addressing an interlocutor—whoever he may be—says neither, "Learn from those who now believe," nor, "Learn from those who have wagered," but, "Learn from those who *now wager*," emphasising his use of the present tense by the adverb *now*. If we accept that the author meant what he said—and any serious study of a writer must surely start out from this as a basic presupposition—these lines ought to be enough to refute most of the traditional interpretations which set out to minimise the role of the wager in Pascal's own religious faith.

There is another passage in the same fragment which I find equally conclusive. Pascal's interlocutor repeats that he cannot believe, and *probably* (the passage can be interpreted in one of two ways) identifies the word "wager" with the word "believe." Pascal's reply, however, identifies them quite unambiguously:

> Yes, but my hands are tied and my mouth is gagged; I am forced to wager, and am not free; they will not release me, and I am so made that I cannot believe. What then am I to do? That is true. But understand at least that your inability to believe comes from your passions, since reason inclines you to believe and you cannot do so.

One might perhaps interpret Pascal's imaginary interlocutor as saying: "I am forced to wager either that God exists or that there is nothing at all," and I cannot believe in His existence. In that case, "believe" and "wager" are not synonymous. However, since Pascal's interlocutor has already accepted Pascal's argument as "obvious," there is a second and more probable interpretation: "I am forced to wager that God exists, and I cannot believe." Here the words "wager" and "belief" become synonymous, and there is no longer any distinction between the wager "written for the free thinker" and the faith of the Christian who does not need to wager. Moreover, the identification between "wager" and "believe" in the rest of the passage containing Pascal's reply seems to me to be quite unambiguous. For we know that, for Pascal, reason does not lead men to believe in the sense required by a Thomistic, Augustinian or Cartesian position. All it does is to lead men to wager that God exists, and nothing more.

This is why, if one gives their full importance to the two passages which I have just quoted and which are normally neglected, it becomes very difficult to deny that the wager occupies a central position in the general scheme of the *Pensées*.

There is, moreover, another text which must be considered by anyone who rejects the idea that the wager argument represents Pascal's own position. It is fragment 234, which Brunschvicg felt to be so similar in inspiration that he placed it immediately after the passage on the wager. The text can be divided into two parts. The first—very significantly—tells us that "religion is not certain," although it is more certain than many other things which influence us and determine our actions. It thus becomes reasonable, and in keeping with the general odds, to commit oneself to a religion which is not absolutely certain.

> If we are to act only on grounds of certainty, we should take no action with regard to religion, for it is not certain. But how many things do we not engage in without being certain, sea voyages or battles! In that case, we should do nothing at all, for nothing is certain. And there is more certainty in religion than in our presupposition that we shall see tomorrow; for it is not certain that we shall see tomorrow, but it is certainly possible that we shall not see it. It is not certain that religion is true, but who can dare to say that it is certainly possible that it is not true? And yet, when men work for tomorrow and for uncertain things, they are acting rightly; for one must work for uncertain things, in accordance with the rules governing the odds.

There is, however, nothing new in this, and critics who interpret the passage on the wager simply as aimed at the free thinker could doubtless interpret fragment 234 in exactly the same way, in spite of the fact that

Pascal now seems to be speaking generally and not addressing any individual person in particular. It becomes much more difficult, however, to defend this interpretation when we come to the second part of the passage, for it is impossible to see how Pascal intended to "convert the free thinker" by setting out such a vehement criticism of Saint Augustine. In fact, this would have been most likely to produce exactly the opposite effect.

Moreover, when one remembers the immense respect which all Jansenists, and especially Pascal, had for Saint Augustine—whose authority was for them almost as great as that of the Bible—one is forced to conclude that Pascal would be most unlikely to have introduced such a passage if he had not been dealing with a point that he considers to be exceptionally important. The fragment—which also shows us Pascal's views on Montaigne—must therefore be considered as representing an essential argument in the work which he intended to write.

One should also note that the ideas which this passage expresses do not stand alone. They continue those expressed in a text of which we unfortunately have only a second-hand version tranmitted to us in the *Mémoires* of Fontaine, the *Entretien avec Monsieur de Saci*, in which Pascal was already putting forward his view of the Christian position and contrasting it with the one-sided approach of scepticism and dogmatism. He took Montaigne as the representative of the first and Epictetus of the second, and showed how Christianity at one and the same time both denied and transcended both positions.

Fragment 234 continues this analysis on a higher, and, I am tempted to say, more dialectical level. Pascal has now come to realise that neither the sceptic nor the dogmatic rationalist adopts a purely one-sided approach, since the sceptic recognises man's need for certainty, and even the dogmatist does not deny that chance and uncertainty play an important role in human experience. Both, however, consider that the element which happens to go against their philosophy—the need for certainty, the importance of chance— is an incidental and not an integral part of the human condition. In Pascal's own words, "they have seen the effect and not the cause." However, there is in fragment 234 a significant change in the thinkers whom Pascal takes as representing the two attitudes. The sceptic is still Montaigne, but the dogmatist has now ceased to be Epictetus and become Saint Augustine.

Saint Augustine saw that men work for things that are uncertain, on the sea and in battles. But he did not see the nature of the odds, which shows that we should do so. Montaigne saw that we are offended at the sight of a mind which cannot think straight, and that custom is all powerful; but he did not see why this should be so. Both these men have seen the effects but have not seen the causes, so that compared to those who have seen the causes they are like those who have only eyes compared to those who also have a mind. For effects are, as it were, sensible to sight, whereas causes can be percieved only by the mind. And although these effects can be seen by the mind, this mind is, compared to the mind which sees the causes, like the bodily senses when compared with the mind.

Pascal thus criticises Saint Augustine very sharply for his failure to recognise both the fundamental role played by uncertainty in man's life, and the "nature of the odds" which shows that man is compelled to work for what is uncertain.

There is perhaps one objection to this interpretation: is Pascal really talking about the wager that God exists, or is he talking about the thousand and one conscious or implicit wagers in the realm of everyday life? For two reasons, I think the former interpretation is the correct one. First of all, because Pascal does acknowledge that Saint Augustine recognises the existence of the daily wagers which we make "on sea, in battle," etc., and, secondly, because fragment 233 reveals Pascal's own awareness of the main "dogmatic" objections to the wager: the statement that reasonable men act only when they are certain and refrain from action whenever they are not. He has already replied to this particular objection of Cartesian dogmatism by the remark: "You must wager, it is not optional, you are embarked."

Now what exactly do these words mean? Certainly not that we are obliged to accept such and such a particular wager in our everyday life, on the sea or in battle, for example. This is simply not true, for the choice of each one of these particular wagers is optional, and we can always reject or accept it precisely because we are never "embarked" in advance. The mistake of dogmatic—or, to be more precise, of Cartesian—rationalism has been to divide man up into small pieces, to consider each act in isolation and then to apply the results of such an analysis to human existence in general.

If, on the other hand, we look upon our life as a whole we shall see that we are in fact "embarked" by virtue of the very quest for happiness which Pascal considers an essential and inevitable part of the human condition. Our freedom is made up of two things: our ability to make a choice in the many wagers that we come across in everyday life, and our need to wager in the one essential choice offered to us between God, on the one side, and nothingness, on the other.

The "nature of the odds" which Saint Augustine failed to recognise shows that man has to "work for uncertain things" only in so far as these odds govern the human condition as such, with man's inevitable quest for happiness and the impossibility of ever establishing this quest on a firm and non-paradoxical basis. A religious hermit who was certain of God's existence could, in the final analysis, deny that man had to work for things that are uncertain.

Thus, the Pascalian texts which identify "wagering" with "believing" speak of those who "now wager" and criticise Saint Augustine for not having seen the "nature of the odds" which show that man must work for things that are uncertain. They criticise him for having, with respect to this truth, been like "those who have only eyes" in comparison with those who "also have a mind." It is for this reason that these texts do, in my view, resist most of the traditional explanations, and [seem] to be serious, if not absolutely decisive arguments in favour of an interpretation which gives the "wager" a central place in the scheme of Pascal's epistemology.

We now have to study the intrinsic significance of the wager and its place both in the *Pensées* and in the general history of philosophical thought.

II

Fragment 233 is presented in the form of a dialogue between Pascal and an interlocutor of whom we know nothing except that he "does not believe" and even that he is "so constituted that he cannot believe." We obviously need to try to identify this man, since he is not only the person whom Pascal addresses in this fragment, but also the reader for whom the whole of the *Pensées* are intended.

The problem is this: does this interlocutor represent a particular type of man—a free thinker, for example—and can we therefore conclude that both fragment 233 and numerous other sections of the *Pensées* are merely part of an apology for Christianity which has no great personal importance for Pascal the believer? Or does this person represent an essential aspect of the human condition, and therefore a potential possibility of Pascal himself?

The same problem can be presented in another, complementary form, in the following question: to what extent are the doctrines of Grace and Predestination accepted by Port-Royal compatible with the very idea of writing an apology for the Christian religion? Scholars have, in fact, often noted the incompatibility between the Jansenist attitude towards Predestination and Pascal's decision to try to bring men to faith by persuading them of the truth of Christianity. They have either criticised him for contradicting his own premises or praised him for having been able to escape from the influence of Jansenism, but they have all nevertheless agreed that the Jansenist doctrine taught that man was completely helpless by himself, so much so that not even prayer could be efficacious unless God intervened by His divine grace.

As Monsieur Gouhier has observed in his unpublished lectures on the *Pensées*, any contradiction in Pascal's work cannot be implicit, since his acquaintances at Port-Royal—especially Barcos and his followers—would certainly have pointed out to him the strong objections which they had to any attempt to bring men to the faith by writing apologiae. Moreover, when one is discussing a thinker of Pascal's status one must accept the idea of a "contradiction" in his thought only when all other possibilities of explanation have been exhausted.

My own view is that there is no contradiction in Pascal's attitude; if he is criticised for acting in a way which, according to his own view, could not be efficacious in itself, then this criticism is valid only if one considers that Pascal was adopting the moral criterion of efficiency and not, as is more probably the case, that of intention.

Let us remember what Kant said in the *Critique of Practical Reason*:

> The judgment which decides whether a thing does or does not fall within the domain of pure practical reason is completely independent of any comparison with our own physical power; the question lies wholly in discovering whether we are allowed to *will* an action related to the existence of an object should it be supposed that this lies within our power.

There is nothing artificial in the comparison between this text and the views adopted by Pascal. Monsieur Gouhier has pointed out that for Pascal, as for all the "Disciples of Saint Augustine," man can in no way whatsoever come to know how God chooses His elect. We have absolutely no means of knowing whether a particular individual is either probably or certainly one of the Elect or one of those whom God has rejected. We are therefore compelled—as Monsieur Gouhier has observed—to act without even considering hypotheses of this nature. We have to accept as a general rule a formal imperative which makes no distinction at all between men, and which, it should be noted, is very similar to the Kantian imperative.

What we now have to decide is what universally valid rule of conduct we should adopt towards all men. Pascal himself tells us what this should be in one of his own texts on Grace:

> That all men in this world are compelled, under pain of eternal damnation and of the sin against the Holy Ghost for which there

is no forgiveness either in this world or the next, to believe that they belong to the small number of the Elect for whose salvation Christ died; and that they should, moreover, believe the same thing about each man and every man who is now on this earth, however wicked and impious he may be; and that for as long as he still has a moment of life; and that all men should leave the distinction between the Elect and Reprobate as part of the impenetrable secret of God.

And in a highly significant variant, Pascal adds that:

All men are compelled to believe, but with a belief mingled with fear and not accompanied by certainty, that they belong to the small number of the Elect whom Jesus Christ wishes to save; and that they should never place any man now alive, however wicked and impious he may be, for as long as he has a moment of life, elsewhere than in the ranks of the Predestined, leaving the distinction between the Elect and the Reprobate as part of the impenetrable secret of God. And that they should therefore do for their fellows everything which can contribute to their salvation.

There is thus no contradiction at all between Pascal's complete acceptance of the Augustinian theories on Grace and Predestination and the fact that he acted as if every man could be saved, doing everything possible to contribute to his salvation (in spite of the fact that, in the final analysis, this depends solely upon the Will of God).

However, these two texts which I have just quoted are not exactly similar, at least at first sight. The first says that "All men are compelled . . . to believe that they belong to the small number of the Elect, and to believe the same about every man," and if we interpret this text absolutely literally it does not really clear up the problem of whether or not it is legitimate to write apologies for the Christian faith. For if I act *as if* each man taken individually belonged to the ranks of the Elect, it becomes unnecessary to write apologiae, for I no longer need to contribute to their salvation.

The second variant text has more nuances, for it first of all tells us that the belief that we are saved should be "mingled with fear" and not "accompanied by certainty." Secondly, it gives a negative twist to the formal imperative mentioned by Monsieur Gouhier: "Never place a man . . . elsewhere than in the number of the Predestined."

Several lines of fragment 194—also quoted by Monsieur Gouhier— express a similar idea:

Since this religion obliges us always to look upon them, as long as they are in this life, as capable of receiving the Grace that will enlighten them, and to believe that they can in a moment of time be fuller of faith than we are ourselves, and that we, likewise, can fall into the blindness where they are now, we must do for them what we would have them do for us if we were in their state, and call upon them to have pity on themselves, and to take at least a few steps to see if they may not find some light.

Thus the formal imperative which justifies the writing of apologiae is this: that we should act as if every man, taken individually, could, in the moments which he still has to live—whether these be many or few—be either saved or damned, and therefore do everything we can to help him "to take pity on himself."

Pascal's own view is certainly that God alone can make our efforts fail or succeed (although, in fragment 233 he once, but only once, mentions the possibility of "believing even naturally"), but this is something which no longer concerns us. In fact, man for us is always a being who can be either damned or saved, and we must act as if, by our action, God is going to assure his salvation.

From the point of view of God there are the Elect who cannot be damned and the Reprobate who cannot be saved. From the point of view of man, on the other hand, the categories of "Elect" and "Reprobate" are in each individual case merely permanent possibilities. Man must think of himself as an intermediate being who brings these two categories together, but who has not yet chosen and who never can make a definitive choice in this life. This, in my view, is exactly the idea expressed not only in the numerous fragments which tell us that man is "neither angel nor beast," that he is "a thinking reed," but also by the two tripartite divisions which make up the very basis of Pascal's thought. One of these divisions is expressed in a text on Grace (the distinction between the Elect, the Reprobate and the Called) and the other in fragments such as the following (257):

There are only three kinds of person: those who, having found God, seek Him; those who, not having found Him, spend their time seeking Him; and those who live without having found Him and without seeking for Him either. The first are both blessèd and reasonable, the last both mad and unhappy, and the second unhappy but reasonable.

For Arnauld and Barcos, of course, there are, from God's point of view, only two kinds of people: the Elect and the Reprobate. To be strictly logical,

Pascal ought to have adopted the same distinction, and seen that, from God's point of view, those who were called but did not persevere in their calling were simply the Reprobate taken after the moment of their fall. However, in his *Ecrits sur la grâce*, Pascal puts these into a third, intermediate category. This is very significant, for he thereby introduces the human point of view expressed in fragment 257 into the divine perspective: while those who are called but do not persevere simply do not exist in the sight of God, who has complete knowledge of reality, they are from the point of view of man nevertheless an essential aspect of the human condition, for man can "know nothing of the impenetrable secret of God" on the subject of "the difference between the Elect and the Reprobate."

Moreover, even a consistent follower of Barcos could only really, from a human point of view, distinguish "hermits" from people who continued to live in the world. Pascal, on the other hand, recognises the existence in every man, whether a believer or a free thinker, of a reason by which he can be led to seek God and to understand the nature of the wager. He constantly recalls, however, that God is not manifest, that He is both absent and present, a Hidden God.

The rest of this text concerns the nature of Divine Grace, whose "impenetrable secret" neither we nor other men can understand in the course of this life.

Both the *Pensées* as a whole and fragment 233 in particular are addressed not to any one individual category of men but to Everyman, Pascal himself included. For in Pascal's view Everyman both can and must be brought by his reason to seek for God, but Everyman also inevitably runs the risk of being mistaken or even of giving up this quest. Yet he must never—and this is true of any authentic human quest—give up hope.

The formal imperative mentioned by Monsieur Gouhier should be expressed like this: "Act towards everyone, whoever he may be, whether the best or worst of men, as if God were to intend to use your action to bring about his salvation." The resemblance between this and the second formulation of the categorical imperative in Kant is obvious, for we see the German philosopher writing:

> Act in such a way as you treat humanity in your own person, as in the person of any other man, always as an end and never as a means.

Thus, in the two tripartite divisions of Pascal's thought the essentially human category is each time the intermediary one, the only one which, as men, we are able to experience in our present life. Similarly, the two people who take part in the dialogue in fragment 233 are, in the last analysis, one and the same person, an indissoluble pair of friends, and this because the one who wagers that nothing exists—although he is not aware of actually making a wager—represents a risk which the man who wagers on God constantly runs but into which he never falls.

One could even go so far as to say that these three types of person go to make up one and the same being, the truly human man. The two extreme categories of the Elect and the Reprobate are, in this respect, the two permanent possibilities between which man must choose. They express, on the plane of the individual, the two possibilities represented by the wager, in so far as to fear to wager that Nothing exists is to fear damnation, and to wager that God exists is to hope for salvation. In this life the human condition lies precisely in this intermediate category made up of the union between hope and fear.

We should never forget that, for Pascal, man is a paradoxical being on every level of existence; that he is a union of opposites; and that, for him, to seek God is to find Him, but to find Him is still to seek after Him. A man who rested and ceased to search, who attained a certainty which ceased to be a wager, would be the complete opposite of the man whom Pascal knew and whom he presented in his work.

III

Before trying to place the wager in the history of philosophy, it would perhaps be useful to see how it fits into the general system of Port-Royal.

Léon Cognet has suggested the possibility of a curious similarity between Pascal's ideas and those accepted by others at Port-Royal by publishing a letter by Mother Angélique de Saint-Jean. This, in fact, recalls a number of views expressed in fragment 233:

> It is like a kind of doubt concerning everything connected with Faith and Providence, but a doubt on which I dwell very little. For, out of fear that reasoning might offer a wider entry to temptation, my mind seems to reject it with a certain attitude that is in itself opposed to faith. Thus, I find myself saying that even if there were to be something uncertain in what I know to be the truth and in what I believe about the immortality of the soul, the best thing for me to do would still be to follow the path of virtue. The very act of writing down such an idea makes me afraid, for I have never before allowed it to present itself so clearly to my

own mind; it is rather something which happens almost without my realising it. But surely there is something lacking in one's faith if one is capable of such thoughts? I have not dared to speak to anyone about them, since I found them so dangerous that I was afraid to even suggest them to anyone to whom I revealed the suffering they caused me.

However, this text seems to me to be rather an indication of the extremes to which a specifically rationalistic and Arnauldian view could lead, rather than a pointer to the tendencies of Port-Royal as a whole. It seems in fact, to put forward two ideas which are basically rationalistic and Stoic in inspiration: that of a doubt that God exists and that of a life given over wholly to virtue. What is peculiar both to Pascal's wager and to Kant's postulate is, however, precisely the opposite view. One can only doubt something if one at least entertains the possibility that it can be approximately or certainly known. For Pascal and Kant, however, theoretical reason can know absolutely nothing about the existence or the nonexistence of God. It would be equally false and equally indefensible to affirm, deny or even doubt it, since all that theoretical reason can do when faced with urgent problems of this kind, which are completely out of its range, is to subordinate itself to a faculty that is capable of going beyond reason because of the ability which it has of making statements in a domain inaccessible to theory. If such a faculty cannot be found, reason must simply content itself with taking note of the radical insufficiency of the human condition.

Now, according to Pascal and Kant, man does possess the synthesising faculty which enables him to eliminate doubt for nontheoretical reasons, and, on the theological plane, to state even the certainly uncertain existence of God.

I have already stated elsewhere that when, in fragment 233 the editors of the Port-Royal edition of the *Pensées* replaced the words "those who now wager" by "those who do not now have any doubt," they were not distorting Pascal's ideas. Although it is a serious thing to do, they were merely trying to avoid scandal by substituting a general type of argument for the particular argument used by Pascal. For, if it is true that all those who wager do not necessarily doubt, it is equally true that most of those who do not doubt do not wager either.

One can nevertheless see in what respects this letter by Mother Angélique de Saint-Jean differs from tragic thought and even contradicts it.

This difference becomes even more apparent when we consider the second element, the idea of a life given over entirely to virtue. For Pascal's wager, like Kant's practical postulate, is based on the idea that such a life is quite impossible. In order to be virtuous, men must wager that virtue and happiness can be linked together, for no one can genuinely choose to give up all attempts to be happy. But, for both Pascal and Kant, there is in this life a fundamental contradiction between virtue and happiness.

The idea of basing one's life solely on virtue is basically Stoical, and one which is quite natural to find either in Mother Angélique or in any thinker who has been either directly influenced by Cartesianism or indirectly affected by the semi-Cartesianism of Arnauld. It is, however, completely opposed to any tragic thought, and we know that both Kant and Pascal unequivocally rejected Stoicism in all its forms.

Thus, in my view we should not look to this letter for the deeper analogies between Jansenist thought and the Pascalian wager. We should look rather in a less obvious but equally essential direction: that of the docrines concerning Grace and Predestination. If, in fact, fragment 233 expresses ideas peculiar to Pascal himself, the text on Grace quoted at the beginning of this chapter reflects a position shared by the rest of the movement. This text, moreover, also implies the idea of a wager based upon the same absolute ignorance of objective reality, but an ignorance that bears not on the existence of God but on the salvation of the individual. In general, the Christian knows that there are many damned and few saved. Nevertheless, everyone should believe that he is "of the small number of the Elect for whose sake Jesus Christ died, and should think the same of the men who live on the earth." And since this belief should remain "mingled with fear" and not "accompanied by certainty," and since this fear and uncertainty stem essentially from man's awareness of the small number of the Elect and of the absense of any theoretical and objective reason for believing that we are included among them, there seems to me to be only one difference between this position and the one expressed in fragment 233: in the text on Grace we are concerned with individual salvation and in fragment 233 with the very existence of God. For Jansenism, in general, God's existence was a certainty and individual salvation a hope. The Pascalian wager extends the idea of hope to the very existence of God, and thereby becomes profoundly different from the views of Arnauld and Barcos. But this is not because Pascal escapes from Jansenism but because, on the contrary, he carries it to its logical conclusions.

I shall conclude this section by quoting a text by Barcos which illustrates the similarity between Jansenist theories on Grace and the Pascalian wager in a peculiarly appropriate manner.

As to the men who say: "If I am one of the Reprobate, why should I act virtuously?" I would reply as follows: "Are·you not

cruel towards yourself if you destine yourself to the greatest of
all evils without knowing whether God has destined you to it?
He has not revealed to you His secret counsel as to your salvation
or damnation. Why do you expect punishment from His justice
rather than forgiveness from His Mercy? Perhaps He will accord
you His grace and perhaps He will not. Why therefore do you
not have as much hope as fear, instead of falling into despair
about a gift which He grants to others who are just as unworthy
as you? By your despair, you infallibly lose what you will probably gain if you hope. And, in your doubt as to whether you are
one of the Reprobate, you conclude that you should act as if you
were damned already, instead of doing what might perhaps save
you from damnation. Surely this is as much against the reason
which you possess as a wise man as against the faith which you
hold as a Christian?" "But," he may reply, "What good will good
works do me if I am not predestined to salvation?" My reply to
him then is: "What do you lose by obeying your creator, by
loving Him, by doing His will? Or, rather, what will you not
gain if you live and persevere in His love? And, even supposing
that you are of the Reprobate,—an idea which I mention with
horror—can you ever, in any condition, free yourself of the ser-
vices which you owe to God? Does not a good and blessèd life
both on earth and in heaven lie in adoring, loving and following
God? Are the sufferings which you undergo by not doing His
will in this world any greater than those which you will incur in
the next?"

IV

As we have seen, there are a number of points of resemblance between
the Pascalian wager and Kant's practical postulate of God's existence, and
the two theories occupy a similar place in the work of the two thinkers.
    In both cases, we find the same basic presuppositions:

1. That no legitimate theoretical arguments can be put forward to
   prove either the existence or the nonexistence of God.
2. That the hope of happiness is an essential and legitimate element
   of the human condition.
3. That it is impossible to achieve this happiness under satisfactory
   conditions in this life (infinite happiness for Pascal, happiness

linked with virtue for Kant) and that it is consequently both necessary and legitimate to state, on the theoretical plane but for nontheoretical reasons, that God exists.

In spite of these striking analogies, there are nevertheless genuine differences between the two thinkers. One of these is quite obvious: Pascal compares the limited happiness offered by terrestrial things to the unlimited happiness promised by religion in the next life, and presents his argument as a calculation of probabilities based on the comparison between what we will win as against what we will lose. Kant, on the other hand, refuses to make any comparison of this nature, and at no time does he think of comparing the happiness of either a Stoic or an Epicurean life centred about the self with the happiness promised by religion. His ethic is quite autonomous, since he teaches that man should in any case act in such a way as to create a moral nature. However, man can do this only if he assumes that reality is such that he can legitimately hope for happiness.

This difference certainly appears considerable from the point of view of a literal analysis which sees these ideas outside the context of the philosophies of which they form part. However, if one examines the problem of the significance of the argument—that is to say, in dialectical terms, if one goes from the abstract empirical appearance to the concrete essence of the text—then this difference seems much less important.

In fact, the concepts of the free thinker and of the calculation of probabilities in Pascal seem to me, like the idea of a nature following universal laws in Kant, to be an accidental element linked to the historical context in which the arguments in question were put forward. When Pascal was writing the *Pensées* the calculation of probabilities and the theory of games of chance were at the centre of men's scientific interests; similarly, the idea of a nature which followed universal and unchanging laws was also fashionable when Kant was writing the *Critique of Practical Reason*. But the proof that the argument based on probability is merely an outward cloak can be found in a passage where Pascal is certainly speaking for himself and which is much closer to Kant's argument:

> Now what harm can come to you if you adopt this course? You will be faithful, honest, humble, grateful, generous, and a sincere and truthful friend. It is true that you will not taste the poisoned fruits of glory and luxury; but will you not have other pleasures? I tell you that you stand to win in this life; and that at each step which you take upon this road you will see such overwhelming evidence of gain and so complete a nothingness in what you are

risking, that you will in the end come to recognise that you have
wagered on a certain and infinite thing for which you have in
fact given nothing at all.

(233)

These lines are not, of course, exactly similar to Kant's approach, for
he makes a distinction between any egotistical pleasure linked to a sensible
object and the respect which we owe to the Law. It does seem to me, however,
that the distinction between the two kinds of pleasure is implicit in the
passage that I have just quoted; moreover, Kant argues exactly as Pascal does
that one cannot separate moral action from the hope of happiness without
inclining it either towards an attitude of laxity or towards one of excessive
enthusiasm.

Thus, both Pascal's admirers and enemies, who have seen the wager
either as an argument aimed at beating the free thinker on his own ground
or as a cunning manoeuvre destined to enable Pascal to defend the position
which best suited him personally, have missed the point of one of the most
important texts in the history of philosophy.

We can neglect its personal or apologetic intention and concentrate on
the two factors which give it this great importance in the history of philosophy: the first of the two ideas which it expresses—that man must wager—
is fundamental to the whole of dialectical thought; the second—that we must
lay our bets in favour of the existence of God and the immortality of the
soul—is characteristic of the tragic vision of the world.

Thus, both rationalists and empiricists attribute no importance at all to
the wager. If the highest value to which man can aspire consists of thinking
clearly and obeying reasonable laws, than the achievement of values depends
upon man and man alone, and on the strength or weakness of his own mind
and reason. The self is at the very centre of rationalistic thought. *Ego Cogito*
wrote Descartes, and faced with Fichtean self the external world loses all
ontological reality. (Pascal, on the other hand, wrote that: "The self is
hateful.") The very idea of help coming to man from outside himself would
be contradictory to any rationalistic ethic, for it is precisely in so far as they
need external help that the thought and will of an individual are inadequate
and fail to come up to the ideal.

Similarly, if it is merely a question of yielding to the invitations of the
senses the situation is, in spite of its apparent difference, in reality analogous
to the one I have just described. For here likewise the individual is sufficient
unto himself. He can work out the advantages and disadvantages of a particular way of behaving, and has no need of any outside help or of any wager.

In the case of dialectical thought, on the other hand, the situation is completely different. The supreme value now lies in an objective and external ideal which man must bring into being, but whose creation no longer depends solely on the thought and will of the individual: infinite happiness for Pascal, the union of virtue and happiness in the Supreme Good for Kant, liberty for Hegel, the classless society for Marx.

Certainly, these different forms of the Sovereign Good are not independent of individual action, for this can help man to reach and achieve them. But the question of whether or not he succeeds goes beyond the individual and depends upon a number of other factors that can either help or hinder his efforts. Consequently, the efficiency or objective meaning of any individual action escapes its author and depends upon factors which, if not foreign to him, at least lie outside himself.

Thus, with Pascal, three elements essential to any action make their way into philosophy, and consequently into the whole of human existence: the elements of risk, of the danger of failure and of the hope of success. However great the will power or intelligence of any individual may be, it is impossible to understand the human condition in its concrete reality without taking these three elements into account.

This explains why, once practical philosophy is no longer centred around an ideal of individual wisdom but comes to deal primarily with external reality, man's life takes on the aspect of a wager on the success of his own action and, consequently, on the existence of a force which transcends the individual. This force must accompany or contribute to the efforts which the individual makes, so that his life becomes a wager that God, Humanity or the Proletariat exists and will triumph.

Thus, the idea of a wager not only occupies a central position in Jansenist thought (wager on individual salvation) or in Pascal's ideas (wager that God exists) or in Kant's philosophy (wager on the practical postulate that God exists and that the soul is immortal). It is also at the very heart of dialectical and materialistic thought under the form of the wager that, in the alternative facing humanity of a choice between socialism and barbarity, socialism will triumph. We also find it expressed quite openly in the most important literary work that expresses the dialectical vision: Goethe's *Faust*.

One could almost analyse the relationship between the tragic and dialectical visions by comparing the wagers of Pascal and Faust in order to bring out their similarities and differences.

Thus, in both Pascal and Goethe the problem presents itself on two levels, that of the divine mind, which in his complete ignorance of the designs of Providence is entirely unknown to man, and that of the human mind.

Similarly, what escapes the individual, what God alone can know, is whether a particular man is damned or saved. On the other hand, on the plane of the individual mind life presents itself both for Goethe and for Pascal as a wager based on the fact that, unless he is to lose his soul, man can never be satisfied with a good that is purely finite.

The differences, which are at least as great as the similarities, lie in the different role attributed to the Devil. For if in Pascal and Kant goodness remains the opposite of evil (while, and herein lies the essence of tragedy, remaining inseparable from it) in Goethe, as in Hegel and Marx, evil becomes the only path that leads to goodness.

God can save Faust only by handing him over to Mephistopheles for the whole of his earthly life. Divine Grace thus becomes, as Grace, a wager which God (who, of course, knows that He will win) makes against the Devil, and the human wager—while still remaining a wager—becomes a pact with the Devil.

We can thus see the whole importance and meaning of the Pascalian wager. Far from merely stating that it is reasonable to chance the certain and finite goods of this world against the possibility of gaining a happiness which is doubly infinite both in intensity and duration (this being merely the external aspect of the argument, aimed at allowing the interlocutor to become conscious of the human condition even on the plane farthest removed from faith), this wager states that the finite goods of this world have no value at all, and that the only human life which has real meaning is that of a reasonable being who seeks God. (And this whether or not he is happy or miserable because he does or does not find Him, which is nevertheless something that he cannot discover until after his death). The only life which has any real meaning is that of the being who places all his goods on the wager that God exists and that He will help him and who shows this by devoting his life to realising a value—that of infinite happiness—which does not depend upon his own strength and of whose final creation he has no certain proof.

From Hegel and Marx onwards, both the finite goods and even the evil of terrestrial life—Goethe's Devil—will receive a meaning inside the framework of faith and hope in the future.

But however important these differences may be, the idea that man is "embarked" and that he must wager becomes, after Pascal, the central idea in any philosophical system which recognises that man is not a self-sufficient and isolated monad but a partial element inside a whole which transcends him and to which he is linked by his aspirations, his actions and his faith. It is the central idea of any concept which realises that man can never achieve any authentic values by his own efforts, and that he always needs some supra-individual help on whose existence he must wager, for he can live and act only in the hope of a final success in which he must believe.

Risk, possibility of failure, hope of success and the synthesis of these three in the form of a faith which is a wager are the essential constituent elements in the human condition. It is certainly not the least of Pascal's titles to glory that he was the first man to bring them explicitly into the history of philosophical thought.

I will add in conclusion that these elements are only another aspect of the two tripartite divisions (those who are called, the Elect and the Reprobate; the men who seek God, the men who do not seek Him and the men who find Him) whose importance in Pascal's thought I have already emphasised.

The two concepts of generalised paradox and of a refusal of the world from within the world have enabled us to understand both Pascal's behaviour in the last five years of his life and the place of the wager in the philosophical system of the *Pensées*.

I shall not here concern myself with the numerous fragments that deal with the positive proof which Pascal found for the truth of the Christian religion. The ideas of the fulfilment of prophecies, of the genuine nature of miracles, of the continuity of the Christian tradition, of the style of the Gospels are still very important for any complete understanding of Pascal's work, but are no longer of any great relevance today. The problem which these texts set for the historian is not peculiar to the study of Pascal, but concerns all forms of tragic and dialectical thought (Kant, Hegel, Marx, Lukács, etc.): that of discovering to what extent someone who has, independently of any theoretical considerations, made an act of faith in the present or future existence of certain values can also, without being inconsistent, make the effort to discover the largest possible number of arguments which, though not finally decisive, do nevertheless contribute towards proving the validity of this faith on theoretical grounds. And, moreover, of discovering whether the act of faith demands such an effort, once it is accepted that both the present existence and the future creation of such values cannot in fact be proved in any absolutely certain manner on the theoretical plane.

There is, in fact, very little difference between the argument that Pascal obviously did not "wager" himself, since he several times mentions the proofs of the Christian religion, and the criticism that Marx "contradicts himself" when he says that socialism will inevitably be produced by the movement of history while at the same time urging men to fight in order to bring it into being. Both criticisms stem from a complete failure, on the part of the rationalist or empiricist thinkers who radically distinguish fact from value judgments, to understand the dialectical nature of human reality.

In fact, the action of wagering the whole of one's fortune or possessions on the present or future existence of certain values means committing oneself to do everything possible to bring them into being. One can do this in order to strengthen one's faith, just as long, naturally, as one does not spoil the true nature of this faith by giving up the demand for absolute truth and as long as one rejects any conscious or half-conscious illusions on this subject. And the quest for probable, though not absolutely definitive, reasons in favour of the future creation of certain values forms an integral part of that commitment of one's whole life to a cause which truly constitutes the wager.

I must add that once the wager is seen as legitimate (since no theoretical argument can ever definitively prove its absurdity) and once it has been seen to be necessary (for practical reasons, for reasons of the heart), then it can no longer be shaken by any purely theoretical difficulty. As Pascal himself remarks in fragment 224: "How I hate these stupidities, not believing in the Eucharist etc. If the Gospel is true, if Jesus Christ is God, what difficulty is there in this particular point of faith?"

Thus, the wager based on the impossibility of conceiving the existence of any finally decisive and compelling argument for or against the present or future existence of values gives central importance to all the probable arguments in favour of this present or future existence and deprives any probable arguments against any of practical importance.

Once this point has been cleared up, however, another difficulty arises. My sketch of Pascal's vision of reality has shown why it leads inevitably to the wager that God exists. But we still have to ask why this God should be the Christian God rather than the God of the Deists or that of any other religious group.

From a purely psychological point of view, it would naturally be very difficult to say exactly what influence the fact that Pascal lived in seventeenth-century France had on his thought. However, I do not think that this is the really important point, since Pascal was too rigorous and exact a thinker to accept the ideology of the society in which he lived in a purely passive manner. On the contrary, he is very mistrustful of this ideology, especially since he himself had far too great a realisation of both the power and the falsity of custom ever to be taken in on such an important point.

Thus, the Christianity of the society in which he lived was important for him merely for its suggestive value, for the way in which it led him to give particular attention to a solution that he would not, however, have accepted if he had not found it valid in itself and if it had not been demanded by the internal consistency of his ideas.

He tells us all this himself, and we can accept everything he says with complete confidence:

> Whatever may be said, it must be admitted that there is something amazing about the Christian religion: "That is because you were born in it," they may say. Far from it: I harden myself against it for that very reason, in case this prejudice leads me into error; but although I was born in it, I still continue to find it marvellous.
>
> (615)

Pascal thus found in Christianity a collection of specific facts which give it the unique position of being able to satisfy all man's needs and which therefore make it true.

It is, of course, possible that in order to reach this result he had to modify somewhat the Christianity of his country and of his own particular environment. It is also possible that by the very fact of doing this he also discovered a Christianity that was more authentic and closer to that of its Founder than the Christianity of his time. I shall not venture to give judgment upon this point, since only a specialist in the general history of religions could hope to be competent in such matters. I shall instead concentrate on one problem: What place did Christianity occupy in Pascal's thought as a whole? In studying it, I shall be obliged to present separately a number of related arguments which, in fact, present the same truth seen from a number of different angles.

For Pascal, Christianity is true because, being made up of a number of paradoxical and apparently absurd statements, it is the only religion which explains the paradoxical and apparently incomprehensible nature of the human condition.

> Original sin is foolishness in the sight of men, but it is not presented as anything else. You therefore have no grounds for reproaching me with the irrationality of this doctrine, since I put it forward as devoid of reason. But this folly is wiser than all the wisdom of man, *sapientius est hominibus*. For without it how could we ever say what man is? His whole state depends on this one imperceptible point. And how could he have become aware of it by reason, since it is something which goes against reason and that his own reason, far from inventing it by its own methods, recoils when presented with it?
>
> (445)

The reasons that make Christianity true are not the rational and positive proofs that can be used to support it, such as the existence of prophecies, miracles, figurative statements, continuity of tradition and so on. What makes it true is, on the contrary, the paradoxical and apparently unreasonable nature of its teaching.

> This religion, although so great in holy, pure and irreproachable miracles; in martyrs; in established kings (David); Isaiah, prince of the blood; and so great in knowledge nevertheless rejects all this and says that is stands neither by wisdom nor signs but by the Cross and folly.
>
> For those who have deserved your belief by these signs and wisdom, and who have proved their character to you, declare that nothing contained in any of this can change us and make us capable of knowing and loving God save only the virtue of the Folly of the Cross, without wisdom or signs; and that without this virtue the signs avail nothing. Thus our religion is folly in respect of the efficient cause, and wise when we consider the wisdom which leads up to it.
>
> (587)

It would be wrong to think that man could be satisfied with a religion that showed him only the greatness of God—or which even gave first place to this greatness—or which promised him sensible happiness. To think this would be the false and one-sided illusion of the rationalists or Epicureans. Man, who is "neither beast nor angel," would not know what to do with a wholly "angelic" religion or with one that promised him merely crude and sensual pleasures:

> The God of the Christians is not simply the God who is author of geometrical truths or of the order of the elements; this is the view of the pagans and Epicureans. He is not solely a God who exercises His Providence over the lives and fortunes of men, in order to bestow long life upon those who worship him; for this is the view of the Jews.
>
> (556)

Similarly, the many who think that Christianity insists on the greatness of God are completely and absolutely wrong about it true nature:

> They take it upon themselves to blaspheme against the Christian religion because they have an inadequate knowledge of it. They

imagine that it consists solely of worshipping a God who is looked upon as great, powerful and eternal, and this is in fact deism, which is almost as far removed from Christianity as atheism, its complete opposite.

(556)

In reality, Christianity is true because it asks us to believe in the existence of a paradoxical and contradictory God, and one whose nature corresponds exactly to everything which we know about man's nature and his hopes: a God who became man, a God who was crucified, and a God who is a mediator:

> All those who seek God apart from Jesus Christ, confining themselves to nature where they find no light to satisfy them and where they manage to know God and serve Him without a mediator, are led to fall into atheism or deism, which are two beliefs which the Christian religion detests almost equally.
>
> This is why I shall not here undertake to prove by natural reasons either the existence of God or the doctrine of the Trinity, or the immortality of the soul, or anything of that kind; not only because I should not feel that I had enough strength to find arguments in nature likely to convince a hardened atheist, but also because such knowledge, separated from Christ Jesus, is useless and sterile. Though a man were to be convinced that numerical proportions are eternal and immaterial truths that depend on a first truth in which they have their being, and which is called God, I should not consider that he had made much progress in his path towards salvation. . . .
>
> If the world existed to reveal God to man, His divinity would everywhere shine forth in an absolutely incontestable manner; but as it exists only through and for Jesus Christ, to reveal to men both their corruption and their redemption, everything stands out as overwhelming proof of these two truths.

(556)

Thus, Christianity, the religion of the God who was made man, of the God who was crucified and who is a mediator, is the only religion whose teaching can have an authentic meaning for a paradoxical being such as man, who is both great and small, strong and weak, an angel and a beast. For such a being, any true and significant message must be paradoxical, so that only Christianity, by the paradoxical nature of each of its dogmas, can explain the contradictory and paradoxical character of human reality.

But this is only a stage in Pascal's argument. If we want another equally important aspect of Christianity we shall find it in the fact that it is the only religion which enables man to achieve his true aspirations: the union of opposites, the immortality of the body as well as that of the soul, and their reunion in the incarnation.

Man would have no use for a religion that promised him merely physical or merely spiritual happiness. For, even if there is no possible link between him and God or between him and Jesus Christ the righteous, his faith in the paradoxical God who was crucified and who became sin, delivers him as of now from the chains of spiritual slavery; spiritual greatness can thus be neither promise nor hope. It is what faith gives the unbeliever from this very moment; or, as fragment 233 puts it, what "he gains in this life" and which is precisely characterised—from the human point of view—by its inadequacy.

Thus, what Christ offers in eternity to Pascal and to the believer is the complement to their spiritual liberty and greatness, and what these need to become wholly authentic: bodily immortality, the true healing which gives immortality not only to the soul but also to the body.

Christianity is thus the only true religion, from among all the other religions upon earth, because it is the only religion which means anything when placed by the side of the authentic needs and aspirations of a man who is conscious of his condition, his possibilities and his limitations, of the man who "goes beyond man" because he is truly human. It is the only religion which explains the paradoxical and double nature of man and of the world, the only one which promises the creation of authentic values, and of the totality which is a reunion of opposites. And, finally, to resume and syn-thesise all these reasons, Christianity is the only religion which not only fully and consistently recognises the ambiguous and contradictory nature of all reality but which also makes this characteristic into an element of God's plan for this earth. For it transforms ambiguity into paradox, and makes human life cease to be an absurd adventure and become instead a valid and necessary stage in the only path leading to goodness and truth.

One could certainly show today that the historical wager on the future existence of the human community (in socialism) also possesses all these qualities; that, like Pascal's Christianity, it is incarnation, the joining up of opposites, and the fitting of ambiguity into a pattern which makes it clear and meaningful.

But Pascal lived in France in the seventeenth century. For him, there was therefore no question of a historical dialect. Indeed, tragic vision knows only one perspective: the wager on the existence of a God who is a synthesis of opposites, and who makes the ambiguous existence of man into a meaningful paradox. This wager assumes the existence of a religion which is not only wisdom but wisdom precisely because of its folly, which is not only clear and obvious but clear because of its very obscurity and true because it is contradictory. Pascal would have had every justification for saying to himself that even the most knowledgable and critical mind would not, in the seventeenth century, have been able to find such a religion anywhere except in Christianity.

Subsequently Hegel, and especially Marx and Lukács, have been able to substitute for the wager on the paradoxical and mediatory God of Christianity the wager on a historical future and on the human community. In doing so, however, they have not given up the main demands of tragic thought, that is to say a doctrine which explains the paradoxical nature of human reality, and a hope in the eventual creation of values which endows this contradiction with meaning and which transforms ambiguity into a necessary element of a significant whole. In my opinion this is one of the best indications which we have of the existence, not only of a continuity in what I would call "classical thought" from Greek times to our own day but also of a more particular continuity in modern classical thought, within whose framework the tragic vision of Pascal and Kant constitutes an essential stage in the movement which goes beyond sceptical or dogmatic rationalism towards the birth and elaboration of dialectical philosophy.

MARTIN PRICE

The Three Orders: Flesh, Spirit, Charity

This kind of opposition between rival world views or orders goes back at least to the classical contrast between the orderly universe of Plato, Aristotle, and the Stoics and the universe of chance, the purposeless world evolving from a fortuitous concourse of atoms, of the Epicureans. This conflict was revived with the growth of Renaissance naturalism. In the seventeenth century the opposition of neo-Stoics and neo-Epicureans renewed the debate between virtue and pleasure as the ends of man, between reason and sense as his instruments of knowledge. Shaftesbury could see all philosophy summed up in this opposition, and Pascal before him played upon the mutual destructiveness of such systems by opposing Epictetus to the modern naturalist, Montaigne. "The evil of one," Pascal is reported to have said, "tends to neutralize that of the other." The Stoic Epictetus frees man of dependence upon external things but induces a pride in the self-sufficiency of reason. Montaigne destroys pride in reason and in moral self-righteousness but tempts man into skepticism and impiety. The opposition, Pascal asserts, shows that only Christian truth can reconcile what is sound in their contradictory views.

Yet it is Pascal who most tellingly states the situation of rival orders:

> There are three orders of things: the flesh, the spirit, and the will. The carnal are the rich and kings; they have the body as their object. Inquirers and scientists; they have the mind as their object. The wise; they have righteousness as their object.

From *To the Palace of Wisdom: Studies in Order and Energy from Dryden to Blake.* © 1964 by Martin Price. Doubleday, 1964.

The three lusts have made three sects; and the philosophers have done no other thing than follow one of the three lusts.

All the glory of greatness has no lustre for people who are in search of understanding. The greatness of clever men is invisible to kings, to the rich, to chiefs, and to all the worldly great. The greatness of wisdom, which is nothing if not of God, is invisible to the carnal-minded and to the clever. These are three orders differing in kind.

(Pensées 460, 461, 793; numbering conforms to Brunschvicg ed.)

Pascal divides men into three discontinuous orders. These could be, and in fact had been, presented as progressive stages of a gradual ascent. But Pascal stresses their discreteness and necessary rivalry. Each order is created by a "lust" (*concupiscence*), in its nature unlimited. What is more important, the order of wisdom is not that of the rulers. Far from being philosophers (although he dreams of the possibility in his letter to Queen Christina), Pascal's kings occupy the lowest of his orders—the order of the flesh.

One of the consequences of this opposition of orders is that each world view must find a way of accounting, in terms of its own ordering of experience, for the mistaken views of its opponents. Typically, the naturalistic neo-Epicurean view places great emphasis on the power of passions—fear, envy, pride—and on their infinitely subtle modes of rationalization. It may assert deliberate deception by priest or king in order to subdue the populace, but the real problem still to be faced is why people should be susceptible to deception, and here the naturalist produces a social psychology that constructs the whole pattern of orthodox belief from a few principles of rudimentary passion. Mockingly, the naturalist may acclaim the grandeur of the social edifice only to remind us of the baseness of the materials.

On the other hand, those who maintain the idea of universal Order can explain the naturalistic view as the contraction of man's godlike reason into a cunning that serves rather than controls his will. The naturalistic account of reality is simply the limited vision of fallen man, which can no longer comprehend the range of experience it knew before the fall. One of the great efforts to dramatize this fallen view was, of course, Milton's Satan; Satan could not persist in his pride without persuading himself that his world was ruled by sheer force, that his obduracy of resentment was the only response to an unjust and selfish punisher, that destruction itself was creative in a world where only force had value. From a Christian point of view, Satan's obduracy can be seen as a travesty of heroic endurance in faith. A passage like this from Kierkegaard's *The Sickness unto Death* catches the Satanic demeanor as the "continuation of sin":

> Just because the demoniac is consistent in himself and in the consistency of evil, just for this cause he also has a totality to lose. A single instant outside of his consistency, one single . . . imprudence, one single glance aside, one instant when the whole thing, or at least a part thereof, is seen and understood in a different way—and with that, he would never more be himself, he says. That is, he has given up the good in despair, it would not help him anyway, he says, but it might well disturb him, make it impossible for him ever again to acquire the full momentum of consistency, make him weak. Only in the continuation of sin he is himself, only in that does he live and have an impression of himself.

This internalizing of order makes of each of the limited orders a peculiar pathologic state which, like paranoia, imposes its special vision upon all that confronts it. Men are locked up in private worlds, and the more order they achieve within them, the greater the disorder in the larger world of which they are members.

The internalizing of orders also produces debate and dialectic. The great exemplars of this kind of conflict are the Platonic dialogues, where the confrontation of Socrates with Callicles or with Thrasymachus is really a confrontation of different orders of experience which have a few key terms wherein they can meet. In Socrates' opponents there is a fundamental inconsistency. They avow a doctrine of unlimited amorality, which allows them to esteem only power; but there is a point at which they admit terms that make that doctrine untenable. Thrasymachus does so in the *Republic* in admitting that there is an art of living, that man has a peculiar virtue or function he alone can fulfill; in doing so, he gives primacy to the soul and to its end of measure or justice. Callicles in the *Gorgias* admits that some pleasures are better than others, and the acceptance of an explicit moral standard follows. In both cases these opponents attempt to account for all experience in terms that would make man a pleasure-seeking animal; their inability to create a consistent, self-contained, comprehensive order on those terms allows Socrates to invert their arguments and to assert his own, moral order, over theirs.

A Socratic paradox occurs, as Dorothea Krook has said, "in the over-lapping area of . . . two worlds; and occurs with the greatest, the most explosive force (knowledge is virtue, for instance) at the points of intersection of the two worlds. And if one may imagine the world of appearances wholly superimposed upon the world of reality (the condition, one must suppose, of the dwellers in the deepest and darkest part of the cave), then the whole field becomes a field for paradox, and there is nothing, literally nothing, the master of dialectic can affirm that is not paradoxical." As Mrs. Krook suggests, the creator of a dialectic like Plato's begins with alternatives that are accepted as exhaustive, and the opponent "always *by definition* chooses the false alternative." The strategy of creating this pattern of dialectic leads us to the problems of ironic satire.

The period . . . from Pascal to Blake, is a great age of irony. Few periods have made such telling use of the dialogue: we see it in Dryden, Prior, Pope, Shaftesbury, Mandeville, Berkeley, Hume—to choose only the more striking figures. And no age has made more striking use of a fictitious narrator or speaker whose peculiar slant of vision is critical to an understanding of the whole work. Swift is the most conspicuous ironist of the age in his use of Lemuel Gulliver and the insouciant teller of *A Tale of a Tub*. But Pope's Socratic use of the Horatian or Juvenalian satirical speaker, Fielding's complex use of the self-conscious narrator, Sterne's Tristram Shandy, and Blake's dramatization in *Songs of Innocence and of Experience* of "the two contrary states of the human soul" are all instances of a literature that demands that we take account of a voice, of a point of view, of a state of the soul that may also imply a world view and a religion. "Without contraries is no progression," Blake wrote in his most overtly dialectical work, *The Marriage of Heaven and Hell*. "Contrary states" in that work exhibit precisely the opposition of orders that I have been trying to present:

> So the Angel said: "Thy phantasy has imposed upon me, & thou oughtest to be ashamed."
> I answer'd: "We impose on one another, & it is but lost time to converse with you whose works are only Analytics."

Blake speaks of the "confident insolence sprouting from systematic reasoning." We may reverse the sequence and see, as Hume does, that the choice of a system may arise from a taste for insolence. This has the value of reminding us of both sides of the transaction; if what a man believes determines his style, his style may also affect his beliefs. Hume speaks of the "sects which secretly form themselves in the literary world" and especially those that take different views of the dignity of human nature.

> The infinite distance between body and mind is a symbol of the infinitely more infinite distance between mind and charity; for charity is supernatural.
>
> All the glory of greatness has no lustre for people who are in search of understanding.
>
> The greatness of clever men is invisible to kings, to the rich, to chiefs, and to all the worldly great.
>
> The greatness of wisdom, which is nothing if not of God, is invisible to the carnal-minded and to the clever. These are three orders differing in kind.
>
> Great geniuses have their power, their glory, their greatness, their victory, their lustre, and have no need of worldly greatness, with which they are not in keeping. They are seen, not by the eye, but by the mind; this is sufficient.
>
> The saints have their power, their glory, their victory, their lustre, and need no worldly or intellectual greatness, with which they have no affinity; for these neither add anything to them, nor take away anything from them. They are seen of God and the angels, and not of the body, nor of the curious mind. God is enough for them. . . .
>
> All bodies together, and all minds together, and all their products, are not equal to the least feeling of charity. This is of an order infinitely more exalted.
>
> From all bodies together, we cannot obtain one little thought; this is impossible, and of another order. From all bodies and minds, we cannot produce a feeling of true charity; this is impossible, and of another and supernatural order.
>
> (793)

This is Pascal's most extensive discussion of the three orders, and they are now ranked in a more traditional way as stages of ascent in a hierarchy. The highest is no longer an order of "will" but one of "charity." The philosophers of "will" take pride in their wisdom: "it cannot be granted to a man that he has made himself more wise, and that he is wrong to be proud: for that is right." Their error lies in assuming that they have made themselves wise, for "God alone gives wisdom, and that is why *Qui gloriatur, in Domini glorietur*" (460). The philosophers have failed to reach true charity: "They have known God, and have not desired solely that men should love Him, but that men should stop short at them!" (463). The order of charity is based upon a hatred of selfhood; it is a true ascent beyond the orders of the flesh and of the mind.

Yet, although Pascal distinguishes between the vertical ascending movement in fragment 793 and the set of horizontal, coequal, and opposed worlds of fragment 460, the two have important resemblances that are distinctive to Pascal's thought. Although the orders of flesh, mind, and charity grow more dignified and more inclusive in their awareness at each stage, they remain discontinuous. There is no graduation by which one moves easily from one to another, nor does one order prepare men for the next above it. Each man is locked in his own order until he has exhausted its possibilities; it is only by finding one order intolerable that he is finally disposed to go beyond it, and nothing he has come to believe in that order can serve him in his movement to the next.

This is an extreme way of stating what is implicit throughout Pascal. The double nature of man is his central theme. Man is at once great and wretched, reasonable and self-deceiving. He participates in two kinds of reality—one governed by his material nature, his passions, and his self-love; the other by his spiritual possibilities, his intuitions of the divine, and his love of God. All of his powers and actions have an ambiguity he can scarcely control; and their very greatness may serve to isolate him all the more from God. It is necessary, therefore, that man have those powers of awareness that can lead him to God, and at the same time that these powers bring him no satisfaction until they are turned to God.

Pascal becomes a vigilant critic of the misuse of these powers, and he makes unremittingly ironic distinctions between the elements that make up the double nature of man and his action. "We make an idol of truth itself; for truth apart from charity is not God, but the image and idol, which we must neither love nor worship; and still less must we love or worship its opposite, namely falsehood" (582). Man must accept his state of semi-darkness, in which God is neither fully revealed nor altogether hidden. "The knowledge of God without that of man's misery causes pride. The knowledge of man's misery without that of God causes despair" (527). "There must be feelings of humility, not from nature, but from penitence, not to rest in them but to go on to greatness. There must be feelings of greatness, not from merit, but from grace, and after having passed through humiliation" (525). Pascal sees all heresies as the reduction of this double truth to a single one:

"unable to conceive the connection of the two opposite truths, and believing that the admission of one involves the exclusion of the other, they adhere to the one, exclude the other, and think of us as opposed to them" (862). The great embodiment of the double truth is, of course, Jesus Christ; he "constitutes the middle course because in Him we find both God and our misery" (527).

No man of his age presented this paradox of man's plight with more thoroughness and intensity than Pascal. The sundering of an Order into orders, and man's necessary blindness to orders other than his own, which Montaigne found evidence for a relativistic view, Pascal interprets as evidence of man's fallen state. He rejoices at such evidence, because it constitutes a reason for man's coming to God. It shows man how intolerable independence from God is, and demands of him that he surrender the self-determination that is inevitable illusion.

The first of Pascal's orders, the order of the flesh, yields a secular world governed by egoism and controlled hatred, a world in which men are ruled by either their desire or their reverence for power. Power stimulates imagination, and imagination creates happiness. But this is imagination in the narrow sense of phantasy; and what it creates is a system of appearance and custom in which men find the stability of a shared dream. Such a world is hateful to the man who can see beyond it; but it is necessary, even providential, for the man who cannot. Man stumbles into a peaceful order, a system he neither earns nor understands. Any society is better than none; in the world of the carnal no society is more just than another, for the idea of justice has no meaning. The keeping of peace, any peace, is sufficient. This is the world of Hobbes's *Leviathan*.

What is striking in the political thought of Pascal and Hobbes alike is the arbitrary and conventional nature of authority. Pascal recognizes man's need for society; it comes of pride, the desire for recognition or esteem, the fear of instability and social disorder. So in Hobbes the competitive quest for grandeur is the source at once of social life and of its disorder; there can be no peace in a world where by his nature each man must overcome every other lest he himself be overcome. Both men see the state as a necessary form of stability, and for Hobbes the undivided authority of a sovereign power is indispensable. Pascal sees the social order as the necessary subjection to power in a fallen world, and Hobbes sees the state as a necessary result of man's inherent selfishness.

Hobbes's *Leviathan* defends any state so long as it is sufficiently strong and stops short of denying its very justification, that is, does not arbitrarily demand of men their lives. Hobbes therefore can make such statements as,

"*Honorable* is whatsoever possession, action, or quality, is an argument and sign of power." All the traditional moral terms, once translatable into denominations of power only because the traditional view of Order assumed that power and virtue are harmonious, are now reduced to terms for simple power. It hardly matters who rules nor by what pretexts so long as the rule is stable.

It follows that the world of the flesh is a world of dress, of red robes and ermine, of cassocks and square caps. The role of Louis XIV, for example, was to become all the more an assertion of power, with the resources of art turned to the creation of effect, as that role lost its greater import. "Beneath the surface, even of Louis's ideas," writes a recent historian, "a certain traditional notion of religious duty is still clearly discernible; but this is emptied of its true content by a new and purely psychological interpretation of the natural self of the ruler and his development—an interpretation which, even at this stage, appears to require scarcely any support from theological and ethical arguments." The surface becomes important, for it alone compels awe where the very nature of the inside becomes at best a problem and at worst an irrelevance. The ceremonious formalities of Louis's court create a dress so blindingly splendid and a management so exquisitely complicated as to exhaust any attention that might be paid to their limitations.

Custom and habit generate the illusion of legitimacy or justice in turn; the survival of power gives it authority and its antiquity seems to confer truth upon it. Pascal's dialectical sense of a double truth leads, finally, to a brilliant fragment on the attitudes toward illusion:

> *The reason of effects.* Degrees. The people honor persons of high birth. The semi-learned despise them, saying that birth is not a personal, but a chance superiority. The learned honor them, not for popular reasons, but for secret reasons. Devout persons, who have more zeal than knowledge, despise them, in spite of that consideration which makes them honored by the learned, because they judge them by a new light which piety gives them. But perfect Christians honor them by another and higher light. So arise a succession of opinions for and against, according to the light one has.
>
> (337)

If the "dignity of man consists in thought," it is in man's mind—in the second order—that we might expect to find his true greatness. The superiority of thought to physical power is clear enough: "By space the universe encompasses and swallows me up like an atom; by thought I comprehend the world." The capacity for knowledge, so thoroughly muffled in the order of the flesh, gives man a kind of dominion over that which outwardly rules him: "man knows that he is wretched . . . but he is really great because he knows it." Still, as we have seen, Pascal resists any Stoical deification of mind. The mind's greatness lies in its ability to see through the impositions of the world; but this penetration does not bring happiness, or even equanimity. It is only the starting point for the upsetting process by which man knows himself a creature of God, for his God is a hidden God who never quite reveals Himself as man might wish.

The theme of the *deus absconditus* or hidden God is Pascal's principal way of asserting the paradox of man's situation: "It is incomprehensible that God should exist, and it is incomprehensible that He should not exist" (230). Every religious choice must, from the point of view of the rational man, be a wager. Later theologians may call it a leap, but Pascal insists upon the power of self-interest which still must govern a man who is not of the order of charity. Such a man must act by calculation, even at the limits of the calculable. God might have disclosed himself in nature, but he leaves men "in a darkness from which they can escape only through Jesus Christ" (242). Jesus "is a God truly hidden; . . . He will be slighted; . . . none will think that it is He; . . . He will be a stone of stumbling, upon which many will stumble, etc. Let people reproach us no longer for want of clearness, since we make a profession of it" (751).

The mysterious double nature of Jesus corresponds to the doubleness of man and nature. For man as man, there is no resolving this doubleness. He must always confront the paradox, "a thesis and antithesis *simultaneously* opposed and inseparable . . . for which there is no hope in this world of solving the irreducibility." As Lucien Goldmann sees Pascal's thought, its tragic aspect lies in the fact that man *is* man to the extent that he asserts the possibility of a synthesis, all the while aware that this assertion itself cannot escape paradox, that the only certainty man can know as man is "an uncertain certainty, a postulate, a wager."

It is man's tragic plight to be placed inexorably in a mean between the extremes where alone he might find peace; this is "not equilibrium but permanent tension, unmoving movement," a tension that can be resolved for Pascal only in the transcendent and mysterious figure of Jesus Christ. Reason can find no certainties on which to rest except the wretchedness of man's condition. If it can discern the intolerable horror of the secular world view of the fleshly, it can only prepare the mind for an assent to more than it can itself understand. "We must know where to doubt, where to feel certain, where to submit. He who does not do so, understands not the force of reason. There are some who offend against these three rules, either by affirming everything as demonstrative, from want of knowing what demonstration is; or by doubting everything, from want of knowing where to submit; or by submitting in everything, from want of knowing where they must judge" (268).

The order of the mind, if it does not know where to submit, tends to become a rationalistic system, which deduces from its first principles all that the world contains or suggests. It claims utter command by thought over the pattern and purpose of human experience. But such command, Pascal shows, is illusory; the reason accepts first principles that fall short of the complexity of nature, and it builds upon them systems that flatter its powers. The infirmity of these systems becomes evident as we approach the limits of our understanding, the double infinity of the inconceivably vast and the infinitesimally small. In one perspective man is nothing, in the other all. "What will he do then but perceive the appearance of the middle of things, in an eternal despair of knowing either their beginning or their end. All things proceed from the Nothing, and are borne towards the Infinite." "Through failure to contemplate these Infinites, men have madly rushed into the examination of nature, as though they bore some proportion to her" (72). Faced with an incomprehensible infinity, man's reason boggles and resists; it defends itself with a fiction. "We represent some [premises] as ultimate for reason, in the same way as in regard to material objects we call that an indivisible point beyond which our senses can no longer perceive anything, although by its nature it is infinitely divisible" (72).

First principles, in so far as they are tenable at all, are given to reason, Pascal insists, not created by it. "We know truth, not only by the reason, but also by the heart, and it is in this last way that we know first principles; and reason, which has no part in it, tries in vain to impugn them." However much it may resent their source and question their authority, "reason must trust these intuitions of the heart, and must base on them every argument" (282). The possibilities of a rational universe are hopeless. We live, after all, and for good cause, less by the slow constructions of reason than by the "easier belief" of custom, which makes us believe "without violence, without art, without argument." Reason can scarcely take account of all that confronts it; it often "wanders, through want of having all its principles present. Feeling does not act thus; it acts in a moment, and it is always ready to act" (252).

The celebration of reason has usually been a celebration of human dignity. Man as rational animal is in command of his nature, both through the self-knowledge that gives him intellectual mastery and the self-government that gives him ethical control. In declaring the limits of reason to be the limits of God as well as man—in assuming that God cannot or will not act against reason—man asserts a continuity between the divine and the human, and constructs a universe that conforms to the powers of the human mind. The greater man's confidence in his rational power, the greater his sense of freedom: he can choose for himself, his choices have authority, and his use of choice is a proper fulfillment of his nature. For Pascal, however, man is neither so free as he dreams nor so wise as he trusts. He is always building, as Blake was to observe later, a mundane shell that shuts out the horror of the void and protects his world from foundering into chaos. But this same shell shuts him off from a knowledge of his full nature. In Blake the shell prevents man from realizing his capacities; it imposes upon him the tyranny of an inert, external nature. In Pascal a similar shell is created by the rationalism that lulls man with a dream of a world in which his mind is master.

Pascal's purpose is to place reason within a self that surrounds and undoes it. The self that acts with intuitive certainty is not anti-rational but irrational. It exists either below or above reason, a creature of custom and automatism on the one hand, of charity and grace on the other. The orders of flesh and charity have curious ways of meeting, and the most ambiguous term in Pascal is *coeur*. The ambiguity arises from the double object of the heart's love: self and God. Our "action is often determined, not by the grounds which we could, or even by grounds which we *do* explicitly assign, but by a fundamental attraction to, or love of, either God or self as the case may be, which may not be actually present to the conscious mind at the moment." The *coeur*, the *automate*, the force of love, the whole rationally groundless basis of behavior are frightening to the rational man and providentially beyond his control.

From this view of man's nature follow conclusions about his universe. His God is not simply the transparent rational Mind that he can know with confident love and easy assurance; nor is He to be sought in the design of nature, like the Pantocrator of Newton. God is at once knowable and unknown. Adequate knowledge of Him cannot be won by reasoning about nature; yet any knowledge that neglects the criticism of reason is likely to be superstition ("submitting to everything, from want of knowing where they must judge"). The universe is susceptible to scientific study (as Pascal, of all men, knew); yet its very mysteries throw us back upon the sense of how arbitrary and limited our scientific constructs are. We are left in desperate need of reason as a guard against self-deception and in desperate danger of the greatest self-deception of all, idolatry of reason.

If the orders of the flesh and the mind are rejected, the ultimate celebration Pascal allows the order of charity is somewhat chilling. First of all, it can be known only in its own terms, and Pascal's movement between will and heart, heart and charity, makes the difficulty of knowing it all the sharper. We can know what it is not, as in our knowledge of God, more confidently than what it is. Second, charity is "of an order infinitely more exalted" than the other two—but so exalted that it is totally divorced from the power of this world:

> The saints have their power, their glory, their victory, their lustre, and need no worldly or intellectual greatness, with which they have no affinity. . . . They are seen of God and the angels, and not of the body, nor of the curious mind. God is enough for them.
>
> (793)

This radical separation between Christ and culture has its sublimity but also its destructiveness; it sets so abrupt a chasm between the orders as to imperil all aspiration. One must admire the power to draw distinctions, to insist upon the discontinuities of our experience and upon qualitative differences. Pascal forbids us those comfortable confusions that allow us to make easy substitutions: political action for personal honor, public service for private devotion, success for self-knowledge. And yet, does he? As soon as he must come to terms with the worldly power from which charity is set infinitely apart, he has lost the means of criticizing or governing it. To renounce the world, he must first submit to it, accede to its power, and accept that power as legitimate in its sphere.

If the world of power is a fallen world in which a hidden God bids man seek his private salvation, there is no principle of resistance. One cannot resist, one can only renounce. For resistance will itself seem further complicity in sin, further self-deception or pride. There is an almost inexorable logic by which the most radical rejection of the world becomes the most conservative submission to it. If all that is of value exists in another order, infinitely separated, which one cannot wed with lower orders, charity has achieved a purity that looks very much like irrelevance. Man can no longer take excessive pride in his reason, but can he trust his mind at all? Is nature merely a source of temptation and subsequent disillusion to the "curious mind"? Can man's moral virtues lead him somehow to spiritual vision, or do they inevitably produce pharisaism? Ronald Knox put the problem well:

> Pascal recognizes the classical proofs of God's existence and admits the force of them, but he dislikes them. You may almost

say that if he had been in a position to do it he would have hushed them up. He *wanted* our fallen nature, left without grace, to be as weak and miserable as possible. . . . his picture of man's misery remained incomplete, lop-sided, if you could think of man un-redeemed as possessing any sky-light, even, that gave on the supernatural.

(Enthusiasm)

The difficulties of Pascal's position arise in part from his rhetorical strategy; he takes much for granted and seeks to shock those men Shaftesbury was later to call "half-thinkers." Historians have observed that sentimentalism arose in England partly from the orthodox refutation of Hobbes's account of man as naturally predatory. Terms that had held together a composite view were split open by the very pressure of argument. So in Pascal we can see terms that have latent within them a celebration of the heart he did not intend, but could hardly control once the terms had been released. The reasons of the heart are invoked against the rationalist, but the heart can move from intuitive rightness to sympathetic artistry, even visionary wisdom.

At the very least Pascal's doctrine of the three orders is a brilliant rhetorical device for making us see false orders replacing true, disorder itself exhibiting a formal pattern that is a parody of what man might achieve or even thinks he has achieved. Yet the very dialectical brilliance produces paradoxes that men need to resolve, and the writers with whom we shall be concerned in [*To the Palace of Wisdom*] sought to resolve them in ways that Pascal illuminates rather than anticipates. Some try to establish a continuity among all three orders; others reconcile two in order to overthrow the third. What gives Pascal a peculiar value for our purposes is the dramatic way in which he raises the question of orders and all but subverts the more traditional idea of Order.

JEAN MESNARD

The Revelation of God

Man cannot reach God by his own powers alone. Reason demonstrates this fact; religion supposes it. Yet man is not condemned to the irrationality of the wager. What does this mean if not that man can count on some powers other than his own? Whence comes this new help if not from God? As soon as God intervenes, His relationship with man is modified. Reason has at its disposal new data, fulcrums from which it can rise to conclusions that seemed inaccessible before. Reason can no longer pride itself of its power, once it has been forced to bow, to accept the loss of initiative; Deism is no longer conceivable. The mind, which remained blind when the will was placed before the restraining exigency of the wager, is penetrated by a new light. The affirmation of God becomes perfectly legitimate and correct only as of the moment when God revealed Himself.

The expression "revelation of God" can be understood in two different ways. It is applied to the delivery of the divine message, to this corpus of knowledge about Himself that God transmits to men, to this body of doctrine to which, through faith, every adept of a revealed religion adheres and which distinguishes revealed religion from natural religion. But in a second sense, God reveals Himself when He manifests Himself as a person, when He imposes the idea of His presence by means of signs accessible to the senses or the intelligence, when He appears among men. In the first case, God defines Himself; in the second, He reveals Himself.

From *Pascal*, translated by Claude and Marcia Abraham. © 1969 by Desclée de Brouwer. University of Alabama Press, 1969.

If Pascal constantly effected this distinction, at least implicitly, he never-theless considered these two aspects of revelation as inseparable and com-plementary. When presenting itself to men the revealed doctrine is always marked with the divine seal and associated with signs that authenticate it. Inversely, when God manifests Himself it is in order to give a teaching, to attest to a truth. Faith is never without proof, and proof is the basis for faith.

> There is a reciprocal duty between God and men. . . .
> Men owe it to God to receive the religion which He sends to
> them.
> God owes it to men not to lead them into error.
> (Pensée 843, Brunschvicg edition)

Pascal thus returned indirectly to an idea that he held dear: when God reveals Himself it is not only so that we may affirm His existence, it is also so that we may embrace His religion. Faith forms a total; it is not acquired through a successive adhesion to each one of the verities of which it is composed (and of which the existence of God is the first). God does not reveal His existence without also revealing His doctrine. In other words, it is not the "God of the philosophers and of the scholars" (*Mémorial*) who reveals Himself—a revelation of which God has no need, since human reason flatters itself of being able to reach Him directly—it is rather "the God of Abraham, the God of Isaac, the God of Jacob" (556; cf. *Mém.*), the God who speaks to Moses through the burning bush and presides over the destinies of the people He has chosen to keep His law; it is the "God of the Christians" (556; cf. 544), whose personality can be defined only in relation to the totality of Christianity; it is the true God, the "only true God" (*Mém.*).

To this supernatural revelation must correspond proofs that are equally supernatural. If God asks reason to submit, He does not leave it without guaranty. On this subject, Pascal had eternal Wisdom speak with a remark-able precision:

> I do not mean that you should submit and believe in me without
> reason, and I do not pretend to dominate over you tyrannically.
> Nor do I claim to explain everything to you. And, in order to
> reconcile these contradictions, I intend to show you clearly, by
> convincing proof, by signs of divinity in me, which will convince
> you of my nature and invest me with authority, by means of
> wonders and proofs which you cannot reject; and that afterwards,
> I mean you to believe the things which I teach you when you

find no other cause to reject them other than that you cannot of
yourselves know whether they exist or not.

(430)

In other words, religious truths can be neither demonstrated nor con-
tested. They are quite beyond the reach of human powers. But they are the
teachings of a God who has given signs of His divinity and to whom it is
therefore reasonable and necessary to submit. God would be tyrannical if
He demanded the adhesion of the mind without the participation of the
mind. Man would show himself to be "superstitious" and not "pious" (255)
if he submitted without reason. But the reasons that man has for submitting
are not found by him. They are proposed by God. Supernatural evidence,
just like natural evidence, invites the mind to bow before it.

Among the revealing signs of God there is one that imposed itself from
the thought to Pascal's reflection: miracles. Circumstances contributed to
this. According to the capital testimony of his sister Gilberte, Pascal was
profoundly moved by the so-called Miracle of the Holy Thorn, by which
on March 24, 1656, his niece and godchild Marguerite Périer was cured of
a lachrymal fistula that had been considered incurable.

> The joy he felt as a result [said Gilberte] was so great that he
> was completely absorbed by it. And as he never turned his mind
> to anything without much reflection, this particular miracle fos-
> tered in him several very important thoughts on miracles in gen-
> eral, both in the Old and in the New Testaments. If miracles
> exist, it follows that there must be something beyond what we
> call nature. The consequence is highly sensible: we have only to
> convince ourselves of the certainty and authenticity of miracles.
> Now, there are rules for this which are equally sensible and these
> rules happen to be right for the miracles which are in the Old
> Testament. These miracles are therefore true: there is therefore
> something beyond nature.
>
> But these miracles have further signs showing that their prin-
> ciple is God, and those of the New Testament particularly have
> signs showing that He who worked them was the Messiah awaited
> by men. Thus, as the miracles of the Old and of the New Tes-
> taments prove that there is a God, those of the New Testament
> in particular prove that Jesus was the true Messiah.

The fragments of the *Pensées* that have come down to us do not contain
the elements of so precise a theory. It is probable that Gilberte was somewhat

mistaken about the deep thought of her brother, who supposedly drew from the miracles of the Old Testament proof not only of the existence of God but of the truth of the entire Jewish religion, first form of the Christian religion that is, in turn, proven by the miracles of the New Testament. On the other hand, Gilberte was right to emphasize that a general reflection emanated from the specific reflection on the Miracle of the Holy Thorn. Among the sheaves that constitute the *Pensées*, the oldest are made up of notes on miracles from which a double orientation manifests itself, one polemical, the other apologetic. On the one hand the fight begun in the *Provinciales* is continued: the marvelous healing of Marguerite Périer furnished new food to the controversies between friends and adversaries of Port-Royal; on the side of the former Pascal invoked the authority of this divine testimony. On the other hand, the constant comparison of the Miracle of the Holy Thorn with the miracles of the Old and the New Testaments, imposed by the necessities of polemics, served as a spark to a reflection directed no longer against the Jesuits but against the libertines. However, the bulk of the thoughts on this subject are connected to controversy rather than to apology.

However limited the object of these thoughts may be, however insufficient their elaboration, they nevertheless allow one to foresee an important aspect that one must be careful not to caricature.

The miracle is a language that God speaks to us. It is not a useless anarchical manifestation of the supernatural; its essence is to signify. It settles contestations: "Miracles, the mainstay of religion. They were the mark of the Jews. They were the mark of the Christians, the saints, the Innocents, the true believers" (851). The miracle distinguishes the true from the false doctrine; it gives assurance to those who are in truth; it invites those who are in error to detach themselves from it. Oftentimes it even symbolizes this doctrine whose mainstay it is. Jesus Christ "proves that He forgives sins by performing a miracle" (808; cf. 643). Thus, the curing of the paralytic reported by Saint Mark expresses, in the bodily order, the healing of the soul procured by the remission of sins. The power of Jesus, manifest in visible things, guarantees this power over the invisible things that He simultaneously attributes to Himself. Generally, "miracles prove the power which God has over hearts by the power which He exercises over bodies" (851). In more profound but also more obscure terms: "Miracles and truth are necessary because man must be convinced entirely in body and in soul" (806).

It is proper for any language to require interpretation, and so it is with the language of miracles. To distinguish the real miracles from the false, to determine what God meant by them—Pascal undertook to propose rules concerning all of these matters. But what he particularly wished to point out was that the most shining and clearest true miracle can be warded off, in a way, by whoever refuses to welcome the declared truth that they consider unpleasant. Thus, for example, the Pharisees could choose to be blind to the prodigies of Jesus Christ. To be understood, all divine signs demand an attitude of submission.

Finally, the significance of the miracle is tied to the circumstances in which it appears. It places itself in a precise manner in time; it constitutes God's answer to the questions of the moment; it aims at certain witnesses and addresses itself to determined interlocutors. Although this privileged manifestation of the supernatural nevertheless maintains a general bearing, Pascal, by considering its relation with the moment, was led to limit the place of the miracle in the permanent principles concerning the approach to God.

Therefore, if Pascal did at first conceive of an apology based exclusively on miracles, he soon went beyond it to adopt a broader perspective. That is what Gilberte suggested indirectly:

> All the different reflections of my brother concerning miracles gave him many new lights on religion. As all truths are derived one from the other, it was enough that he applied himself to one, the others would come crowding in, and he analyzed them in such a way that he was carried away, according to what he often told us. And it was on this occasion that he felt so aroused against atheists that, seeing in the insights which God had given him means to convince them and reduce them irremediably, he applied himself to this work whose parts, which we have gathered, make us so regret that he was unable to assemble them himself.

Thus, in tackling his *Apologie* head-on, Pascal nevertheless did not abandon the notion of miracles. Any revelation of God, any insertion of the supernatural into the human, any sign proving the truth of religion, can legitimately be called miracle. "I would not be Christian without miracles, said Saint Augustine" (812). This thought expresses only the very general idea that God cannot demand faith if He has not revealed Himself.

In the same sheaf of the *Pensées*, Pascal affirmed very clearly that miracles, in the restrictive sense of the word, are necessary only at certain stages of revelation. During the time of Jesus Christ, for example: "People would not have sinned had they not believed Jesus Christ without miracles" (811).

Now, to lead to God, we have at our disposal another sign of a more permanent range:

> Jesus Christ performed miracles, and the Apostles after Him, and the first saints in great numbers, because, as the prophecies were not yet fulfilled and were being fulfilled by them, only miracles testified. It had been foretold that the Messiah would convert the nations. How would this prophecy have been accomplished without the conversion of the nations, and how could the nations have been converted to the Messiah had they not seen this final effect of the prophecies which prove it? Therefore, before His death, rise from the dead, and conversion of the nations, all this was not accomplished and thus miracles were necessary during all of that time. Now they are no longer necessary against the Jews because the fulfilled prophecies are a continuing miracle.
>
> (838)

> The greatest proofs of Jesus Christ are the prophecies. That is also where God was most lavish; for the event that has fulfilled them is a miracle subsisting from the birth of the Church until the end. Therefore God has raised up prophets for sixteen hundred years; and for four hundred years thereafter, He scattered all these prophecies with the Jews who bore them to all the corners of the earth. Such was the preparation for the birth of Jesus Christ, whose Gospels having to be believed by everyone, it was necessary not only that there be prophecies to make people believe it, but that these prophecies be spread throughout the world so that the Gospel should be believed by everyone.
>
> (706)

Thus, the realization of the prophecies became for Pascal the great sign of the truth of Christianity—a sign that is constantly offered to the eyes of all men and one that, by virtue of this fact, is self-sufficient.

This sign is more intimately associated with the doctrine of which it constitutes the proof than in the case of miracles. By accomplishing His earthly mission, Jesus Christ has realized the prophecies. At the same time, through His life as well as His word, He has expressed the divine message, the content of which has been registered in the Gospels. With the coming on earth of the Incarnate Word, the revelation of God, in the two meanings of the word "revelation," reaches a pinnacle that will not be transcended in this world. It is only by means of the eternal life, by means of the "glory" (233), that man will obtain a more total revelation.

The prophecies are essentially a proof of Jesus Christ. But this does not limit their range. All Christian truths are contained in Jesus Christ; it is impossible to reach any of them without passing through Jesus Christ:

> We know God only through Jesus Christ. Without this Mediator all communication with God is removed; through Jesus Christ we know God. All those who have claimed to know God and to prove His existence without Jesus Christ had only inadequate proofs. But as proofs of Jesus Christ, we have the prophecies which are solid and palpable proofs. And these prophecies, having been accomplished and proven true by events, attest to the certainty of these truths and therefore are proof of the divinity of Jesus Christ. In Him and by Him we therefore know God. Outside of that and without Scripture, without original sin, without the necessary Mediator who was promised and who came, God cannot be proved absolutely nor can either a good doctrine or a good morality be taught. But through Jesus Christ and in Jesus Christ one can prove God and teach morality and doctrine. Jesus Christ is therefore the true God of men.
>
> (547)

Pascal supported his conviction that the prophecies constitute a total proof by yet another line of argument. The writings of the prophets are a part of the Old Testament, and the accomplishment of the prophecies is attested to by the New Testament—whence the following reasoning: *"Proof of the two Testaments simultaneously.*—To prove the two at the same time, we have only to see if the prophecies of the one are realized in the other" (642). The Old and the New Testaments having been constituted in an independent manner, their convergence is miraculous and attests to the divine origin of both. Now, these two books together constitute the Bible, the sum total or revelation, and thus is the divine seal affixed on the divine doctrine.

But this second way of looking at the prophetic argument is, in fact, identical to the preceding one. Scripture "has only Jesus Christ as its object" (548), "Jesus Christ, whom the two Testaments consider, the Old as its expectation, the New as its model, both as their center" (740).

The putting of the prophecies into operation forces us to ascribe a grand design to God. The entire mission of the Jewish people has been to prophesy. It is from within this people that God has chosen the prophets who, inspired by His spirit, announced the coming of the Messiah. But it was not enough

that this announcement be made; it was further necessary that it be dissem-
inated everywhere. On this score the Jewish people have further served the
plan of God, who dispersed them throughout the world, dispersing with
them the Holy Books, which they revered and which were thus brought to
the attention of the world:

> Even if a single man had compiled a book of the prophecies
> concerning Jesus Christ, concerning the time and the manner,
> and if Jesus Christ had come in accordance with these prophecies,
> it would be an infinite force.
>
> But there is much more than that. It was a succession of men
> who for four thousand years, constantly and without variation,
> came one after the other to foretell this same coming. It was an
> entire people who proclaimed it, and one that had existed for four
> thousand years in order to bear witness as one body to their
> certainty about it, and from which they were not to be diverted
> by whatever threats and persecutions to which they were sub-
> jected: this is something far more considerable.
>
> (710)

Thus an entire concept of history is involved in Pascal's reflection on
the prophecies. But in an apologetic perspective, what is especially important
is that such a reflection can be imposed on any man, the convincing value
of the sign constituted by the prophecies. Now if the authors of the New
Testament, then the ancient apologists, have constantly appealed to the
prophetic argument to show the divinity of Christianity, it is nevertheless
true that the argument was not decisively imposed and, notably, that most
of the Jews did not recognize in Christ the Messiah announced by their
prophets. How can this difficulty be resolved?

The method that appears simplest would consist of envisaging the prophecies one by one and to give for each one a manifest proof of its realization.
Pascal rejected this method except for one category of predictions: those that
announce the time of the coming of the Messiah. Their meaning is particularly clear and applies itself exactly to the time of the coming of Jesus
Christ:

> That during the fourth dynasty, before the destruction of the
> second temple, before the domination of the Jews was taken away,
> in the seventieth week of Daniel, during the period of the second
> temple, the pagans would be instructed and led to the knowledge
> of the God worshipped by the Jews; and those who love Him
> would be delivered from their enemies and filled with the fear
> and the love of God.

And it happened that during the fourth dynasty, before the destruction of the second temple, etc., the pagans in mass adored God and led an angelic life; the girls consecrated their virginity and their lives to God; the men renounced all pleasures. What Plato could not persuade a small number of chosen and educated men to accept, was accepted by a hundred million ignorant men when coming from a secret force made manifest by a few words.

(724)

With this one exception the prophecies are obscure. The contradiction appears obvious between the Messiah awaited by the Jews and the one recognized by the Christians. The foretold Messiah was to be a powerful and glorious king who would vanquish the enemies of Israel. Jesus Christ accomplished nothing of the sort. He lived poor and gained no temporal success; in the realm of human achievements His life was a failure. He himself defined His realm as being spiritual and claimed power only over souls. Is this contradiction not insurmountable? For Pascal, in fact, the contradiction did not exist. The prophecies are ambiguous; they are expressed in a figurative language; in it, the material is the image of the spiritual. In fact, the prophets attributed only a spiritual royalty to the Messiah; the victory that they announced had to be won over evil and sin—the only true enemies of the people of Israel (as of all men). This principle, applied to the details of the prophetic writings, allows us to have the aspects of the foretold Messiah coincide with the face of Jesus of Nazareth.

To show that the prophecies were realized, it is therefore sufficient to demonstrate in a rigorous manner that the prophets were in fact expressing themselves figuratively. Pascal applied himself at length to this task:

To show that the Old Testament is only symbolic, and that the prophets meant other goods when they spoke of temporal goods, the arguments are:

First, that this would be unworthy of God.

Secondly, that their pronouncements express very clearly the promise of temporal goods and that they nevertheless say that their pronouncements are obscure and that their meaning will not be understood at all. Whence it becomes apparent that this secret sense was not that which they expressed openly, and that consequently they meant other sacrifices, another savior, etc. They say that this will be understood only at the end of time. Jer. xxx, *ult*.

The third proof is that their pronouncements are contradictory and cancel out, so that there is an obvious and flagrant contra-

diction if one assumes that they meant nothing other than those
of Moses when they spoke the words of law and sacrifice. Therefore, they meant something else, contradicting themselves sometimes in a single chapter.

Now, in order to grasp the meaning of an author . . .(659) . . .
it is necessary to reconcile all the conflicting passages.

                                                          (684)

Thus, among other arguments, the very declarations of the prophets
prove that their language has a double meaning and that "the Old Testament
is a cipher" (691). It is not possible to be satisfied with the literal; it is
necessary to go to the spiritual. That is a search that, as we shall see, is
essential to the discovery of religious truth.

Is the lack of evidence of the prophecies of a nature to diminish their
value as a sign? In no way. It even brings about a consequence that reinforces
it. These prophecies, which the Jews carried throughout the world, remain
incomprehensible to them. They did not see their realization, and their
descendants, keeping up their error, continue to await the promised Messiah
and to conceive of Him as a glorious and liberating sovereign. Ever since
they began to bear the prophecies, the Jews have been testifying in favor of
the Christians, but their testimony is involuntary and, as a result, rigorously
impartial. This situation is in conformity with the plan of God; the Jews
have had "the two qualities which it was necessary for them to have had: to
be very much like the Messiah in order to symbolize Him, and very unlike
Him in order not to be suspect witnesses" (663).

It nevertheless remains true that, if the ambiguity of the prophecies can
be removed through reasoning, it remains no less a possible obstacle to the
understanding of the sign by any man. But once more, is it not the very
nature of a sign to demand an interpretation?

By the prophecies, it is not isolated facts that are called upon to testify,
it is a "whole people" (710) that, by an essential aspect of its history, has
revealed the presence of God in the world. But the perspective can be further
broadened to the point where it embraces all of history. The Christian
religion then draws a new proof from the ascertaining of its "perpetuity," a
new revealing sign of God.

Perpetuity consists of the permanence of the true religion during all
times.

> This religion, which lies in believing that man has fallen from a
> state of glory and communication with God into a state of sadness,
> of penance and estrangement from God, but that after this life

we shall be restored by a Messiah who was to come, has always
existed on earth. All things have passed and this one has remained
for which all things exist.

(613)

Pascal conceives this permanence in the most rigorous manner possible.
He literally considers "that the true Jews and the true Christians have but
one and the same religion" (610).

In its original form, the idea is nothing more than a corollary of the
prophetic argument. "There has always been a belief in the Messiah" (616).

> Let us consider that, since the beginning of the world, the ex-
> pectation or worship of the Messiah has subsisted without inter-
> ruption; that there have been men who said that God had revealed
> to them that a Redeemer who would save His people would be
> born; that Abraham came afterwards to say that it had been
> revealed to him that He would be born of him by a son that he
> would have; that Jacob declared that among his twelve children
> He would be born of Judah; that Moses and the prophets came
> afterwards to announce the time and the manner of His coming;
> that they said that the law which they had was valid only until
> the coming of the Messiah's; that until then it would be perpetual,
> but that the other would endure forever; that thus their law, or
> that of the Messiah of which it was a promise, would always be
> on earth; that in fact it has always lasted; that finally Jesus Christ
> came in all the foretold circumstances. That is admirable.
>
> (617)

Since the beginning of the world and to the end of time, "Jesus Christ is
the object of everything and the center to which everything is drawn" (556).

But it is not only through hope that the "true Jews" communicated with
the "true Christians"; it is also through faith. The Jewish law was the image
and the promise of the religion of Jesus Christ. Just as the prophecies express
in a material, "carnal" language the spiritual good that the Messiah was to
bring, so the religious practices of the Jews, their "carnal" rites, the circumcision for example, their material sacrifices, the formalism of their law, are
all to be considered as symbolic of the "circumcision of the heart" (683; cf.
610), of the inner sacrifice demanded of the Christian, of a law which can
be synopsized in the single word "charity," that is to say, love. This deep
sense of the Jewish religion is demonstrated by a method similar to the one
applied to the prophecies:

If the law and the sacrifices are the truth, they must be pleasing
to God and not displeasing. If they are symbols they must please
and displease.

Now throughout Scripture, they please and displease.

It is said that the law will be changed, that the sacrifice will
be changed; that they will be without law, without princes, and
without sacrifices; that a new covenant will be made; that the law
will be renewed; that the precepts which they received are not
good; that their sacrifices are abominable; that God did not demand any.

It is said, on the contrary, that the law will last forever; that
this covenant will be forever; that the sacrifice will be forever;
the the scepter will never leave them, since it must not leave them
until the coming of the eternal King.

Do all these passages mark that this all be reality? No. That
it be symbolic? No; rather that it is reality or symbol. But the
first, excluding the literal, show that it is only symbolic.

All these passages together cannot be said to be literally true;
all can be considered symbolic: therefore, they are not considered
literal but symbolic. *Agnus occisus ab origine mundi juge sacrifictum.*

(685)

The Jewish religion was not to be interpreted literally. The rites it had
prescribed had no intrinsic value; they formed a type of envelope to be
penetrated. The "true Jews" perceived the truth beyond the symbol; their
faith was not [different] from that which Jesus Christ defined. "The God of
Abraham, the God of Isaac, the God of Jacob" is also "the God of the
Christians" (556).

The "saints" (613) of the Old Testament also knew how to see beyond
the events they witnessed and to read in the history of their people the
history of the salvation of the world. It is not only the religion, it is also the
entire destiny of the Jews that must be considered as symbolic. Such is the
meaning of the great miracles of the Old Testament:

> God, wishing to show that He could create a holy people, with
> an invisible holiness, and to fill it with eternal glory, made visible
> things. As nature is an image of grace, He made among the good
> things in the realm of nature what He was to do among those of
> the realm of grace, so that the people would see that He could
> create invisible things since He readily made visible ones.
>
> He thus saved this people from the flood; He caused them to

be born of Abraham; He redeemed them from their enemies and gave them rest.

The aim of God was not to save from the flood and to give birth to an entire people of Abraham simply to lead them into the promised land.

. . . God has therefore shown the power He has of giving invisible rewards by demonstrating the power He has over the visible.

(643)

What realizes perpetuity is therefore not, properly speaking, the fact that the Jewish religion found its accomplishment in the Christian religion; it is that there have always been Christians, the "saints" of the Jewish people being perfectly similar to the "true Christians," while the "carnal Christians" (607), who think they they are able to do without loving God and who put all their hope in the material rites of the sacrifices, are no less perfectly similar to the "carnal Jews" of the old law.

Now these "true Jews" and "true Christians" were able to preserve and transmit the torch of truth only at the price of unheard of difficulties in the face of which any merely human enterprise would have crumbled:

At the beginning of the world, men were carried away by every type of disorder, and yet there were saints such as Enoch, Lamech, and others, who waited patiently for the Christ who had been promised from the beginning of the world. Noah saw the wickedness of men carried to the highest degree; and he deserved to save the world in person through the hope of a Messiah whose symbol he was. Abraham was surrounded by idolators when God revealed to him the mystery of the Messiah whom he hailed from afar. At the time of Isaac and Jacob, abominations were widespread over all the earth; but these saints lived their faith; and Jacob, dying and blessing his children, cried out in an ecstasy that made him interrupt his speech: "I await, o my God, the saviour which you have promised: *Salutare tuum exspectabo Domine*."

The Egyptians were infected with idolatry and magic; God's people themselves were led astray by their example; and yet Moses and others believed in Him they did not see and adored Him, looking to the eternal gifts which He was preparing for them.

The Greeks, and the Romans after them, caused false gods to

reign; the poets created a hundred diverse theologies; the philosophers split into a thousand different sects. And yet there were
always, in the heart of Judea, chosen men who foretold the advent
of this Messiah who was known only to them.

He finally came in the fullness of time; and since then so many
schisms and heresies, so many overthrowings of states, so many
changes of every sort have taken place; and this Church, which
adores Him who has always been adored, has subsisted without
interruption. And what is admirable, incomparable and completely divine is that this religion, which has always endured,
has always been fought. A thousand times it was on the eve of
total destruction; and, every time that it was in this state, God
restored it by extraordinary strokes of His might. For what is
astonishing is that it has maintained itself without yielding or
bending to the will of tyrants. For it is not strange that a state
endures when its laws have to give way to necessity.

(613)

But religion never suffered or made use of such a thing. Therefore
these compromises, or miracles, are necessary. It is not strange
to preserve oneself by yielding, and it is not properly speaking
to maintain oneself; and yet do they perish entirely: none has
lasted a thousand years. But that this religion has been able to
always subsist, and inflexible, that is divine.

(614)

Furthermore, it is not only because of outside obstacles, but because of
its inner nature, that the Christian religion has not been able to subsist
without paradox and without miracle. "The only religion against nature,
against common sense, against our pleasures, is the only one which has
always been" (605).

The idea of perpetuity, like the analysis of the prophecies, permits the
maintenance of a narrow tie between the revealed doctrine and the sign that
authenticates it. But the divine intervention is less obvious, and it is only
the solidity of the work that attests its supernatural character. That is without
a doubt the reason that prompted Pascal to develop the prophetic argument
with such emphasis.

Thus it is through the Bible that the double revelation of God operates,
and this book, which contains the divine doctrine, also bears the mark of its
supernatural origin. Pascal carried his reflections on this subject very far.
His exegesis, elaborated at length, is of a remarkable originality. And yet

this part of the *Pensées* has been very much neglected by most of the commentators, whether believers or unbelievers, although such neglect clearly renders impossible any precise and coherent synthesis of a religious thought whose general equilibrium disappears as soon as an element is lacking.

One should not believe that the essential part of this thought consists in what appears to us notoriously caducous. That Pascal did not apply a critical and historical method to the interpretation of the Bible, that he did not foresee the difficulties that a Richard Simon would raise—that is certainly true. But several considerations force us to regard this as of only limited importance.

First of all, it is not out of a desire to conform or out of timidity that Pascal omitted this critical study. Without a doubt he did not suspect, any more than his Port-Royal friends did, the magnitude of the task that presented itself. But how would he not have been ready to assimilate the conquest of a rigorous critique, he who fundamentally posited that nothing that is accessible to reason could be the domain of faith? In biblical criticism, just as in the revision of Scholastic physics, Pascal would have seen not a threat to faith, but a means to purify it, to establish it on its real ground.

What remains is that the problem did not occur to him. In point of fact, his attention was focused in an entirely different direction. The literal meaning of the Bible attracted him hardly at all; he became particularly interested in the symbolic exegesis. Now such an exegesis remains always legitimate, whatever the size of the critical work to which the literal commentary will have given birth. Having been abandoned for two centuries, this way of approaching the sacred text today enjoys a remarkable return to favor. It may perhaps be said that it could never impose itself on someone devoid of faith. It seems to us, however, that in many cases the symbolic or allegorical value of certain parts of the Old Testament can be suggested by the analysis of the intentions of the author, that is to say, by Pascal's very own method. Undoubtedly, this very method, applied today, would not lead to the same conclusions. But the important thing is that its use can still be justified. Of course, if from exegesis we pass over to spirituality and to the idea of the "hidden God," on which we shall have more to say, the permanent value of the Pascalian reflection is even more evident.

More than the use of the symbolic interpretation, what bothers us in this part of the *Pensées* are the extremes and the systematizing spirit that it contains. The almost total suppression of the literal sense of the prophecies, the refusal to grant any value to the Jewish religion literally considered, the refusal to grant any religious import to the march of the Jews towards the promised land, the idea that the real Jews and the real Christians have exactly the same religion—all of these deal too gratuitously with this great law of history, that is, the law of evolution. In his thirst for the absolute, in his conviction that there can be no religious truth other than a total one, Pascal excluded any idea of progress in the revelation of God. Does this mean that the introduction of this idea is of a nature to ruin the argumentation of the *Pensées* concerning prophecies and perpetuity? Far from it. Pascal essentially wanted to seize religion through the intermediary of history. This is as perfectly legitimate a step for the believer as for the unbeliever, and one that responds to a profound tendency of the modern mind. The fact that we have a different concept of history than Pascal did obliges us to revise, but not to challenge his method. Thus the idea of perpetuity remains if one considers, with the modern Christian, that the Jewish religion and history constitute not the first form of the Christian religion but rather the preparation for it; that revelation passes through successive stages, gaining each time in precision and scope; that God acts as a "pedagogue," so to speak, progressively leading His people towards a truth too high to be directly attained—if one substitutes for the idea of an integral revelation reserved to a few the idea of a partial revelation offered to all.

Fundamentally, Pascal's entire argumentation concerning the Bible rests on two main ideas, and it is only by attacking these that one reaches the basis of the principles of the doctrine of the *Pensées*. The first one consists of maintaining above all that the Christian truth is a revealed truth. While a widespread tendency among theologians urges them to make revelation enter as much as possible into the categories of reason, Pascal on the contrary argues vehemently for the autonomy of revelation and considers that it must be assimilated not through a rational incorporation but by the submission of the mind to the fact that revelation constitutes. The second idea, which directly commands the apologetic method, can be expressed thus: the proof of revelation is furnished by the history of revelation. God reveals Himself by revealing His doctrine. This God, present in history, is a living God, a God who infinitely transcends the universe that He has created and whose laws of nature could not exhaust the being, a truly personal God who enters into time and constantly speaks to men. These two ideas are in no way harmed by the evolution of biblical criticism, and they can be developed in ways different from those of Pascal without losing their profoundly Pascalian character.

Using these two ideas as points of departure, it is possible to understand the place held in the *Pensées* by the person of Jesus Christ. The "Word" has come to bring revelation to men. God has sent Him to preach His doctrine, to remove the veil which covered the truth in the Old Testament, to give the "key to the cipher" (681). Moreover, there is no revelation other than that of Jesus Christ. Everything that God has made known of Himself through other means is only a promise or symbol of what has been announced through the only true way. This we have already amply ascertained. The totality of revelation is concentrated in the mission of Jesus Christ. At the same time, Jesus Christ is God Himself descended upon earth; He is the Son testifying for His Father. Never had the "living God" better deserved His name; never had He appeared more visible; never had He become a fact to this point. Jesus Christ is therefore the sign par excellence of the truth of Christianity. The Bible, we have said, works the double revelation of God. It is permissible to take up again the same formula, in a still more precise sense, concerning the one who is the "center" (740) of the two Testaments.

But Jesus Christ is not only God; He is man. His message is not only the truth of God, but the truth of man. This message, even before it was announced by His word, was proposed by His person. Jesus Christ Himself signifies the total truth since "the Christian religion . . . properly consists in the mystery of the Redeemer who, uniting in Himself the two natures, human and divine, has taken men out of the corruption of sin to reconcile them to God in His divine person" (556).

This is why Jesus Christ is the indispensable Mediator. Between the corruption of man and the perfection of God, the distance may be crossed only by passing through Him who has assumed the misery of man to make it rise again to God. "It is not only impossible but useless to know God without Jesus Christ . . ." (549). Impossible: God can be known only if He has revealed Himself; now, it is His Son who has revealed Him to us. Useless: the knowledge is not meant to satisfy our curiosity, but to procure our salvation; now, there is no salvation for anyone who does not also know his misery.

> The knowledge of God without the knowledge of one's misery leads to pride.
> The knowledge of one's misery without the knowledge of God leads to despair.
> The knowledge of Jesus Christ represents the middle, because therein we find both God and our misery.
>
> (527)

Jesus Christ is therefore the location of all truth:

> Not only do we know God only through Jesus Christ, but we know ourselves only through Jesus Christ. We know life and

death only through Jesus Christ. Outside of Jesus Christ, we do
not know what is either our life or our death or God or ourselves.

Thus, without Scripture, which has only Jesus Christ for its
object, we know nothing, and we see only darkness and confusion
in the nature of God or in nature itself.

(548)

Truth thus revealed is not merely the object of knowledge or of contemplation. It is a principle of action and a source of salvation since it offers
to man, through the union with Jesus Christ, the means of overcoming his
misery and of finding again the greatness that he derives from his divine
origin.

Jesus Christ, the Man-God, is by Himself, as the Gospel puts it, "the
way, the truth and the life." By investing Himself with humanity He has
realized in His person the fullness of revelation. But by the same token He
has renounced the manifestation of His divinity in an obvious manner. He
has dissimulated this divinity under a veil "by covering Himself with humanity" (*Lettres à Mlle de Roannez*); this is a veil that is all the more difficult
to penetrate since He refused even the greatness proper to man: "He did not
invent; He did not reign" (793). The people were "disappointed by the
ignominious and poor advent of the Messiah" (571) and refused to recognize
Him. Assuming the human condition to the very end, Jesus chose not to
distinguish Himself from the common man.

According to the permanent plan of God, however, the revelation
brought by the Son was authenticated by signs. To His contemporaries Jesus
Christ revealed His divinity through miracles. It is by basing himself on
those miracles that Pascal, as we have seen, had first envisaged the construction of an apologetic edifice. But he finally adopted a totally different perspective. Considering the miracles of Jesus Christ as a proof of efficacy limited
in time, by virtue of the very plan of God, he directed his entire effort to
the argumentation through the prophecies. The latter having only Jesus
Christ as their object, the grandiose vision is offered to us of a Christ placed
in the center of history, on whom all light converges, but who possesses of
Himself no radiance. The Man-God maintains Himself in a state of humility
that is suitable to His human nature, and it is God alone who glorifies Him
by ordering all things in relation to His coming:

What man ever had greater fame? The entire Jewish people predicted His coming before He came. The Gentiles adored Him
after His coming. Both peoples, Gentile and Jew, considered Him
as their center.

And yet, what man ever enjoyed this fame less? Of His thirty-three years, He spent thirty without appearing. [Then] for three years, He was considered an impostor: the priests and the leaders rejected Him, His friends and closest kin despised Him. Finally, He died betrayed by one of His own, denied by another, and abandoned by all.

What share then had He in His fame? Never has a man had as much glory; never has a man suffered greater ignominy. All this fame was only for our sake, to make Him recognizable to us; and He gained nothing out of it for Himself.

(792)

Such is the paradox of Jesus Christ. It was contrary to the mission of Him who was bringing total revelation to come bathed in an entirely divine glory; to do this would have been to betray His human condition. To fill His role of Mediator well, He had to make His humanity burst forth no less than He had to reveal Himself as God.

It is, moreover, the acceptance of His human condition that is at the basis of His glorification. When He had gone to the utmost of the tests, which are the lot of mankind, by accepting death, He deserved to have His divinity made manifest in a most dazzling manner by His resurrection. To this resurrection Pascal evidently granted a prime place in his argument, for he was careful to show the value of the testimonies that establish it:

The hypothesis of fraudulent Apostles is quite absurd. Let us follow it to its conclusion; let us imagine these twelve men assembled after the death of Jesus Christ, plotting to say that He had risen from the dead. By so doing they attack all the powers. The heart of man is strangely prone to levity, to change, to promises, to riches. If a single one of them had changed his mind because of these attractions, and more likely because of prisons, torture and death, they would have all been lost. Follow that conclusion.

(801)

But the resurrection remains semisecret. It leaves Jesus Christ in the state of obscurity in which He wished to appear. Is not this obscurity, the sign of His humanity, also in a way a sign of His divinity? The power is obviously an attribute of God; it is this power that is made manifest in the miracles, in the prophecies, in the "conduct of the world" (289). But holiness, though less visible, is an even more essential attribute of God. Jesus Christ possesses this attribute to the highest degree and in a particularly pure manner, since He renounced all other forms of greatness:

> It is really ridiculous to be scandalized by the lowliness of Jesus Christ, as though this lowliness were of the same order as the greatness which He had just revealed. Let us consider that greatness in His life, in His passion, in His obscurity, in His death, in the choice of His disciples, in their desertion of Him, in His secret resurrection and in the rest, and we shall see that it is so great that there is no reason to be scandalized by a lowliness which is not there.
>
> (793)

Can this refutation of the "Judaic" attitude which leads to a disregard of the Messiah because of His so-called "lowliness" be transformed into a positive argument? Is the holiness apparent in Jesus Christ an effective sign of His divinity? The *Pensées* offer the beginning of several reasonings in that direction. However, the sign constituted by holiness is really perceptible only "to the eyes of the heart which perceive wisdom" (*Ibid.*). But when all is said and done, is such not the case with all divine signs? Revelation is of the same nature as the mystery of God.

JAN MIEL

Pascal and Theology

The historicity of man's condition is certainly one of the most difficult of all theological principles to discuss and keep firmly in mind. Rational thought is by its nature opposed to historical truth, aiming as it does at a truth that transcends historical vicissitudes. Yet, as we have seen [elsewhere], every important element of Pascal's analysis of man must be defined historically. There is no human nature separable from the story of a mankind that was created sane, just, and free, and which lost those attributes through Adam's Fall. The attempt to define a nonhistorical human nature is the worm in the apple of Thomism which the Jesuits swallowed whole and brought forth as the viper's tangle of casuistry and the new morality. And the attempt to interpret the *Pensées* as a description of such a permanent human nature leads to the idea of the "sublime misanthrope" or the anguished preromantic, or other mistaken views of their author.

It may seem untoward to insist so on the historical nature of Pascal's thought when one of his most distinguished modern critics has taken him to task exactly for lacking a sense of history. The question raised by M. Béguin [in *Pascal par lui-même*] is in fact several questions which we must try to keep distinct. There is the first and fundamental question as to whether the unfolding of time plays an essential role in his thought, or whether Pascal's vision is classical, timeless, nonhistorical. Here, it seems to me, we must insist most strongly on the essentially historical nature of his vision. In an age of philosophical systems, and a physical mechanism that transcended

From *Pascal and Theology*. © 1969 by the Johns Hopkins University Press, Baltimore/ London.

and destroyed time, Pascal more than anyone in his age and society—even among his Augustinian friends—upheld the Augustinian vision, not only against the Jesuits, but against Thomists and Cartesians, scientists and mathematicians: "Dieu d'Abraham, Dieu d'Isaac, Dieu de Jacob, non des Philosophes et des savants" (*Mémorial*). The revelation of Christianity is essentially a Sacred History, and the events of that history from the Creation and the Fall of Adam to the Incarnation and the awaited Second Coming are, for Pascal, more important and more enlightening than any philosophical system known or possible; philosophical systems are in fact shown to be themselves mere temporal manifestations and are seen in the light of an historical development that transcends them. It is hardly necessary to emphasize the role of this "theology of history" in Pascal's thought: it was to play an enormous part in the Apology, and the ramifications of it fill only slightly less than half of the total pages of the *Pensées*. And one of the main points of the rest of the Apology was to show that man is a "monstre incompréhensible" as long as he tries to understand himself in purely philosophical terms without reference to his historical situation. But this is of course always with reference to Sacred History; Béguin's criticism is rather that Pascal's thought seems to have no place in it for secular history, or rather to describe secular history as pure vanity—an enormous waste motivated by concupiscence and doomed to damnation.

Once again a distinction must be made between two questions: the first would concern the individual's attitude toward secular life, i.e., to what extent the Christian is called to participate in the society of his time and in the better aims of that society; we shall return to this question shortly. The other question is the intellectual question of how we conceive secular history, particularly in its relation to the History of Salvation. Here, as Béguin recognizes, we are outside the scope of the Apology and consequently need not expect to find very many helpful texts, but there are nonetheless indications of Pascal's position. As Béguin says, there is none of the meditation on the density and mystery of historical becoming that characterizes some thinkers since the nineteenth century, and also perhaps certain passages of St. Augustine. But the elements of the Augustinian view are all there: the emphasis on the Mystical Body and the insistence on the invisibility of election, which we saw developed in the *Ecrits sur la grâce* as an essential difference between Jansenists and Calvinists; this doctrine sees God's intentions as hidden and mysterious until the end of time: a doctrine which in fact puts considerable weight on an historical development which cannot exclude secular history, since it cannot really distinguish it from the History of Salvation. And finally there is the generosity and justice of God toward all men (not just the elect) and the desire of Christ for the salvation of all.

This last position, involving the fifth condemned proposition of Jansenius, has led some commentators to see Pascal as abandoning the Jansenist position on this point. However, this is difficult to maintain: the position in the texts in the *Pensées* is exactly that of the *Ecrits sur la grâce* and of the *Abrégé de la vie de Jésus Christ*, namely, that the statement "Christ died for all men" can be understood in two ways depending on whether you are considering Christ as a man or Christ as God. This is merely a matter of common sense; Pascal goes further, however, and finds fault with those who emphasize the fact that his death did not benefit all men, rather than the fact that it was offered for all. It is possible that he has in mind some of his Jansenist friends, but possible also that, as in the *Ecrits sur la grâce*, he means the Calvinists, and wishes to preserve the Augustinian doctrine from the gloomy air they seem to give it. In any case, it is clear that although all humanity will not finally be saved, only God's judgment will discern, at the end of time, the Elect from the damned. So, what Henri Marrou says of the Augustinian doctrine could also express the conception of Pascal: "Nous possédons le sens de l'histoire, mais par la Foi, c'est-à-dire d'une connaissance qui demeure partiellement obscure. C'est le sens global de l'histoire qui nous est révélé; non le détail, les modalités de sa réalisation." Although the unbeliever must be made to see the vanity of the ideals of secular society, the Christian, enlightened as to the ultimate direction of history, will look for the hand of God at work even through the vanity of men, drawing good out of evil. Pascal was more concerned to lead the unbeliever to the point where he could receive this vision than to produce meditations upon it which might please the mind but leave the heart untouched. For a philosophy of history remains always a philosophy and therefore is itself ahistorical; but an apology that rejects philosophy and attempts rather to move its readers into a religion that is in its very essence historical hardly deserves the reproach of lacking a sense of history. In the History of Salvation, Pascal is undoubtedly more interested in the salvation than in the history, but the one cannot exist without the other, and Pascal was one of the very few in an age of philosophy and science to see this clearly and to base all his thinking on it.

Finally, concerning the question as to what extent the Christian is called to participate in the society of his time and in general to contribute to the better aims of society, it seems incredible that anyone familiar with Pascal's life could suppose that he somehow rejected society or life in the world. It is true of course that he admired and encouraged those who chose to withdraw for the sake of the religious life—his sister Jacqueline and Charlotte de Roannez are notable examples. But his attitude on the question of the signature also made it clear that he did not consider even the religious as exempt from the cares and obligations of other Christians, and indeed in the seventeenth century they were not. In any case, although Pascal must have considered the religious life for himself, he not only rejected such a withdrawal but seems to have accepted his worldly condition with an equanimity bordering on lightheartedness.

Nor do the *Pensées* anywhere contradict such an attitude. On the contrary, near the end of the wager he reminds his interlocutor of the advantages of choosing God and losing oneself: "Vous serez fidèle, honnête, humble, reconnaissant, bien faisant, ami sincère, véritable" (Pensée 233, Brunschvicg edition). And elsewhere he says, "Nul n'est heureux comme un vrai chrétien, ni raisonnable, ni vertueux, ni aimable" (541). The import of these statements is clearly that the Christian convert does not withdraw from human society, but becomes more truly human. He has of course undergone a change of heart: his activity is no longer mere diversion or distraction, motivated by concupiscence and egoism—although these are never in this life entirely absent; his motivation is now primarily charitable, done not for his own gain or glory, but for others, and so for God. Conversion, for Pascal, was never a refusal of society or history, of the world as our scene of operations, our very condition of life. It was rather a reentry into human society with purified motives, an entry into history with a fuller understanding and acceptance of its process. And to return to our old question of freedom, the true Christian's activity in the world will actually be freer. Because, although it is always possible for him to fall from grace, he is yet free from the anxiety of having to merit his salvation. His most characteristic virtue is hope, a virtue that presupposes existence in time and precludes both a fatalistic attitude and also a Pelagian one, for, as Pascal notes, if we could truly earn our salvation, "le juste ne devrait donc plus espérer en Dieu, car il ne doit pas espérer, mais s'efforcer d'obtenir ce qu'il demande!" (514).

The very real contrast between the outlook of Pascal and that of the "humanisme dévot" of the sixteenth and seventeenth centuries has led too many to suppose that Pascal is a sort of antihumanist. The following passage, besides giving us a clear picture of Pascal's goal as apologist, also shows much about his assessment of man.

> Contrariétés. Après avoir montré la bassesse et la grandeur de l'homme.—*Que l'homme maintenant s'estime son prix. Qu'il s'aime, car il y a en lui une nature capable de bien; mais qu'il n'aime pas pour cela les bassesses qui y sont. Qu'il se méprise, parce que cette capacité est vide; mais qu'il ne méprise pas pour cela cette capacité naturelle. Qu'il se haïsse, qu'il s'aime: il a en lui la capacité de connaître la vérité et d'être heureux; mais il n'a point de vérité, ou constante, ou satisfaisante.*

Je voudrais donc porter l'homme à désirer d'en trouver, à être prêt, et dégagé des passions, pour la suivre où il la trouvera, sachant combien sa connaissance s'est obscurcie par les passions; je voudrais bien qu'il haït en soi la concupiscence qui le détermine d'elle-même, afin qu'elle ne l'aveuglât point pour faire son choix, et qu'elle ne l'arrêtât point quand il aura choisi.

(423)

This passage summarizes much of what I have tried to bring out already: man's true nature as a "capacité vide," the need to both love and hate oneself, and so forth. It also shows the precise limits of Pascal's ambition, not just for his Apology, but for self-knowledge and the efforts of human reason. It has been said that Pascal's vision is essentially discontinuous, there being no communication between the three orders of body, mind, and heart; and that there exists likewise an unbridgeable abyss between man and God. One author says that Pascal wished to "couper les ponts de l'homme à Dieu sans renoncer à les faire exister l'un pour l'autre." Such a notion, however, presupposes that outlook, characteristic of Renaissance Humanism, in which man sets out to reach God and can do so only by deeds of valor or towers of intellect. The ideal of a St. Ignatius, at least in the early stages of his conversion, was totally that of the heroic deeds to be done to reach God, and the ideal of the chivalrous saints does not seem so far from that of the chevalier of metaphysics, Descartes. The bridges built in the name of an all too human rationalism and "gloire" had to be destroyed. Yet Pascal did not accept the total lack of communication that seems to be characteristic of both Calvinism and the fideism of Montaigne; they are accused of fostering despair or a "nonchalance du salut." The true way to God, then, was not through building great edifices, which could only be towers of Babel, nor in despairing of all communication, but, as the above passage says, in being ready and alert and wanting to find the bridge that God built to man. So the "humanisme dévot" of the Renaissance depended on a notion of man as fundamentally independent of God but with the power to reach God through his efforts. Pascal, on the other hand, notes that "l'homme n'est ni ange ni bête, et le malheur veut que qui veut faire l'ange fait la bête" (358). Man's efforts to scale the heights are doomed, but once he recognizes his radical dependency on God and accepts God's efforts to reach him through Jesus Christ, he is more truly human in this life and destined for a glory greater than that of the angels. Pascal's humanism thus lies more in his hope for humanity than in his confidence in man's powers; but his decriptions of the spiritual life of the true Christian show far more than a narrow theologism. Hatred for self is counterbalanced by a new self-acceptance, and, as one no longer feels endangered by other Egos, one's relations to others are also transformed in the direction of self-effacement and generosity. And even one's relation to nature is affected; as one learns to abandon the "esprit de système" and live in the present, nature is no longer merely an object to be subjected to laws, but speaks directly to the heart in a relation that approaches intersubjectivity. There is no doubt a dimension that is properly mystical involved here, though this is a debated point; the relation to a recognized Christian mystical tradition is not so clear. But there are points in Pascal that suggest closer parallels may be found in oriental mystical doctrines, in particular that of Zen Buddhism with its emphasis on an immediate and mindless relation to the world, however different may be the paths that lead to this new awareness.

Theology, as I have tried to show throughout [*Pascal and Theology*], played a far more important role in the development of Pascal's thought than is usually supposed. His interest in theology and his efforts to acquire a serious understanding of its implications date from the time of his first conversion (1646), and his interest, his study and meditation of the Bible, and even the presumption that he understood some aspects of theology better than the professionals: all can be traced to this early period. Further, there is no reason to suppose that this interest was lost even in the so-called mundane period; and there is no justification at all for supposing that when he came to the writing of the *Lettres provinciales* he was still theologically naïve and had to have his theology dictated to him by Arnauld and Nicole

As to what his theology was, there is not the slightest doubt that it was the Augustinian theology as interpreted by Jansenius and Saint-Cyran and their followers. Difficulties over Pascal's Jansenism invariably arise out of the habit of regarding Jansenism as some sort of bugbear, a pernicious and monolithic heresy that taints all associated with it. A sensible historical perspective reveals that it is merely a label given to a group of defenders of the Augustinian doctrine of grace as that doctrine was undermined and threatened with extinction in the Renaissance. Nor is this to say that the Jansenists were right and the Molinists wrong: both groups can claim their ancient authorities—the Molinists echoed not only Pelagius but also the almost unanimous sentiment of the pre-Augustinian Fathers. And if the Jansenists can claim the weight of Conciliar support, Molinists nevertheless represented something like a new mind of the Church struggling against Augustinian conservatism.

Pascal claims to have looked at both sides of these questions and opted most decisively for the Augustinian view, for reasons that may originally have had more to do with the question of reason and revelation than with questions concerning grace and free will; our knowledge of Pascal's early thought is too sparse to allow any definite conclusions on that point. In any case he clearly never abandoned the basic Augustinian doctrines but rather proceeded to elaborate on them in his own way with a view, perhaps again dating from soon after the first conversion, to the writing of an Apology for Christianity. In both the projected Apology and in the *Lettres provinciales* the Augustinian (or Jansenist) theology is not only very much present, but supplies the real intellectual basis for both works, being at the source of all the apparently diverse discussions and attacks in the *Provinciales*, and supplying the framework for understanding the whole anthropology of the *Pensées*. Even the tactics of the Apology presuppose a Jansenist view of man, and not only as regards the role of reason. For example, Pascal offers us no vision of damnation such as we find in a Dante or a Bernanos, and the reason is that fear was not considered, in the Jansenist theory of "delectatio," to be an adequate motive force to turn the heart toward God.

But in looking at Pascal's own attempts to write real theology—the so-called *Ecrits sur la grâce*—we discover that although the doctrine is Jansenist, the style is not. Here Pascal shows not just a clairty and conciseness which contrast strongly with the style of an Arnauld, but as always an originality of approach. His emphasis on linguistic analysis is virtually unique in theological writing before the twentieth century. It is not at all the same sort of thing that occupied the Scholastics, who were concerned with precision of concepts; Pascal was keenly aware that theological statements, even those of a Pope or a Council, were made by men who meant something by them in a particular historical, intellectual context; so although their truth is *not* therefore relative, their meaning is.

And this characteristic of his theological writing carries over into all his writing, especially into the *Pensées*. It is an almost unparalleled ability to rethink man's problems entirely from within the limitations of our condition. So when writing against the vanity even of philosophers, who are after all only seeking their own glory, Pascal adds, "Et ceux qui écrivent contre veulent avoir la gloire d'avoir bien écrit; et ceux qui les lisent veulent avoir la gloire de les avoir lus; et moi, qui écris ceci, ai peut-être cette envie; et peut-être que ceux qui le liront" (150). Denouncing "amour-propre" does not make one exempt from it; quite the contrary. Of course, as a thinker who saw that a fly could disrupt a metaphysical proof, that a pretty face or a kidney stone could change the course of history, and who considered a sneeze to be as worthy of philosophical reflection as deeds of valor, Pascal was not so original; the example of Montaigne was always before him. But Pascal refused the Montaignian shrug of the shoulders ("que sais-je?") and sought always to get as near to the truth as the condition of our language and our reason allow. Questions such as that of the existence of God and of the immortality of the soul are real questions of vital importance to every man; but philosophical answers are not real answers, because philosophers assume they can be answered in the abstract, out of time, free from the passions which animate us, ignoring the role of the questioner. This, then, is the primary characteristic of that strange argument, the wager, which has enticed but often repelled philosophers: that it tries to give the best answer possible to these questions without attempting to rise above the conditions of human existence to do it. So much of what seems to be paradoxical in the *Pensées* arises out of the same point of view. It is not, as M. Goldmann would have it, a refusal of the world from within the world: it is rather a total acceptance of the world in the knowledge that all our aspirations are other-worldly; it is the application to our intellectual life of the mystery of the Incarnation.

Yet this also echoes, and for Pascal probably arises out of meditation on the Augustinian doctrine of grace. For man's will is free, but he cannot freely will his salvation unless predestined to do so, and God's predestination is entirely beyond our grasp. In fact it was the aspiration toward freedom as independence that lost us our freedom in the Garden of Eden, and which still distorts our notions of freedom so that we cannot abide grace. For even grace does not restore the absolute freedom Adam enjoyed, but only a present sense of radical dependency on God's will which enables one to reason in good faith, to live in hope, and to act in charity. We become, at best, free as the birds are free, that is, in harmony with a nature that is the always actual expression of God's will.

The Augustinian theology would seem to me then the only basis for a consistent interpretation of Pascal's thought, for that thought is largely theo-logical in it origins and in its continued inspiration. It is a theology which, in Pascal's version, leaves a large place to observation, because events are direct expressions of the will of God and because "les choses corporelles ne sont qu'une image des spirituelles." Behind the observations of human nature and society in the *Pensées*, however, there is almost always a theological understanding which alone supplies their coherence. And it is because of this underlying unity of his thought that Pascal never feared to stretch his ideas to their limits, for in doing so he felt neither contradiction nor anguish but only the omnipresence of a central and substantial Truth.

PHILIP LEWIS

Dialogic Impasse in Pascal's Provinciales

The frequent recourse to dialogue in the *Provinciales* and the *Pensées*, doubt-less revealing a penchant toward a polemical appropriation of Socratic di-alectics, strikes the reader as a pervasive phenomenon in Pascal's writing, one which his reflections on the art of persuasion justify in rhetorical terms. For both the participating interlocutor and the witness or reader, the ex-perience of dialogue can afford the coexistence of demonstrative understand-ing and pleasureful discovery. It is from the necessary opposition and combination of these distinct modes of discernment and principles of truth that the problematics of persuasion emerges in "De l'Art de persuader." Given "un balancement douteux entre la vérité et la volupté," the cornerstone of Pascalian rhetoric becomes psychological knowledge of the addressee: "il faudrait . . . connaître tout ce qui se passe dans le plus intérieur de l'homme . . . [Q]uoi que ce soit qu'on veuille persuader, il faut avoir égard à la personne à qui on en veut, dont il faut connaître l'esprit et le coeur, quels principes il accorde, quelles choses il aime." A successful dialogue, directed by a speaker attentive to the ways of both mind and heart, leads the interlocutor to the self-satisfying recognition of his own truth, latent within the self, and thus into an affectionate "communauté d'intelligence" with the perceptive speaker: "on trouve dans soi-même la vérité de ce qu'on entend, laquelle on ne savait pas qu'elle y fût, de sorte qu'on est porté à aimer celui qui nous la fait sentir, car il ne nous a point fait montre de son bien mais du nôtre" (fragment 652; Pascal references cite the Lafuma edition). In tracing a con-

From *Canadian Review of Comparative Literature* 3, no. 1 (Winter 1976). © 1976 by Philip Lewis. University of Toronto Press, 1976.

version of the truth which is spoken into a possession which is felt, and therewith of an intellective encounter into an affective bond, this observation describes the process of mutual appropriation which underlies the positive function of dialogue, its formidable rhetorical (or polemical) potential for mediation and conciliation. The exchange of words can engender far more than the formulation or demonstration of logical truth; it can also serve to identify the truth discovered in dialogue as the shared property of the interlocutors. Their personal investment in that truth exceeds the immediate product of dialectical reflection as it engages the whole of each person in the complex of an integrally human relationship, a union of knowledge and desire embracing the love of truth and the truth of love.

Taken as an existential medium which embodies and reveals the deeply human and proprietary cast—at once personal and interpersonal—which truths acquire in the process of discovery and formulation, the constructive dialogue envisioned by Pascal may be situated within a humanistic tradition which accentuates the value of a relatively free, manipulable, dynamic discourse, open to the play of interrogation, objection, digression, and improvisation. The shifting and plurivocal movement of dialogue runs counter to the predominatory and univocal discourse of authority; it works against the reimposition of fixed ideas which, if they are blindly received without contestation, interpretation, and modernization, threaten to prevent the recipient from appreciating the originality and priority of his own insights, and thus to alienate the individual from his own thought through the subordination of experiential truth to an autonomous world of ideas. Above all else the humanist's task is to insist upon dialogue in his relation with the past, upon reappropriation of truths in the light of individual experience. In this context, moreover, Pascal falls squarely within the lineage of one of his most prominent adversaries, Montaigne (whose "skepticism" is the principal object of the *Entretien avec M. de Saci*, a rather curious dialogue recorded by a secretary whose introductory remarks on Saci's flexibility as an interlocutor serve to remind us of the suppleness of the genre).

In adopting the form of the essay, Montaigne clearly drew upon and moved beyond the similarly open and pliable forms of the letter and the dialogue, forms which Pascal employs in the *Provinciales* and specifically envisions as devices to be exploited in his Apology (cf. the notations specifying the letter-form in fragments 2, 4, 5, 7, etc., and the passages of dialogue in several important fragments: 131, 132, 149, 418). For Montaigne, settling upon the form of the essay meant disallowing the affectation of the letter-form, with its fictional addressee and its common tendency toward stylistic modishness, while at the same time consolidating and expanding the opening

toward a personal, subjective discourse which the epistolary form had illustrated; similarly, it meant exploiting the capacity of dialogue to facilitate
the variation of subjects and changes of perspective, while discarding the
fiction of a multi-personal encounter in favour of a more immediate articulation of individual self-expression and self-interrogation which the dialogue
is apt to diffuse or to mask. In Pascal's stinging attack on Montaigne ("Le
sot projet qu'il a de se peindre . . ." [780; cf. 649]), we may read not simply
his disdain for Pyrrhonistic arguments, but also an aversion to the intro-
verted, reflexive form of the essay, a self-satisfied transcription of the mind's
dialogue with itself. By contrast, the insistent intervention of dialogue in
Pascal's polemical and apologetical writing systematically reflects his inter-
subjective focus, an outgoing concern for the *other*—notably the ecclesiastical
adversary in the *Provinciales*, the nonbeliever in the *Pensées*.

   Yet Pascalian dialogue is by no means just a didactic tool for engineering
agreement. An authentic dialogue never functions simply as a discursive
form which allows the participants to exchange views, to elicit information,
to argue opposing positions, to reduce differences and attain a meeting of
minds and hearts. As the prefix *dia* (variously signifying "one with another"
and "apart from") suggests, dialogue is a double-edged instrument, for it is
at once the medium of union and separation, concord and discord, revelation
and deception, at once the communal appropriation and the combative ex-
propriation of a *logos* which one speaks for oneself, as a subject, from the
inside, only to propel it outward, to be apprehended by the other as an
object, on the outside. Potentially, the rhetorical strength of dialogue—the
subtly compelling force with which the act of communication affects the
participant or witness—is also its weakness, for the human relationship which
undergirds the process of verification can also undermine it:

> Qu'il est difficile de proposer une chose au jugement d'un autre
> sans corrompre son jugement par la manière de la lui proposer.
> Si on dit: je le trouve beau, je le trouve obscur, ou autre chose
> semblable, on entraîne l'imagination à ce jugement ou on l'irrite
> au contraire. Il vaut mieux ne rien dire et alors il juge selon ce
> qu'il est, c'est-à-dire selon ce qu'il est alors, et selon que les autres
> circonstances dont on n'est pas auteur y auront mis.
>
> > (529; cf. the celebrated definition of eloquence,
> > Brunschvicg ed., 16)

Yet, Pascal adds, silence itself can be a compromising gesture. The point is
that the open form of dialogic communication entails a risk, envisaged here
as the corruption of judgement by the imagination and detailed massively

in the *Pensées* by the analyses of the *puissances trompeuses*, of man's susceptibility to error, distraction, and self-deception. The risk of a counterproductive response, such as a reaction against a proposition on account of its form, or the speaker's manner, or the listener's bias, or circumstance, etc., inheres in the humanity of the interlocutor, whose freedom in dialogue is the freedom to pursue discussion indefinitely, or to break it off arbitrarily. The risk, in short, of irresolution, of inconclusiveness. If the dialogues which we encounter in Pascal's polemical writing are typically inflected by the apologist's pressure toward a statement of agreement, their movement is also that of a confrontation which enacts a struggle of the form against itself—against the polymorphous play of reflection and the values of openness and of contestation which adherence to the dialogic form implies. Over and beyond the persuasive power of dialogue which Pascalian rhetoric discloses, it is this irrepressible ambivalence—as the play of difference with and against unification—which Pascal's texts invite us to measure.

The composition of the *Provinciales* inevitably reflects the polemical circumstances which motivated Pascal to come to the defence of the Jansenist position: the work is unfinished, reflects the episodic composition of a text which developed in response to a protracted controversy, cannot be regarded as an integrally conceived whole. From a formal standpoint, the superstructural division of the text would also seem to temper pretentions to artistic unity: the collection of letters to the provincial friend (letters 1–10) constitutes, strictly from a retrospective viewpoint, a dynamically constructed unit which is decisively detached from the succeeding letters to the Jesuit fathers (11–19). The point of juncture between these two sections (letter 10) prepares a shift from satire to straightforward refutation and denunciation, from irony to absolute seriousness, from the perspective and tone of inquiry to those of authority, from the intriguing narration of dialogues which explore the confrontation of the Jansenists and their adversaries to the uncompromising pursuit of a critical monologue in which the writer, having shed his narrative guise, argues the case with which he has become fully identified. In short, the central change in the letter-writer's addressee from friend to foe marks the culmination of an increasingly intense experience of *engagement*—the conversion of a narrator, who exploits the epistolary form as an artful, spontaneous device, into an author, who has reverted to the austere prosaic voice of the treatise or tract.

In the fragmentary notations of the final letter, the predominant motif remains the resignation of the Jansenists which their admiring defender has underscored at the end of the eighteenth letter while explaining his own refusal to accede to it. By abandoning the unfinished text, however, he appears to grant implicitly that, as the evolution of the *Provinciales* suggests, the positions of the antagonists have been fully revealed in their hopeless rigidity. Consequently, the undeveloped notes of letter 19 stand as a final step in a polemical trajectory which runs from investigation through the taking and defending of a position to the collapse of that defence, and finally into the unassailable posture of wilful silence, the ultimate gesture in the rejection of compromise. "J'ai vu enfin en eux le caractère de la piété chrétienne qui fait paraître une force" (letter 19). The last published letter attempts to justify the writing of a defence which has proved to be futile and which, carried on, could only be taken as a sign of weakness. The force of truth that Pascal has *seen* in the Jansenists is the force that he can attain only by ceasing—in an act of solidarity with his allies—to write on their behalf.

Thus, if their historical background precludes a resolutely literary account of the *Provinciales*, the work appears to inscribe the logic of a communicative failure in the passage from the narrative mode of satire through the overtly polemical mode of apology to the isolation of righteous force in silence. To a considerable extent, moreover, the *Provinciales* occasion an evolution in the relationship of author to reader which reproduces the descent from the two or more voices of dialogue to the one voice of monologue to the zero of a communicative impasse. In the letters to a provincial friend, our sympathy with the Jansenist position and the satirical project is engaged, engendering the sense of an artistic and argumentative success. In contrast, the subsequent letters, insofar as they convey the author's self-appreciative concern with defending his own polemical project and his one-sided inattentiveness to the context in which the Jesuit outlook acquires its relative validity, tend to undermine that sympathy, to expose the Jansenist position to critical scrutiny. As the author's distance from his position vanishes, the reader's reappears. In terms of Pascalian rhetoric, the preemptory voice of monologue denies to the reader the possibility of discovering the truth in an experience which he shares with the writer. Thus the very failure of the *Provinciales* may be detected in the abandonment of a practice of dialogue which the initial letters of the collection inaugurate and points to the crucial status of that practice in Pascal's writing.

The first section of the *Provinciales* appropriates the epistolary form—which itself posits a dialogue relationship in the exchange between the fictional correspondents, Montalte and his provincial friend—to the narration and interpretation of a series of dialogues. These encounters initially represent the narrator's attempt to inform himself about the disputes preoccupying the learned doctors of the Sorbonne, or more precisely, to determine the grounds of the disagreement between the Jansenists and the Jesuits. The problem of dialogue is rapidly reduced to that of terminological confusion: the lexical field surrounding the theological notion of grace generates a kind of conceptual background noise, exemplified by the mystifying terms *pouvoir prochain* (letter 1) and *grâce suffisante* (letter 2), which must be filtered out in order for a meaningful discussion to take place, i.e., at first the dialogues appear to involve not so much the substance of the discord as the conditions which govern the possibility of a dialogue concerning that discord. The third letter, exploiting a dialogue between neutral parties, explores the meaning of heresy, exposing the Molinists' tactic of combining censure ("ils n'ont fait autre chose que prononcer ces paroles: *Cette proposition est téméraire, impie, blasphématoire, frappée d'anathème, et hérétique*") and silence, a flat refusal to respond to Arnauld's propositions at face value. Jansenists and Molinists are divided either by the Molinists' refusal to debate in common language, or else their refusal to debate at all.

With the fourth letter, however, the dialogues move into a vein of greater urgency. To be sure, problems of definition, distinction, and interpretation will recur incessantly and the function of language as the vehicle of reflection and as an instrument of ethical positioning will remain crucial (often as an explicit motif) in every exchange. Moreover, the composition still follows the outlines of the preceding epistles, starting out with yet another problematic term, *la grâce actuelle*, around which a rudimentary argumentative structure is formed, and playing off the narrator's dialogues with representatives of the opposing parties (first on a concordant note with the Jansenist friend; then, discordant with a Jesuit friend) against one another. Nevertheless, the overall focus begins to shift away from the doctrinal arguments concerning the notion of grace toward the issues of ethics, from the status of words and formulae as such toward a substantive concern with the individual's spiritual condition. Also in the letter, the second of the two dialogues brings on stage for the first time a Jesuit father, whose appearance prefigures the installation—in the second dialogue of letter 5—of a single Jesuit informant as the ongoing interlocutor for the narrator in what will be henceforth a single dialogue, involving just the two characters, which serves as the framework of each letter (i.e., 6–10).

This narrowing of focus also signals the transformation of the narrator from investigator-reporter into aggressive protagonist and self-confident judge who, no longer relying on the explanations of his Jansenist friend, will recognize himself in the text as a clandestine public figure whose letters are circulating widely and are directed, in effect, to a collective addressee. As the text expresses more openly its own fictive design, Montalte's role will be still more clearly that of the critical analyst whose task is to resist the casuist's manipulation of language ("tout ce bandinage," letter 10), to oppose to the proliferation of magical words and formulative artifice the straight-forward speech of the *honnête homme*. Throughout the encounters with the Jesuit which served to discredit the ethics of intention and the practice of casuistry, it is precisely the futility of conversing in incompatible languages—and thus the impossibility of meaningful dialogue—which are ceaselessly reconfirmed. For the Jesuit, the dialogues with the indictive Montalte are not occasion for responding personally and spontaneously, they are simply challenges to authority which he must answer by citing the appropriate refutation. The process of quotation, the backtracking recourse to authorization, can go on indefinitely, for the Jesuit is bound to the assumption that somewhere in the canons of his order a response can be found to any problem or objection. Indeed, the scholastic corpus of the Society constitutes a kind of textual interference, comparable in function to the mystifying terminology which impedes the dialectical process of mutual understanding in letters 1–4. The casuistic text, a licentious deviation form the Scriptures and writings of the saints, always intervenes so as to shield the Jesuit from the force of direct address or from direct responsibility for his own replies ("je ne dis jamais rien de moi-même," letter 9), to maintain a gap between the inter-locutors, to uphold the negative dialogic function of separation.

Although the Jesuit tactics—recurrent appeal to esoteric language and to a labyrinthine textual authority—are by nature quite resilient in the face of attack ("on accorde toujours ces contradictions prétendues," letter 6), the Pascalian protagonist does manage in each letter to box his adversary into an untenable position. In so doing, he not only impresses upon the reader of his narrative the validity of his own views; he also reinforces the Jesuit's retrenchment in the position—alien to dialogue—of authority. Through the dialogues with the Jesuit father, Pascal presents a remarkably subtle, yet unmistakable enactment of an overriding political principle, enunciated from the outset in a brutally unequivocal rejoinder which cuts off the series of several dialogues in the first letter: "Vous le [the word *prochain*] direz, ou vous serez hérétique, et M. Arnauld aussi; car nous sommes le plus grand nombre; et, s'il est besoin, nous ferons venir tant de cordeliers, que nous l'emporterons." Each of the first three letters marks trenchantly the status of numerical superiority, the basis of ecclesiastical dominance, as the court of last resort, and the depth of the threat which the *Provinciales* pose to the Jesuits clearly lies in the vigour with which the work represents the Jesuits' ultimate allegiance to power in the conflict of power and truth. In Montalte's final conversation with his Jansenist friend, the latter articulates with consummate strategic acumen the relation between the Society's program of aggrandizement and its disregard for evangelical truth:

> Ils ont assez bonne opinion d'eux-mêmes pour croire qu'il est utile et comme nécessaire au bien de la religion que leur crédit s'étende partout et qu'ils gouvernent toutes les consciences. Et parce que les maximes évangéliques et sévères sont propres pour gouverner quelques sortes de personnes, ils s'en servent dans ces occasions où elles leur sont favorables. Mais comme ces mêmes maximes ne s'accordent pas au dessein de la plupart des gens, ils les laissent à l'égard de ceux-là, afin d'avoir de quoi satisfaire tout le monde.
>
> (letter 5)

All of the conversations with the Jesuit reflect this policy—the subordination of truth to power—in the violence which the casuistic extension of authority works simultaneously upon the truths of Christian doctrine and the logic of common sense.

Thus the dead end of the dialogues with the Jesuit—as well as their static, repetitive cast—is anticipated from the outset, for the opposing poles of political authority and evangelical truth are not subject to dialectical articulation. As the Jesuit emphasizes in the final exchange upon learning that Montalte is reading casuist literature, the discourse of authority is not meant for independent study, should be read only along with an initiated guide, only with *direction*, only as an act of acquiescence and submission. Entering into dialogue on the Jesuit's terms would mean assuming the dependency of his position in relation to the Society, to ecclesiastical supremacy, and it is that very dependency—moral abjection in lieu of Christian humility—which Montalte condemns in a final admonition which expresses his immediate concern for the well-being of his adversary. The dialogues terminate at this point, in a scene mingling pathos and revulsion, where the protagonist resorts to a personal accusation, addressed directly to the Jesuit, whom he exhorts to break away from his complicity with the crimes of the casuists. This indictment marks and culminates a dianoetic stand-off: the Jesuit's institutional commitment to his order is simply not commensurable with the protagonist's insistence on fidelity to the truths of Christian tradition. The impasse both instigates the switch to the monophonic idiom of the subsequent letters and anticipates the breakdown of the polemic at the end of the work. Having experienced the impossiblity of achieving a dialogic convergence, the protagonist falls back, in his last words, on the hope for a divinely inspired conversion.

Within the *Provinciales*, the letters which narrate a certain communicative success are, then, the initial ones, those which focus upon the obstacles to dialogue and thereby forecast the immutably antithetical positions which the letters can only delineate in their mutual exclusiveness. The very first discussions in the work, which turn upon the term *pouvoir prochain*, draw attention to the dialogical import of the doubly fictional play of the text—as epistolary dialogue, addressed through an imagined addressee to a collective audience, and as dialogues narrated within that discursive framework. When the term *pouvoir prochain* surfaces in the opening investigation, it creates confusion and consternation for the narrator, whose project is transformed into the unraveling of a mystery ("il m'en fit un mystère"), or, as it were, into an initiation into the mystical power of the expression. The difficulty lies in the elusive modifier *prochain* (indicative of close proximity in space, imminence in time, a minimal differential in logic), encountered in two conflicting definitions of *pouvoir prochain:* "c'est avoir tout ce qui est nécessaire pour la [an action] faire, de telle sorte qu'il ne manque rien pour agir"; "quand vous dites que les justes ont toujours le *pouvoir prochain* pour prier Dieu, vous entendez qu'ils ont besoin d'un autre secours pour prier, sans quoi ils ne prieront jamais." In the first case, *prochain* signifies the reduction of the gap between the potential and the real, serves only to recall the possibility of nonrealization, whereas in the second case, *prochain* signifies the reopening of the gap between the potential and the real, indicates that the realization remains dependent on a supplemental factor which must intervene to provide what is lacking. Each proposition defines power as a function of the *lack* ("il ne *manque* rien"; "*besoin* d'un autre secours") of what is necessary, the *lack* being the differential factor required for thinking the concept of power.

With the contradictory definitions of *pouvoir prochain* firmly in place, the final dialogue of the letter brings together the representatives of the two definitions, who nonetheless concur—in joint opposition to the Jansenists— on the use of the word *prochain:* "Ne sommes-nous pas demeurés d'accord de ne point expliquer ce mot de *prochain*, et de le dire de part et d'autre, sans dire ce qu'il signifie?" Through this conspiratorial agreement, meaning is suppressed in favour of nonmeaning, semantic difference overridden with vocalic indifference: speech is posited as adequate by virtue of its audible presence, in its syllabic reality; the detached signifier becomes the instrument of paradoxic union. Since disregarding the signified suspends the adjective's supplemental function of specifying the presence or absence of a *lack*, it is ultimately the notion of power itself which is lost in the "liberation" of the signifier. Now governed only by the meaningless vocable *prochain*, *pouvouir* is magically set adrift, laid open to redefinition.

At this point the Pascalian narrator, responding to the dialogic exposition of contradiction by enunciating his own fundamentally conservative view of language, nonetheless detonates the action of the signifier *prochain* in his own discourse:

> Car, quand on aurait décidé qu'il faut prononcer les syllables *pro*, *chain*, qui ne voit que, n'ayant point été expliquées, chacun de vous voudra jouir de la victoire? Les Jacobins diront que ce mot s'entend en leur sens. M. Le Moine dira que c'est au sien; et ainsi il y aura bien plus de disputes pour l'expliquer que pour l'intro- duire. Car après tout, il n'y aurait pas grand péril à le recevoir sans aucun sens, puisqu'il ne peut nuire que par le sens.

Here at the very moment when the political import of suppressing the meaning of the pivotal word is unveiled, the textually spectacular splitting of the component sounds *pro/chain* regenerates the differential process of meaning. The interrogation bears directly on what is to be *seen* in the separate syllables *pro* and *chain*: the division of the factions of Molinists is reinscribed as a division within the very word which links them together. While that link (which, moreover, is semically re-marked by the combination of *pro* plus *chain*, for the *linkage* [of the factions to/in *pouvoir*]) is restored by pronunci- ation—the momentary act of *unison*—of the word *prochain*, the word remains the sign of the division which it masks, points to the meaning hidden inside its meaninglessness. The commentary on the word represents the meaning of that supposed meaninglessness as the *intention* of the respective parties in suppressing the signified: their desire is to subject the word to the meaning they wish to attribute to it, to affirm their own power (victory) in their control over language. The entire critique of the ethics of intention (notably in letters 6–8) is grounded in this elemental correlation of meaning with intention.

As the ensuing dialogue reiterates, the Molinists' intent is quite literally to impose, by force if necessary, adhesion to their own language: "Il faut, me dirent-ils tous ensemble, dire que tous les justes ont le *pouvoir prochain*, en faisant abstraction de tout sens." This statement, at once reaffirming and carrying out the conspiratorial policy, indicates explicitly what the Molinists make visible by manipulating *prochain* so as to rework, to their advantange, its relation to *pouvoir*—that is, that the speaker exercises power in his dictation of and over language, that in playing with the word *prochain* the Molinists are literally playing with *power*. By remobilizing the process of meaning within the texture of the word, the protagonist asserts the power of his own linguistic strategy. He has effectively foiled his opponents' tactic by showing that their duplicity has only displaced and concealed the distinction which continues to divide them, by revealing the irrepressibility of the *lack*, which reemerges in the *lack of meaning* as the differential factor that restores the play of difference—a play which is embodied in the commentary itself by the opposition of *sans aucun sens* to *par le sens*. The opposition of meaning to its lack corresponds precisely to the original contradiction between the Molinist definitions of *pouvoir prochain*, opposing power to its lack. The encounter with Montalte is doubly injurious to the Molinists insofar as they are confronted not only with external attack, but also with the persistence of their internal dissension.

The mystery of *pouvoir prochain* having been explained, the dialogue with the Molinists, the last one of the first letter, moves quickly to a cut-off stemming from the narrator's refusal to adopt the language which his interlocutors seek to impose. The characteristic impasse of the *Provinciales* is, then, already delineated here in the opposition of linguistic strategies which the text exposes in their political connotations. The articulation of the *word* with *power* is reinforced, moreover, in the closing of the first letter, where an ironic suggestion that the members of the Academy "bannissent par un coup d'autorité ce mot barbare de Sorbonne" is followed by a glaringly paronomastic conclusion—as if the text could not fail to release the signifying thrust of the term *prochain* which the dialogue had "unchained": "Je vous laisse cependant dans la liberté de tenir pour le mot de *prochain*, ou non; car j'aime trop mon prochain pour le persécuter sous ce prétexte." In view of the insistent reemphasis on the word throughout the letter, this wordplay must be taken seriously. At the close of a letter in which the narrator's recurrently abortive attempts at dialogue with the adversary are prefigured and elucidated, the salient constrast of *le mot de prochain* and *mon prochain*— of the adjectival sign of a lack and the substantive sign of a human presence— resumes the diacritical opposition of the improper use of the word as a vehicle of power (a *pretext* for *persecution*) to its proper use as the vehicle of unambiguous meaning (the correct use of *mon prochain*, positing a relation of closeness, equality, shared humanity, precludes the relation of oppression or subordination which is enacted by the imposition of the word without regard for its meaning). Since *mon prochain* embodies the actualization of the meaning which is lacking, and which is only potential in the empty, equivocal *mot de prochain*, the contrast effectively restates the narrator's preference of truth—as that which cannot be *imposed* on the addressee who is invoked in his freedom of choice—to force.

This same revealing contrast effects the return of the independent interlocutor who has been missing from the dialogue with the Molinists. *Mon prochain* designates the fictional correspondent whom the letter-writer addresses, not as an automatic ally, but as an interlocutor prepared to ply language to truth rather than to search for its power. The crucial function of the epistolary form of the first ten letters of the *Provinciales* consists in maintaining—against the foreground of communicative failure—the silent presence of that other *prochain* with whom dialogue remains possible. *Mon prochain* is the fundamental textual inscription of the crucial lack which articulates meaning and power with the practice of dialogue; it is the differential factor which requires that the successful dialogue (the *realization* of truth through the mutual appropriation of language) with the correspondent be predicated upon the failure of the narrated dialogue with the adversary, just as the meaning of truth must be predicated upon its differentiation from power. The relation of the narrator and his audience is consolidated by the relegation of the Jesuit interlocutor to the position of the excluded third party, by the recognition of the will-to-power as an intolerable interference which must be suppressed by the parties to a meaningful dialogue. Thus the *Provinciales* communicate their truth and establish a basis for dialogue through a lack of dialogue. The work represents with masterful cogency a dialogical vision in which truth occupies the position of the lack in relation to power (and *vice versa*): incommensurable with a power that it lacks irrevocably and whose meaning it governs, truth is nonetheless caught up in an endless struggle with that power. Hence the interdependence of positive and negative dialogue in the *Provinciales* leaves intact the fundamental problem of conciliating truth and power. What is finally anticipated here, in this consummate prefiguration, is the entire problematics of truth which is regenerated by the necessarily fragmentary writing of the *Pensées*.

PAUL DE MAN

Pascal's Allegory of Persuasion

Attempts to define allegory keep reencountering a set of predictable problems, of which the summary can serve as a preliminary characterization of
the mode. Allegory is sequential and narrative, yet the topic of its narration
is not necessarily temporal at all, thus raising the question of the referential
status of a text whose semantic function, though strongly in evidence, is not
primarily determined by mimetic moments; more than ordinary modes of
fiction, allegory is at the furthest possible remove from historiography. The
"realism" that appeals to us in the details of medieval art is a calligraphy
rather than a mimesis, a technical device to insure that the emblems will be
correctly identified and decoded, not an appeal to the pagan pleasures of
imitation. For it is part of allegory that, despite its obliqueness and innate
obscurity, the resistance to understanding emanates from the difficulty or
censorship inherent in the statement and not from the devices of enunciation:
Hegel rightly distinguishes between allegory and enigma in terms of allegory's "aim for the most complete clarity, so that the external means it uses
must be as transparent as possible with regard to the meaning it is to make
apparent." The difficulty of allegory is rather that this emphatic clarity of
representation does not stand in the service of something that can be
represented.

The consequence, throughout the history of the term *allegory*, is a
recurrent ambivalence in its aesthetic valorization. Allegory is frequently

From *Allegory and Representation: Selected Papers from the English Institute, 1979–1980*,
edited by Stephen J. Greenblatt. © 1981 by the English Institute. Johns Hopkins
University Press, 1981.

dismissed as wooden, barren (*kahl*), ineffective, or ugly, yet the reasons for its ineffectiveness, far from being a shortcoming, are of such all-encompassing magnitude that they coincide with the furthest reaching achievements available to the mind and reveal boundaries that aesthetically more successful works of art, because of this very success, were unable to perceive. To remain with Hegel a moment longer, the aesthetic condemnation of allegory, which becomes evident in the assumed inferiority of Virgil with regard to Homer, is outdone, in Hegel's own allegory of history, by its assignation to the meta-aesthetic age of Christianity, thus making the triadic procession from Homer to Virgil to Dante characteristic for the history of art itself as the dialectical overcoming of art. The theoretical discussion of the uncertain value of allegory repeats, in the *Aesthetics*, the theoretical discussion of the uncertain value of art itself. In the wavering status of the allegorical sign, the system of which the allegorical is a constitutive component is being itself unsettled.

Allegory is the purveyor of demanding truths, and thus its burden is to articulate an epistemological order of truth and deceit with a narrative or compositional order of persuasion. In a stable system of signification, such an articulation is not problematic; a representation is, for example, persuasive and convincing to the extent that it is faithful, exactly in the same manner that an argument is persuasive to the extent that it is truthful. Persuasion and proof should not, in principle, be distinct from each other, and it would not occur to a mathematician to call his proofs allegories. From a theoretical point of view, there ought to be no difficulty in moving from epistemology to persuasion. The very occurrence of allegory, however, indicates a possible complication. Why is it that the furthest reaching truths about ourselves and the world have to be stated in such a lopsided, referentially indirect mode? Or, to be more specific, why is it that texts that attempt the articulation of epistemology with persuasion turn out to be inconclusive about their own intelligibility in the same manner and for the same reasons that produce allegory? A large number of such texts on the relationship between truth and persuasion exist in the canon of philosophy and of rhetoric, often crystallized around such traditional philosophical topoi as the relationship between analytic and synthetic judgments, between propositional and modal logic, between logic and mathematics, between logic and rhetoric, between rhetoric as *inventio* and rhetoric as *dispositio*, and so forth. In order to try to progress in the precise formulation of the difficulty, I turn to what I find to be a suggestive example, one of the later didactic texts written by Pascal for the instruction of the pupils at Port-Royal. The text, which dates from 1657 or 1658 (Pascal died in 1662), remained unpublished for a long time, but did not pass unnoticed, since Arnauld and Nicole incorporated parts of it in the *Logique* of Port-Royal. It has since been mentioned by most specialists of Pascal and has been the object of at least one learned monograph. The text is entitled *Réflexions sur la géométrie en général; De l'esprit géométrique et de l'Art de persuader*, a title rendered somewhat oddly, but not uninterestingly, in one English edition of Pascal as *The Mind of the Geometrician*. It is an exemplary case for our inquiry, since it deals with what Pascal calls, in the first section, "l'étude de la verité" or epistemology and, in the second, "l'art de persuader" or rhetoric.

Ever since it was discovered, *Réflexions* has puzzled its readers. Arnauld's and Nicole's way of excerpting from it to make it serve the more narrowly traditional Cartesian mold of the *Logique* considerably simplified and indeed mutilated its Pascalian complexity; the Dominican Father Touttée, who was the first to unearth it from among Pascal's papers, expressed great doubts about its internal coherence and consistency. Despite strong internal evidence to the contrary, the text has often not been considered as a single entity divided in two parts, but as two entirely separate disquisitions; Pascal's early editors, Desmolets (in 1728) and Condorcet (in 1776), gave it as separate fragments, and not until 1844 did it appear more or less in the now generally accepted form of one single unit divided into two parts. The history of the text's philology curiously repeats the theoretical argument, which has compulsively to do with questions of units and pairs, divisibility, and heterogeneity.

The argument of the *Réflexions* is digressive, but not at all lacking in consistency. If it indeed reaches dead ends and breaking points, it does so by excess of rigor rather than for lack of it. That such breaking points are reached, however, cannot be denied. Recent commentators have valiantly tried to patch up the most conspicuous holes by attributing them to historical indeterminations characteristic of Pascal's time and situation. In a text that is historically as overdetermined as this one—and that contains echoes of an almost endless series of disputations which, in the wake of such philosophers as Descartes, Leibniz, Hobbes, and Gassendi, mark the period as one of intense epistemological speculation—the temptation is great to domesticate the more threatening difficulties by historicizing them out of consciousness. Even after this operation has been performed, some anomalies remain that pertain specifically to the nature rather than the state of the question. The most conspicuous break occurs in the second part, in the section on persuasion. Pascal has asserted the existence of two entirely different modes by which arguments can be conducted. The first mode has been established in the first section, in polemical opposition to the scholastic logic of syllogisms, as the method of the geometricians, and it can be codified in the rules that

Arnauld and Nicole incorporated in the *Logique*. When these rules are observed, it is the only mode to be both productive and reliable. Because of
the fallen condition of man, however, it cannot establish itself as the only
way. Though man is accessible to reason and convinced by proof, he is even
more accessible to the language of pleasure and of seduction, which governs
his needs and his passions rather than his mind. In their own realms, the
language of seduction (*langage d'agrément*) and the language of persuasion can
rule or even cooperate, but when natural truth and human desire fail to
coincide, they can enter into conflict. At that moment, says Pascal, "a dubious
balance is achieved between truth and pleasure (*vérité et volupté*), and the
knowledge of the one and the awareness of the other wage a combat of which
the outcome is very uncertain." Such dialectical moments are, as the readers
of the *Pensées* well know, very common in Pascal and function as the necessary
precondition for insights. No such resolution occurs at this crucial moment,
however, although the efficacy of the entire text is at stake. Pascal retreats
in a phraseology of which it is impossible to say whether it is evasive or
ironically personal: "Now, of these two methods, the one of persuasion, the
other of seduction (*convaincre . . . agrées*), I shall give rules only for the former
. . . [the geometrical persuasion]. Not that I do not believe the other to be
incomparably more difficult, more subtle, more useful, and more admirable.
So, if I do not discuss it, it is because of my inability to do so. I feel it to
be so far beyond my means that I consider it entirely impossible. Not that
I do not believe that if anyone is able to do so, it is people whom I know,
and that no one has as clear and abundant insight into the matter as they
do." The reference appears to be to Pascal's friend the Chevalier de Méré,
who had already been present by polemical allusion at an earlier and delicate
moment in the first part of the treatise, thus enforcing the impression that,
at the moment in the demonstration when we are the most in need of clear
and explicit formulation, what we get is private obfuscation. For, as is clear
from many testimonials and, among many other instances, from the prose
of the *Lettres provinciales*, Pascal's claim at being incompetent in the rhetoric
of seduction is certainly not made in good faith. The concluding paragraphs
of the text never recover from this decisive break in a by no means undecisive
argument. What is it, in this argument, that accounts for the occurrence of
this disruption? What is it, in a rigorous epistemology, that makes it impossible to decide whether its exposition is a proof or an allegory? We have
to retrace and interpret the course of the argument, as it develops in the first
section of the *Réflexions* and as it finds its equvalent in the underlying logical
and rhetorical structure of the *Pensées*, in order to answer this question.

"De l'esprit géométrique," part 1 of the *Réflexions*, starts out from a

classical and very well known problem in epistemology: the distinction between nominal and real definition, *definitio nominis* and *definitio reo*. Pascal
insists at once that the superiority and reliability of the geometrical (i.e.,
mathematical) method is established because "in geometry we recognize only
those definitions that logicians call *definitions of name* (*définitions de nom*), that
is to say, giving a name only to those things which have been clearly designated in perfectly known terms." Nothing could be simpler, in Pascal's
exposition, than this process of denomination, which exists only as a kind
of stenography, a free and flexible code used for reasons of economy to avoid
cumbersome repetitions, and which in no way influences the thing itself in
its substance or in its properties. Definitions of name are, says Pascal, "entirely free and never open to contradiction." They require some hygiene and
some policing. One should avoid, for example, that the same signifier designate two distinct meanings, but this can easily be assured by public con-
vention. Real definitions, on the other hand, are a great deal more coercive
and dangerous: they are actually not definitions, but axioms or, even more
frequently, propositions that need to be proven. The confusion between
nominal and real definitions is the main cause of the difficulties and obscurities that plague philosophical disputation, and to keep the distinction
between them clear and sharp is in Pascal's own terms, "the (real) reason for
writing the treatise, more than the subject with which I deal." The mind of
the geometrician is exemplary to the extent that it observes this distinction.

Can it really do so? As soon as it is enunciated, the apparently simple
definition of definition runs into complications, for the text glides almost
imperceptively from the discussion of nominal definition to that of what it
calls "primitive words," which are not subject to definition at all, since their
pretended definitions are infinite regresses of accumulated tautologies. These
terms (which include the basic topoi of geometrical discourse, such as motion,
number, and extension) represent the natural language element that Descartes
scornfully rejected from scientific discourse, but which reappear here as the
natural light that guarantees the intelligibility of primitive terms despite their
undefinability. In geometrical (i.e., epistemologically sound) discourse, primitive words and nominal definition are coextensive and blend into each other:
in this "judicious science . . . all terms are perfectly intelligible, either by
natural light or by the definitions it produces."

But things are not quite so simple. For if primitive words possess a
natural meaning, then this meaning would have to be universal, as is the
science that operates with these words; however, in one of the sudden shifts
so characteristic of Pascal and which sets him entirely apart from Arnauld's
trust in logic, this turns out not to be the case. "It is not the case," says

Pascal, "that all men have the same idea of the essence of the things which I showed to be impossible and useless to define . . . (such as, for example, time). It is not the nature of these things which I declare to be known by all, but simply *the relationship between the name and the thing*, so that on hearing the expression *time*, all turn (or direct) the mind toward the same entity . . . (*tous portent la pensée vers le même objet*)." Here the word does not function as a sign or a name, as was the case in the nominal definition, but as a vector, a directional motion that is manifest only as a turn, since the target toward which it turns remains unknown. In other words, the sign has become a trope, a substitutive relationship that has to posit a meaning whose existence cannot be verified, but that confers upon the sign an unavoidable signifying function. The indeterminacy of this function is carried by the figural expression "porter la pensée," a figure that cannot be accounted for in phenomenal terms. The nature of the relationship between figure (or trope) and mind can only be described by a figure, the same figure that Pascal will use in the *Pensées* in order to describe figure: "Figure *porte* absence et présence, plaisir et déplaisir" (Pensée 265; Pascal references cite the Lafuma edition); this is a sentence to which we will have to return later on. This much, at least, is clearly established: in the language of geometry, nominal definition and primitive terms are coextensive, but the semantic function of the primitive terms is structured like a trope. As such, it acquires a signifying function that it controls neither in its existence nor in its direction. Another way of stating this is to say that the nominal definition of primitive terms always turns into a proposition that has to, but cannot, be proven. Since definition is now itself a primitive term, it follows that the definition of the nominal definition is itself a real, and not a nominal, definition. This initial complication has far-reaching consequences for the further development of the text.

The discussion of denomination and of definition leads directly into Pascal's more fundamental and systematic statement about the intelligibility and coherence of mind and cosmos: the principle of double infinity, which also underlies the theological considerations of the *Pensées*. From a traditional point of view, the interest of the *Réflexions* is that it spells out, more explicitly than can be the case in the apologetic and religious context of the *Pensées*, the link between this central principle, so often expressed, in Pascal himself and in his interpreters, in a tonality of existential pathos, and the geometrical or mathematical logic of which it is actually a version. The text helps to undo the tendencious and simplistic opposition between knowledge and faith which is often forced upon Pascal. The *logos* of the world consists of the "necessary and reciprocal link" that exists between the intrawordly dimensions of motion, number, and space (to which Pascal also adds time), the principle asserted in the only quotation from Scripture to appear in the text: *Deus fecit omnia in pondere, in numero, et mensura.*

Pascal is indeed in conformity with his age of science in making the cohesion of arithmetic, geometry, and rational mechanics the logical model for epistemological discourse. He is also in essential conformity with that age, the age of Leibniz and the development of infinitesimal calculus, in designating the principle of double infinity, the infinitely large and the infinitely small, as the "common property (of space, time, motion, and number) where knowledge opens up the mind to the greatest marvels in nature." Thus, when the burden of Pascal's text becomes the assertion of the infinite divisibility of space and of number (it being assumed that infinite expansion is readily granted, but that the mind resists the notion of infinite divisibility), one is not surprised to find the first four of the five arguments designed to overcome that resistance to be traditional assertions that do not stand in need of development. They reiterate such fundamental principles of calculus as the impossibility of comparing finite and infinite quantities and, in general, move between spatial and numerical dimensions by means of simple computation (as in the instance of the irrational number for the square root of two), or by experimental representations in space, without the intervention of discursive language. The text starts to proliferate and to grow tense, however, when it has to counter an objection that is to be attributed to Méré and that compels Pascal to reintroduce the question of the relationship between language and cognition. Méré argued that it is perfectly possible in the order of space to conceive of an extension made up from parts that are themselves devoid of extension, thus implying that space can be made up of a finite quantity of indivisible parts, rather than of an infinity of infinitely divisible ones, because it is possible to make up numbers out of units that are themselves devoid of number. Méré uses the principle of homogeneity between space and number, which is also the ground of Pascal's cosmology, to put the principle of infinitesimal smallness into question. Pascal's retort marks the truly Pascalian moment in the demonstration. It begins by dissociating the laws of number from the laws of geometry, by showing that what applies to the indivisible unit of number, the *one*, does not apply to the indivisible unit of space. The status of the *one* is paradoxical and apparently contradictory: as the very principle of singleness, it has no plurality, no number. As Euclid said, *one* is not a number. It is a mere name given to the entity that does not possess the properties of number, a nominal definition of nonnumber. On the other hand, the one partakes of number, according to the principle of homogeneity enunciated by the same Euclid who decreed the one not to be a number. The principle of homogeneity ("magnitudes are said to be of the same kind or species, when one magnitude can be made to exceed another by reiterated multiplication") is mathematically linked to the principle of infinity in this proposition. *One* is not a number; this proposition is correct, but so is the opposite proposition, namely, that *one is* a number, provided it is mediated by the principle of homogeneity which asserts that *one* is of the same species as number, as a house is not a city, yet a city made up of houses that are of the same species as the city, since one can always add a house to a city and it remains a city. Generic homogeneity, or the infinitesimal, is a synechdocal structure. We again find in the fundamental model of Pascal's cosmos, which is based on tropes of homogeneity and on the notion of the infinite, a system that allows for a great deal of dialectical contradiction (one can say $1 = N$ as well as $1 \neq N$), but one that guarantees intelligibility.

The interest of the argument is, however, that it has to reintroduce the ambivalence of definitional language. The synechdocal totalization of infinitude is possible because the unit of number, the *one*, functions as a nominal definition. But, for the argument to be valid, the nominally indivisible number must be distinguished from the *really* indivisible space, a demonstration that Pascal can accomplish easily, but only because the key words of the demonstration—indivisible, spatial extension (*étendue*), species (*genre*), and definition—function as real, and not as nominal, definitions as "définition de chose" and not as "définition de nom." The language almost forces this formulation upon Pascal, when he has to say: "cette dernière preuve est fondée sur la *définition* de ces deux *choses*, indivisible et étendue" or "Donc, il n'est pas de même genre que l'étendue, par la *définition* des *choses* du même genre" (italics mine). The reintroduction of a language of *real* definition also allows for the next turn in the demonstration, which, after having separated number from space, now has to suspend this separation while maintaining it—because the underlying homology of space and number, the ground of the system, should never be fundamentally in question. There exists, in the order of number, an entity that is, unlike the *one*, heterogeneous with regard to number: this entity, which is the *zero*, is radically distinct from one. Whereas one is and is not a number at the same time, zero is radically not a number, absolutely heterogeneous to the order of number. With the introduction of zero, the separation between number and space, which is potentially threatening, is also healed. For equivalences can easily be found in the order of time and of motion for the zero function in number: instant and stasis (*repos*) are the equivalences that, thanks to the zero, allow one to reestablish the "necessarily and reciprocal link" between the four intra-wordly dimensions on which divine order depends. At the end of the passage, the homogeneity of the universe is recovered, and the principle of infinitesimal symmetry is well established. But this has happened at a price: the coherence of the system is now seen to be entirely dependent on the introduction of an element—the zero and its equivalences in time and motion—that is itself entirely heterogeneous with regard to the system and is nowhere a part of it. The continuous universe held together by the double wings of the two infinites is interrupted, disrupted *at all points* by a principle of radical heterogeneity without which it cannot come into being. Moreover, this rupture of the infinitesimal and the homogeneous does not occur on the transcendental level, but on the level of language, in the inability of a theory of language as sign or as name (nominal definition) to ground this homogeneity without having recourse to the signifying function, the real definition, that makes the zero of signification the necessary condition for grounded knowledge. The notion of language as sign is dependent on, and derived from, a different notion in which language functions as rudderless signification and transforms what it denominates into the linguistic equivalence of the arithmetical zero. It is as sign that language is capable of engendering the principles of infinity, of genus, species and homogeneity, which allow for synechdocal totalizations, but none of these tropes could come about without the systematic effacement of the zero and its reconversion into a name. There can be no *one* without zero, but the zero always appears in the guise of a *one*, of a (some)thing. The name is the trope of the zero. The zero is always *called* a one, when the zero is actually nameless, "innomable." In the French language, as used by Pascal and his interpreters, this happens concretely in the confusedly alternate use of the two terms *zéro* and *néant*. The verbal, predicative form *néant*, with its gerundive ending, indicates not the zero, but rather the one, as the *limit* of the infinitely small, the almost zero that is the one. Pascal is not consistent in his use of *zéro* and *néant*; nor could he be if the system of the two infinites is to be enunciated at all. At the crucial point, however, as is the case here, he knows the difference, which his commentators, including the latest and most astute ones, always forget. At the end of the most systematic exposition of the theory of the two infinites, at the conclusion of part 1 of the *Réflexions*, we find once again the ambivalence of the theory of definitional language, which we encountered at the start.

The unavoidable question will be whether the model established in this text, in which discourse is a dialectical and infinitesimal system that depends on its undoing in order to come into being, can be extended to texts that are not purely mathematical, but stated in a less abstract, more phenomenally or existentially perceivable form. One would specifically want to know whether the principle of homogeneity implicit in the theory of the two infinites, *as well as* the disruption of this system, can be retraced in the theological and subject-oriented context of the *Pensées*. Since this would involve an extensive reading of a major and difficult work, we must confine ourselves here to preliminary hints, by showing first of all how the principle of totalization, which is implicit in the notion of the infinite, underlies the dialectical pattern that is so characteristic of the *Pensées*. Once this is done, we should then ask whether this pattern is at all interrupted, as the numerical series are interrupted by zero, and how this disruption occurs. As a general precaution, we should be particularly wary not to decide too soon that this is indeed the case, not only because the consequences, from a theological and an epistemological point of view, are far-reaching but also because the remarkable elasticity of the dialectical model, capable of recovering totalities threatened by the most radical contradictions, should not be underestimated. The Pascalian dialectic should be allowed to display the full extent of its feats, and, if a disjunction is to be revealed, it can only be done so by following Pascal in pushing it to its eventual breaking point.

What is here called, for lack of a better term, a rupture or a disjunction, is not to be thought of as a negation, however tragic it may be. Negation, in a mind as resilient as Pascal's, is always susceptible of being reinscribed in a system of intelligibility. Nor can we hope to map it out as one topos among topoi, as would be the case with regular tropes of substitution. It is possible to find, in the terminology of rhetoric, terms that come close to designating such disruptions (e.g., *parabasis* or *anacoluthon*), which designate the interruption of a semantic continuum in a manner that lies beyond the power of reintegration. One must realize at once, however, that this disruption is not topical, that it cannot be located in a single point—since it is indeed the very notion of point, the geometrical zero, that is being dislodged—but that it is all-pervading. The anacoluthon is omnipresent, or, in temporal terms and in Friedrich Schlegel's deliberately unintelligible formulation, the parabasis is permanent. Calling this structure ironic can be more misleading than helpful, since *irony*, like *zero*, is a term that is not susceptible to nominal or real definition. To say then, as we are actually saying, that allegory (as sequential narration) is the trope of irony (as the one is the trope of zero) is to say something that is true enough but not intelligible, which also implies that it cannot be put to work as a device of textual analysis. To discover, in the *Pensées*, the *instances de rupture*, the equivalence of the zero in Pascal's theory of number, we can only reiterate compulsively the dialectical pattern of Pascal's own model or, in other words,

read and reread the *Pensées* with genuine insistence. Pascal himself has formulated the principle of totalizing reading, in which the most powerful
antinomies must be brought together, in the pensée headed "Contradiction"
(257): "One can put together a good physiognomy only by reconciling all
our oppositions. It does not suffice to follow a sequence of matched properties
without reconciling contraries: in order to understand an author's meaning,
one must reconcile all the contradictory passages" (*pour entendre le sens d'un
auteur il faut accorder tous les passages contraires*). Applied to Scripture, which
Pascal here has in mind, this reconciliation leads directly to the fundamental
opposition that underlies all others: that between a figural and a true reading.
"If one takes the law, the sacrifices, and the kingdom as realities, it will be
impossible to coordinate all passages (of the Bible); it is therefore necessary
that they be mere figures." The question remains, of course, whether the
pair figure-reality can or cannot be itself thus reconciled, whether it is a
contradiction of the type we encountered when it was said that one is a
number and is not a number at the same time, or whether the order of figure
and the order of reality are heterogeneous.

For all the somber felicity of their aphoristic condensation, the *Pensées*
are also very systematically schematized texts that can be seen as an intricate
interplay of binary oppositions. Many of the sections are, or could easily
be, designated by the terms of these oppositions, as is the case for our first
and simplest example, two of the *Pensées* (125 and 126), which could properly
be entitled "Nature" and "Custom": "What are our natural principles if not
the principles we have grown accustomed to? In children, they are the
principles they have learned from the customs of their fathers, like the hunt
in animals. A different custom will produce different natural principles. This
can be verified by experience, by observing if there are customs that cannot
be erased. . . . Fathers fear that the natural love of their children can be
erased. What kind of nature is this, that can thus be erased? Custom is a
second nature that destroys the first. But what is nature? Why is custom
not natural? I am very much afraid that this nature is only a first custom,
as custom is a second nature." This passage turns around a saying of common
wisdom (*La coutume est une seconde nature*), as is frequently the case in Pascal,
and it thus sets up a very characteristic logical or, rather, rhetorical pattern.
A set of binary oppositions is matched in a commonsensical order in terms
of their properties: here, custom and nature are matched with the pairs first/
second and constant/erasable (*effaçable*), respectively. Nature, being a *first*
principle, is constant, whereas custom, being second or derived from nature,
is susceptible to change and erasure. The schema, at the onset, is as follows:

| nature | first | constant |
| custom | second | erasable |

The pattern is put in motion by a statement (also based, in this case, on common observation) that reverses the order of association of the entities and their properties. It is said that fathers fear, apparently with good reason, that natural feelings of filial affection can be erased, thus coupling the natural with the erasable and, consequently, with secondness. A first (nature) then becomes a first second, that is, a second; a second (custom) becomes in symmetrical balance, a second first, that is, a first:

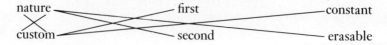

The properties of firstness and secondness have changed places, which results in the undoing or the deconstruction of the binary opposition from which we started. It has now become impossible to decide whether a given experience can be called natural or customary. Since they are able to exchange or cross over, in a chiasmic reversal, their properties, nature and custom have been brought together to the extent that their opposition has been inscribed into a system of exchange which is structured like a trope (chiasmus). Nature and custom are united within a single system, which, although experienced as negative by the author ("I am afraid that . . ."), is nevertheless a cognition.

The same pattern, with increased complications, reappears time after time and underlies some of the most famous and thematically suggestive of the *Pensées*. Consider, for example, the section on the nature of man (131). It starts out from an opposition that, this time, is historical and, to that extent, empirical: the philosophical debate—to which Pascal has gained access through his closest predecessors, Montaigne and Descartes—between sceptical and dogmatic philosophy, *pyrrhoniens* and *dogmatistes*. The establishment of the original grid, which was obvious in the case of nature and custom as first and second, is more complex in this case, in which scepticism and dogmatic faith have to be matched with truth and nature, respectively. The argument goes back to the example and the logic used by Descartes in the first two meditations. It established the claim for the cognitive value of doubt by reference to the polarity of sleeping and waking, of dream and reality. One normally assumes that the condition of waking is the true condition of man, the first norm from which sleep and dream are derived and displaced, secondary versions. Sleep is grafted upon the condition of

awakeness like a secondary upon a primary quality. The original pattern is
as follows:

wake	perception	first
sleep	dream	second

Since we think that we are awake when we dream, it follows that the properties can be ordered according to the same symmetrical pattern we encountered in the Pensée on nature and custom. Like Keats at the end of the
"Ode to a Nightingale," we should each ask: Do I wake or sleep? For it is
no longer certain that our primary consciousness is awake at all, that consciousness is not a palimpsest of dreams, some of them individual, some
shared with others, all grafted upon each other. "Is it not possible that this
half of our life (day) is itself a mere dream on which the other dreams are
grafted, and of which we will awake at death?" This suspicion, which undoes
the natural polarities of day and night, wake and sleep, is clearly the product
of the sceptical mind and justifies the pairing of scepticism with knowledge.
The sceptical position always had knowledge on its side, and the only thing
the dogmatists can oppose to this knowledge is the natural conviction that
infinite doubt is intolerable. "What will man do in this condition? Will he
doubt of everything, doubt that he is awake, that he is being pinched or
burned, will he doubt that he doubts, doubt that he is? One cannot reach
this condition, and I assert as a fact that there never has been a perfectly
consistent and actual sceptic. Nature supports our feeble reason and shelters
it from such extravagance." Scepticism and dogmatism are now firmly paired
with truth and nature, respectively.

Scepticism	Truth
Dogmatism	Nature

But this original configuration is not a stable one. As is clear from the
preceding quotation, one cannot be consistently sceptical, but it is just as
impossible to be consistently natural, for however "extravagant" the sceptical
position may be, it is nevertheless the only mode of truth accessible to us,
and it deprives all claims to natural truth of authority. To the belief "that
one cannot doubt natural principles," the sceptics counter "that the uncertainty of our origin includes that of our nature." This argument cannot be
refuted: "The dogmatists have been trying to refute it ever since the world
began."

The situation is not only unstable, but coercive as well. At this point in the *Pensées*, one moves from the logic of propositions, statements as to what is the case, to model logic, statements of what should or ought to be the case. For one cannot remain suspended between the irreconcilable positions: it is clear that, by not choosing between the two poles of the polarities, one is adopting the sceptical position. The predicament is that of the undecidable: propositional logic is powerless to decide a conflict that has to find a solution, if this logic is to survive.

In a first dialectical reversal, the answer will be to give the predicament a name, which, in this case, will be "man," the being who stands in that predicament. "Man" is then not a definable entity, but an incessant motion beyond itself. "L'homme passe l'homme" says Pascal, in a phrase that has received many pseudo-Nietzschean interpretations of existential transcendence and transgression. Perhaps more important is the numerical formulation of the "definition" of man, which takes us back to the *Réflexions*. For it follows, says Pascal, that man is double, that the one is always already at least a two, a pair. Man is like the *one* in the system of number, infinitely divisible and infinitely capable of self-multiplication. He is another version of the system of the two infinites; immediately after having stated that man surpasses man, and that man is double, Pascal can add that Man *infinitely* surpasses man, "l'homme passe *infiniment* l'homme." As a metaphor of number, man is one and is not one, is a pair and is infinite all at the same time.

The dialectic of the infinite, which starts in the initial doubt, is thus able to unfold itself consistently. For the double, and hence infinitesimal, condition of man, this becomes the key to the knowledge of man's nature. "For who fails to see that without the knowledge of this double condition of nature man was in an irrevocable ignorance of the truth of his nature?" This ruse of reason is purely Cartesian: doubt is suspended by the knowledge of doubt. One sees that the original structure, pairing scepticism with truth and dogmatism with nature, has been chiastically crossed, since now the true knowledge of radical scepticism is paired with nature, through the mediation of the concept of man, standing by implication for the system of double infinitude. The rhetorical pattern that underlies this system is the same as in the previous example.

It is legitimate to "pair" this Pensée with another and more rigorously schematized one, which states the same tension, but empties it of the existential pathos of totalization (122). It is headed by the binary opposition "Grandeur et misère": "Since misery is derived from greatness, and greatness from misery, some have decided in favor of misery all the more decisively, since they have taken greatness to be the proof of misery, and others have decided for greatness with all the more power, since they derive it from misery itself. All they were able to say in support of greatness has served as an argument for the others to demonstrate misery, since the higher the station from which one falls the more miserable one will be, and vice versa. They are carried upon each other (*portés les uns sur les autres*) in a circle without end, it being certain that as men gain in enlightenment, they find both greatness and misery in themselves. In a word: man knows he is miserable. He is therefore miserable, since that is what he is, but he is also great because he knows it." (*En un mot, l'homme connait qu'il est misérable. Il est donc misérable puisqu'il l'est, mais il est bien grand puisqu'il le connait.*)

The end of the text telescopes the chiasmus in a particularly condensed form, starting from the pairing of misery with (self-) knowledge and of greatness with being: "Man *is* great because man *knows* misery" (*l'homme connait qu'il est misérable*). The final sentence has reversed the pattern: misery is paired with being, in the tautology "il est misérable puisqu'il l'est," and greatness with knowledge, the self-knowledge of misery. The mediation is carried out by the apparently deductive prepositions in the sentence: "il est *donc* misérable *puisqu'*il l'est," where the cognitive power is carried by the logical articulations *donc* and *puisque*, and the ontological power by the tautology of the assertion. The dialectic has been flattened out into tautology, in the endlessly circular repetition of the same, and the teleological form of infinite transcendence has been replaced by this monotony. All the same, despite the thematic and tonal difference between the two Pensées on man, the rhetorical pattern remains the same, grounded in the infinitesimal symmetry of the chiasmic reversal. Here, in one of the bleakest of the *Pensées*, this pattern appears perhaps in the purest form.

The transition from self-knowledge and anthropological knowledge to teleological knowledge often passes, in Pascal, through the dimension of the political. Louis Marin is right to insist on the close interconnection between epistemology, political criticism, and theology, in the sequence of *Pensées* entitled "Raison des effets." This sequence deals primarily with a distinction between popular and scientific knowledge and thus returns to the question that underlies the *Réflexions* as well: the antinomy between natural language and metalanguage. The polarities in Pensées 90–101 oppose the language of the people (vox populi) to that of the mathematicians; moreover, Pensée 91 contains a good description of Pascal's own writing style, in its peculiar mixture of popular, nontechnical diction with redoutable critical rigor: one must have what Pascal calls "une pensée de derrière" (which sees behind the apparent evidence of things), yet speak like the people. Whereas the man of science possesses true knowledge (*episteme*), the people follow the vagaries of opinion (*doxa*). The starting position, then, will be:

| people | doxa | false |
| geometrician | episteme | true |

It would be a mistake, however, to dismiss popular opinion as simply false. In a way, the (popular) saying "Vox populi, vox dei" is sound, as are, according to Pascal, the various popular opinions of which he enumerates a rather baffling catalogue of examples. This being the case, a first chiasmic reversal takes place, in which popular opinion has some claims to truth, and the mind of the geometrician, in his scorn for popular wisdom, some taint of falsehood.

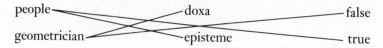

This first chiasmus, however, is only the beginning. Although it is true that the people have sound opinions, it is not really true that they possess the truth. For the people can be counted on to provide the wrong reasons for their sound opinions. "They believe" says Pascal, "that truth is to be found where it is not. There is truth in their opinions, but not where they imagine it to be." This knowledge of error, which is true, is no longer a popular knowledge, but the privileged knowledge of the man who has benefited from the critical rigors of scientific reasoning. A second reversal now associates popular opinion, which to some extent is true, with epistemological false-hood, whereas the knowledge of this falsehood is again true. "We have shown that men are vain in their respect for trivial matters; this vanity reduces all their opinions to nought. We have then shown these opinions to be altogether sound; consequently, the self-esteem of the people is quite legitimate, and the people are not at all as inestimable as one believes. And thus we have destroyed the opinion that destroyed the opinion of the people. But we must now destroy this final proposition and show that it remains true that the people are in error, although their opinions are sound, because they don't locate their truth where it belongs, and by thus locating it where it is not, their opinions are again very erroneous and very unsound."

Many more instances could be listed in an order than would cover the thematic scale of topoi taken up in the *Pensées*, from the most trivial to the most sublime. The same structure, the same "continual reversal from pro to contra" (*renversement continuel du pour au contre*) would reappear in an endless set of variations on chiasmic crossings of binary oppositions. In the process, a wealth of thematic insights would indicate the universal effectiveness of what is a fundamentally dialectical pattern of reasoning, in which oppositions are, if not reconciled, at least pursued toward a totalization that may be infinitely postponed, but that remains operative as the sole principle of intelligibility. Our question remains whether some of the texts from the *Pensées* explicitly refuse to fit this pattern—not because they are structured along a different tropological model (which would diversify but not necessarily invalidate the dialectical model), but because they disrupt the motion of what is demonstrably the same pattern. Consider Pensée 103, headed "Justice, Power" (Justice, force).

> "It is just that what is just should be followed; it is necessary that what has the most power should be followed.
>
> Justice without power is impotent, power without justice is tyrannical.
>
> Justice without power is open to contradiction, because there always are wrongdoers. Power without justice stands accused. Justice and power must therefore be brought together, by making the just strong and the strong just.
>
> Justice is subject to dispute. Power is easily recognizable and without dispute. [Thus it has been impossible to give power to justice, because power has contradicted justice and said that it is unjust, and said that it is itself just.
>
> And thus, not being able to make the just strong, one has made the strong to be just.]
>
> [Ainsi on n'a pu donner la force à la justice, parce que la force a contredit la justice et a dit qu'elle était injuste et a dit que c'était elle qui était juste.
>
> Et ainsi ne pouvant faire que ce qui est juste fût fort, on a fait que ce qui est fort fût juste.]

It is at once clear, on hearing the passage, that, although the chiasmic structure is the same as before, the crossing is no longer symmetrical, since it takes place in one direction but not in the other. A new complication has been introduced and is observable in an opposition that gives each of the key words a double register that is no longer, as in the previous passages, an opposition between two modes of cognition. The opposition is stated at the start in the contrast between "il est juste" and "il est nécessaire," in which the first assertion depends on a propositional cognition, but the second on sheer quantitative power, as in the proverb "La raison du plus fort est toujours la meilleure" or, in English, "Might makes right." Propositional statements line up on the side of cognition, model statements on the side of performance; they perform what they enunciate regardless of considerations of truth and falsehood. Consequently, all words used in the demonstration acquire this ambivalent status: the verb *suivre*, for instance, can be read in its deductive and cognitive sense, in which the necessity is the necessary deductiveness of reason, but it can also be read in the sense of pure coercive power, as in the phrase "la femme doit suivre son mari."

"Suivre" is thus distributed in its double register in the first two sentences of the Pensée. The same is true of justice, which can on the one hand be read as cognitive *justesse*, as the precision of rational argument, but which is clearly also to be read in the sense of the judicial praxis of a court of law. In this latter capacity, it clearly lacks the persuasive power of sheer argument which it possesses in the first sense; it is open to uncertainty and contradiction and therefore lacks power. For the proper of justice to be power, and for the proper of power to be justice, they must be able to exchange the attributes of necessity and of innocence which characterize them. Justice must become necessary by might, might innocent by justice. This would accomplish and demonstrate the homogeneity of propositional statements as cognition and of modal statements as performance. But, unlike all other previous examples from the *Pensées*, the exchange does not take place. Justice refuses to become justesse; it remains pragmatic and inconsistent, "sujet à dispute," unable to fulfill the criterium of necessity as cognitive persuasion. Might, however, has no difficulty whatever satisfying the criterion of necessity; it is "sans dispute" and can therefore *usurp* the consistency of cognition without giving anything in return. The usurpation occurs in the double register of the locution "sans dispute," a quality that pertains to mathematical proof as an indication of epistemological rigor, but which, as in "right makes might," also pertains to force by sheer intolerance and tyranny. Force, which is pure performance, usurps the claim to epistemological rightness. It does so because it can become the subject of the sentence of enunciation and can be said to speak: "la force a contredit . . ." and "la force a dit . . ."; it can pronounce on the lack of epistemological "rightness" of justice, and it can proclaim its own epistemological infallibility. The performative declares itself declarative and cognitive. The "on" in the final sentence: "on a fait que ce qui est fort fût juste" can only be "might," which belongs indeed to the order of the "faire" and not of "savoir." But the unilateral victory of force over justice, if it is to be enunciated, as is the case in this passage, still can only be stated in the mode of cognition and of deduction, as is evident from the use of the deductive "ainsi" coupled with "faire" in the sentence "ainsi on a fait. . . ." The status of this "ainsi" is now very peculiar, however, for the pure act of force is entirely arbitrary and not cognitively consequential at all. The "ainsi" does not belong to Descartes, but to any despot who happens to be in power.

The discomfort one should experience on the reading of this final sentence is the same one should experience on hearing the zero assimilated to the one and thus being reinscribed into a system of cognition in which it does not belong. For at the very moment that might has usurped, by imposition and not by transgression, the authority of cognition, the tropological field of cognition is revealed to be dependent on an entity, might, that is heterogeneous with regard to this field, just as the zero was heterogeneous with regard to number. The break is immediately reinscribed as the knowledge of the break in the "ainsi on a fait . . . ," but this "ainsi" must now be said to be ironical, that is to say disruptive of its own deductive claim. The dialectic starts again, but it has been broken in a way that is essentially different from the transgressive reversals we encountered in the other instances. It is in the realm of practical and political justice, and not of Christian charity, that the equivalence of the mathematical zero reappears in the text of the *Pensées*. What is of considerable importance, from a linguistic point of view, is that the break that in the *Réflexions* was due to the complications of definition is now seen to be a function of the heterogeneity between cognitive and performative language. Language, in Pascal, now separates in two distinct directions: a cognitive function that is right (*juste*) but powerless, and a modal function that is mighty (*forte*) in its claim to rightness. The two functions are radically heterogeneous to each other. The first generates canonical rules of persuasion, whereas the second generates the eudaemonic values that are present as soon as one has to say that the claim to authority is made "at the *pleasure* of" the despot. The first is the language of truth and of persuasion by proof, the second the language of pleasure (*volupté*) and of persuasion by usurpation or seduction. We now know why it is that, in the second half of the *Réflexions*, Pascal had to dodge the question of the relationship between these two modes. To the extent that language is always cognitive and tropological as well as performative at the same time, it is a heterogeneous entity incapable of justice as well as of *justesse*. Even in the transcendental realm of revealed language in Holy Writ, the necessary choice between seduction and truth remains undecidable. Pascal's "definition" of figure retains this complication: when it is said that "Figure porte absence et présence," we recognize the infinitesimal structure of cognitive dialectics, but when it is also said that "Figure porte plaisir et déplaisir," it will be impossible to square, to inscribe the four terms *présence/absence* and *plaisir/déplaisir* into a homogeneous "geometrical" structure. The (ironic) pseudo-knowledge of this impossibility, which pretends to order sequentially, in a narrative, what is actually the destruction of all sequence, is what we call allegory.

ROBERT J. NELSON

The Convert

Pascal's younger sister helped him to see the crucial role of pride as a motor of his own behavior in the period just before his so-called second conversion. Both Gilberte and Marguerite testify to the catalytic role of Jacqueline at this juncture.

> God [writes Gilberte] who asked of him a greater perfection, did not wish to leave him there in the world a long while, and on that used my sister to withdraw him from it, as he had formerly used my brother to withdraw my sister from the commitments in which she found herself in the world . . . she could not suffer that the one to whom she was indebted through God for the graces that she enjoyed was not in possession of the same graces; and, as my brother saw her often, she often spoke to him of this, and in the end she did it with such force that she persuaded him of that which he had first persuaded her, to leave the world and all the conversations of the world, of which the most innocent are but continual uselessness, altogether unworthy of the holiness of Christianity to which we are all called and of which Jesus Christ has given us the example.

Yet, we know too well the extent to which Blaise had resisted Jacqueline's desire to withdraw from the world to use this passage for its insight into the grounds on which Blaise finally did end his "worldly period." Marguerite

From *Pascal: Adversary and Advocate*. © 1982 by the President and Fellows of Harvard College. Harvard University Press, 1982.

Périer's account is more consistent with the complexity of her uncle's temperament and spiritual outlook at the time. Her report also gives continuing evidence of the special relation between the younger Pascal children. Gilberte would have the frequency of contact between Blaise and Jacqueline be a somewhat general matter, without specific cause. Given the bitterness with which they had encountered each other just prior to Jacqueline's final vows, given Pascal's plunge into the worlds of science and the court, this seems a pietistic whitewashing of a relation that was especially strained by his feelings that Jacqueline had abandoned him. Marguerite's report that he went to see Jacqueline precisely on the matter of his projected marriage seems more consistent with the pattern of their stormy relationship.

He was his own man at this time. In his relations with his sisters after his father's death, particularly with respect to Jacqueline, he had conducted himself as pater familias (albeit a role he may have used, with Jacqueline, as a surrogate for the role of lover whose imperatives may have unconsciously caused him great anguish). If he was going to confer with any member of the family on a projected marriage, one would have thought it would be with the older sister on at least two counts: she was the older sister and she was experienced in the married state into which he presumably intended to enter. Instead, it was to the younger sister that he addressed himself, perhaps because of geographical convenience, both being in Paris. The motive would be pretextual. He could have conferred with Gilberte by mail, as he so often had before. He would thus have gone to tell Jacqueline of his proposed marriage out of an old longing and an old resentment. "See, now," his first conversation could be seen to have told her beneath its surface message, "what you have reduced me to by forsaking me." It was after this first conference, as Marguerite reports this juncture, that the "frequency" of visits started: "She exhorted him often to renounce it, but the hour was not yet come." She goes on to report that the hour did not come until the feast of the Immaculate Conception—which is to say December 8, 1654, a fortnight after the brother's night of fire, November 23, 1654, the date of his second conversion from which tradition has marked his supposedly absolute break with the world. That the break was not so absolute, particularly in the hold of reason in the *Provincial Letters,* will be the sense of my analysis of much of that famous work. In the delay between the night of fire and his renunciation of the world two weeks later, one can already see the inadvisability of maintaining the simplistic, univocal conception of Pascal's character that has characterized both the hagiological mainstream of Pascal scholarship and the usually hostile liberal, skeptical, tradition that has relied on the hagiological simplicities chiefly in order to point to Pascal as a religious fraud, moral hypocrite, a schizophrenic, or even a psychopath.

Conversions are not simple affairs, especially in the stringencies of the Christian tenets to which Pascal himself converted. One of the principal tenets of the projected *Apology* as of the writings attendant upon it (particularly the *Writings on Grace* and his letters to Charlotte de Roannez) is the imperfection even of the elect, of the possibility and even probability that the elect will himself or herself be unable to continue in the assurance of salvation so long as one is in the world, even in monastic retreat from the world. Thus it is not surprising or disappointing, and certainly not scandalous, that the recently converted Pascal should cling to the world. Nor is it unexpected that it should require, through the catalytic influence of his younger sister, an occasion as extraordinary in its timing and as personal in its content as the one reported by Marguerite to bring Pascal to as complete a break with the world as he or any believer of his persuasion could attain.

The occasion was a sermon at Port-Royal on the feast of the Immaculate Conception, in which the preacher spoke on

> the beginnings of the life of Christians, and on the importance of rendering them holy, in not committing oneself, as do almost all people of the world, by habit, by custom, and by reasons of a very human proper behavior, in offices and marriages; he showed how it was necessary to consult God before thus committing oneself, and to examine well whether one could thereby work one's salvation and whether one would therein find obstacles thereto. As that was precisely his state and disposition, and this preacher preached that with a great vehemence and solidity, he was deeply touched, and, believing that all that was said for him, he took that way, and making serious reflections on this whole sermon while he heard it, he saw my aunt immediately afterward and noted to her that he had been surprised by this sermon because it seemed that it had been made only for him, and that he was all the more reassured that, having found the preacher in the pulpit, she had let nothing on to him [the preacher]. My aunt encouraged as much as she could this new fire, and in a very few days, he determined to break entirely with the world; and for that he went to spend some time in the country in order to disaccustom himself and break the stream of the great number of visits that he had been making and receiving; that worked for him, for since then he saw no more of his friends whom he had been seeing only in connection with the world.

There is undoubtedly some romanticizing here, at least, if we are to understand "world" to mean more than the order of the flesh and of social or political ambition. In the order of the mind, Marguerite and Gilberte not-withstanding, we know that Pascal would continue to concern himself with such things as the mathematical problem of cycloids and the five-penny bus. But the psychological acumen of this report is nonetheless great. It records the by now familiar pattern of Pascal persisting in a chosen pattern with great fixity, going far down the path before reverting to its opposite and then pursuing that opposite with all the intensity of which he was capable.

Conversions are not simple affairs, either theologically or psychologi-cally. His new state would be one that represents a redirection of energy rather than the substitution of one energy for another, a shift in emphasis; he would rely more on one current, the other still making its force felt. This pattern is manifest not only in his behavior after his conversion, completed as we have seen through the intercession of Jacqueline, but in the moment of conversion itself as he recorded it in the *Memorial*:

The year of grace 1654
Monday, 23 November, Saint Clement's day, pope
and martyr, and others in the martyrology.
Eve of Saint Chrysogonus, martyr, and others.
From about half past ten in the evening until
around half past midnight.
Fire
God of Abraham, God of Isaac, God of Jacob.
Not of philosophers and scholars.
Certitude, certitude feeling, joy, peace.
God of Jesus Christ.
Deum meum et Deum vestrum, my God and your God
Your God will be my God.
Forgetting of the world and everything, except God.
He can be found only by the ways taught in the Gospel.
Greatness of the human soul.
Righteous Father, the world has not known Thee,
but I have, O Righteous Father, known Thee.

Joy, joy, joy, tears of joy.
I separated myself from Him.
Delinquerunt me fontem aquae vivae, they have
forsaken me, the fountain of living waters.
My God, will you abandon me?
Let me not be separated eternally from Him.
And if this is life eternal, that they might

know Thee, the only true God, and Jesus Christ
Whom Thou has sent
Jesus Christ.
Jesus Christ.
I separated myself from Him. I fled, renounced,
crucified Him.
Let me never be separated from Him.
He can be kept only by the ways taught in the Gospel.
Total and sweet renunciation
etc.

I have translated here the version of the *Memorial* in Pascal's hand written on a small fold of paper that was itself inserted in a parchment on which according to his nephew, Louis Périer, Pascal had written a slightly different version of the lines I have given here and which contained at the end the following lines:

Total submission to Jesus Christ and to my
director
Eternally in joy for one day of effort on earth
Non obliviscar sermones tuos [I will not forget Thy
Word]
Amen

During his life Pascal carried both parchment and insert in the lining of his jacket. It was obviously what Condorcet called it in the next century, a "mystic amulet." We need not accept Condorcet's derisive overtone, however, for we can understand that the imperious self who had "separated himself from Him" carried this amulet close to his heart throughout his life not out of some superstitious faith in any mystical powers. Rather, he carried it as an act of self-discipline or, more exactly, in the spirit of the text of the *Memorial* itself, of *anti-self* discipline. Pascal had come to know himself, his *self* in all its imperious narcissism. As much the record of a conversion, the *Memorial* is the record of a deconversion from self-regard by this son who has rebelled in his heart against his father and who had known the anguish of separation from that father. In the "God of Jesus Christ," in God through Jesus Christ, who had also seemed to rebel against the Father ("O My God, why has Thou forsaken me?"), Pascal became reconciled to the father. He thus found the certitude to appease the anguish of ambivalence, the love, and the respect for the father warring with the need for self-definition and transcendence of the father's influence. With certitude came "feeling" to buttress "reason," the feelings of joy and peace that assuaged trouble and confusion.

I say to *buttress* reason for the *Memorial* does not attack reason. Rather, its content, like the very act of carrying it through the rest of his life, shows a new relation between reason, the order of mind, and feeling, the order of the heart. This relation emerges most clearly in considering the differences between the version on the folded paper and the version on the pouch of parchment. The version on the folded paper in itself shows the operation of Pascal's memory, a cognitive function related to rational learning and intelligence. The biblical and liturgical texts, some in Latin, some in French (italicized in my translation) undoubtedly sprang to Pascal's spirit in the fire of grace that had moved him. But the meditative form of the *Memorial* shows that the fire of grace had not dampened the fires of reason. It had put them to its own votive use.

In neither version is the *Memorial* an adumbration of the romantic or surrealist form in which it was long believed Pascal later wrote the fragments of the *Thoughts:* acts of inspired or automatic writing in which the reflective self plays no part. In those parts that both versions have in common we clearly have the record of an experience that has been consummated and that is being recorded in a two-part meditation: a first part with a reflective exactness about date, time, and religious setting; a second part (beginning with the titular "Fire" in the center of the page on its own line) in which reflective ("God of . . . not of") and objective (biblical and liturgical references) elements are orchestrated into a poem with three movements with distinct but related motifs. In the first movement (lines 7–16) the poet-convert identifies primarily with God the Father ("God of Abraham," and so on) but sounds the motif of the Son ("God of Jesus Christ . . . the ways taught in the Gospel"), which will later emerge as the principal motif of another movement. The second movement (lines 17–24) is intensely personal, a joyous affirmation of reconciliation with the "Righteous Father," an affirmation nonetheless haunted by the intense personal anguish of having been separated by his own doing ("Je m'en suis séparé"—the reflexive form of the verb has both personal and theological significance). In the third movement the poet reconciles the antithetical modes of the first two movements. The positive feelings of identification with the Father and the attendant feeling of certitude, joy, and peace are reconciled with the anguish at having denied the Righteous Father, an anguish compounded by the fear that the Father will now deny the poet-convert. In this movement there is not only reconciliation on the subjective level, that of feeling, but an important thematic shift: it is not the God of Abraham (first movement) nor the Righteous Father (second

movement) but Jesus Christ (subordinated in the first movement to the God
of Abraham) that the poet-convert apostrophizes.

The two-part meditation is common to both the fold of paper and the
pouch of parchment. On the latter Pascal has varied certain lines through
additions and omissions. Some additions give biblical references in conventional hermeneutic fashion, giving books of the Bible (line 12: Jeh. 20:17;
line 13: Ruth; line 18: Jeh. 17); some lines omit words (line 9 omits the
second preposition of *des*; line 26 omits the name "Jesus Christ"), while others
vary (line 10 reads: "Certitude, joy, certitude, sentiment, sight [*vue*], joy";
line 19 adds "and" after the third "joy"). Most important, of course, the
parchment adds six lines that provide an even more reflective frame than the
first. The preoccupation with the self is found here again, as in the poem
itself, particularly in the second and third movements. Yet, whereas the
lyrical dominated those personal moments in which the poet-convert and
the Divine lived in the order of charity, in the last addition to the parchment
it is more the convert than the poet, more the man of reason than the man
of feeling who prevails. In line 34 the connotations of self-abnegation have
shifted from the poetic to the reflective: "total and sweet renunciation" has
become "total submission." *Renunciation* connotes an awareness of the world
that the poet-convert was leaving behind and the oxymoronic play between
it and "sweet" emphasizes the paradox of the conversion itself. *Submission*
connotes an apodictic relation between signifier and signified. This becomes
even more apparent as the line adds "and to my Director." The addition
replaces "sweet," in fact, and thus suggests an awareness of the world to
which the convert was returning, for, in the Port-Royal tradition, spiritual
directors served principally to reinforce the lesson of the difference between
this world and the other world to which Pascal had been lifted in his
conversion.

Like certain editors of the *Memorial* (the most recent, Sellier, for example)
I speak of the *additions* on the parchment, as if that version were the second.
Both the content of these differences and the circumstances of the two texts
justify this interpretation. The largely referential and grammatical character
of the differences suggest the reworking of an initial text of the *Memorial*: the
version in Pascal's own hand that has survived. The idea of carrying it with
him as a memorial, a *reminder* of moral discipline, occurred to him later
(perhaps immediately after writing the versions on paper) and he saw the
chemical necessity of protecting it and even of having two copies of it, one
on the more durable parchment, to safeguard its disciplinary value to him.
This double guarantee of specifically disciplinary intent would explain the
addition of the three lines at the end of the parchment version. If the rational

faculties stand forth in their reflective aspect in the first of the three lines added, they stand forth just as clearly in their reflective *and voluntaristic* aspects in the last two added. The play between "eternally" and "one day of effort on earth" in line 36 returns us to the Pascal of probability theory and looks forward to his more extended application of that theory in the famous wager fragment of the *Thoughts*. He would have been the first to take his own bet. This is not to say that he thus could testify to prospective other bettors that he could guarantee success. He could not guarantee that to himself either in writing the fragment on the wager or even in writing the *Memorial*. This is clear from the third line of the addition at the end of the text here (line 37): "I will not forget Thy Word." He thus reminds himself that he has at times forgotten that Word and that both by knowledge of his own temperament and according to Jansenist doctrine, it is the human condition to forget the Word of God.

Forget it he would, as his recalcitrance before Jacqueline's exhortations to him at Port-Royal two weeks later show. Perhaps he had been aware of forgetting and thus sought to concentrate on *not* forgetting even before the night of fire. In his last letter to Fermat on the theory of probability, we perhaps have the sign of the conversion he was to undergo less than a month later. In a letter of August 9, 1654, to their mutual correspondent on the matter, Carcavy, Fermat had proposed a three-way collaboration in the publication of some of their researches and reflections. On October 27 Pascal wrote to Fermat to thank him but declined, saying, "For my part, that is far beyond me." The formulation may be purely scientific in intent, although given Pascal's acumen, both in Fermat's and his own eyes, this seems unlikely. As he declined Fermat's invitation he may have already begun the kind of self-defense, defense against himself, that he would have to continue even after his conversion.

LOUIS MARIN

Discourse of Power—
Power of Discourse: Pascalian Notes

Discourse of power—power of discourse: the chiasmus affecting the two terms, power and discourse, points to a problematic in order to elicit a demonstration. However, simply to posit a definition of power and a definition of discourse, on which to base a subsequent examination of the double and inverted relationship linking them in this chiasmus would be the surest way to overlook, forget or misread this problematic. I would suggest a contrary procedure: to find out—or to invent—what happens to power and to discourse within the chiasmus that joins them. What happens to discourse when it is the discourse of power, or when it is itself power? What happens to power when it is spoken by discourse, or when it defines itself? Is there, in the universe of forms of discourse, a discourse specific to power, when discourse in general possesses in and through itself a power "peculiar" to itself? And what is the relationship between *this* power, "peculiar" to discourse in general and power in general, with its taking over of an existent discourse and its enunciation within a discourse "peculiar" to itself?

Two propositions:
1. Discourse is the ideological mode of existence of force, an imaginary known as power.
2. Power is the imaginary of force at the moment that it is enunciated as the discourse of justice.

In order for discourse, power and the chiasmus linking them in my original formulation to come into play, I have introduced into these two propositions

From *Philosophy in France Today*, edited by Alan Montefiore. © 1983 by Cambridge University Press.

the terms "force" and "justice," terms that produce a shift in those of power and discourse. The momentum of this displacement, its driving force, is imagination.

How does force turn into power? How can it survive as power except by *taking over* a discourse of justice? How does this discourse of justice then turn into power, *taking the place* of the effects of force? How does discourse in general produce effects of force which are *taken* to be just, to be justice itself?

Taking over the discourse of . . . taking the place of . . . to be taken for . . . these are the three stages by which the imagination has transformed discourse into power, that is to say, discourse strong of itself.

It was from this angle that I came to Pascal, and in particular to this *pensée* (on which the rest of my text is no more than a commentary):

> *Justice, force.* It is just that what is just should be followed; it is necessary that what is the strongest should be followed. Justice without force is impotent; force without justice is tyrannical. Justice without force is contradicted, because there are always wicked men; force without justice is denounced. Justice and force must therefore be brought together, and to that end let us make it the case that that which is just be strong, and that which is strong be just.
>
> Justice is open to dispute; force is easily recognizable and beyond dispute. Thus was force bestowed upon justice; because force has contradicted justice, and has said that it was unjust, and that it was force itself which was just. Thus, being unable to make what is just to be strong, we have made what is strong to be just.
>
> (Pensée 103)

The text which follows is to be taken as a "philosophical" parable—or rather, since it is not a narrative but a discourse, as an allegory: at first sight a mere contemporary gloss of another man's thought of more than three centuries ago. Yet is could well be that for those with ears to hear, the thought of 1658 as it appears through this commentary speaks essentially of the present day. There is, to my mind, no way of speaking of and with both justice and force *today*, or of fortifying justice *now*, other than by the detour or distantiation here called allegory (elsewhere known as the history of philosophy, history of ideas, critique . . .). Otherwise, to speak in such a way will, *volen nolens*, always turn out to be the speaking of the discourse of power, and he who speaks it, the spokesman of a tyrant.

"It is just that what is just should be followed"; this is a categorical imperative, since justice prescribes its decrees by no other authority than itself. A just prescription is not deduced from the nature of Being, or of the Good, or from some theoretical or speculative proposition. A just prescription is just, without reference to considerations of utility or what is agreeable. There are no degrees of justice, no more or less just: it is a matter of all or nothing. "Justice and truth are two points so fine that our instruments are too blunt to touch them exactly. If ever they succeed, they flatten the point and press all around, covering more of what is false than what is true" (82). Whatever does not coincide with the fine point of justice is unjust. Indiscernible though it may be, it admits of no gradual shading from the just to the unjust.

"It is necessary that what is the strongest should be followed." Force is a matter of necessity. It is impossible to do otherwise than to follow the strong, by virtue of a necessity at once material, mechanical and physical. Force does not carry any imperative—it generates no obligation. Force is absolute constraint and violence (or else we are dreaming, imagining, fantasizing). There are, however, degrees of force: only the strongest is necessarily followed, and even then he must first manifest his strength. How shall he do this other than by confronting the other forces and annihilating them? Thus the strongest demonstrates, without words, that he is, necessarily, the strongest. He achieves this position only at the close of the war of forces that leaves him sole force in the field, having reduced all other forces to naught. The strongest is only the strongest at the pure point of the actual manifestation of his strength, the abstract moment of the annihilation of all the other forces. Such would be the moment of the genesis of society, at once originary and instantaneous, according to the fiction of a state of nature.

> The bonds securing the respect of men for one another in general
> are bonds of necessity: there must be varying degrees of respect,
> since all men seek to dominate while not all, but only a few, are
> able to. Imagine, then, that we can see them beginning to take
> shape. It is certain that men will fight one another until the
> strongest party has subdued the weakest.
>
> (304)

"Justice without force is impotent; force without justice is tyrannical." It is just that what is just should be followed. But whence comes the obligation—how, indeed, can one make it obligatory even for oneself, by some act of autonomous self-obligation—to follow justice? For a just prescription has no authority to prescribe other than that inherent in its own justice. Justice is essentially impotent, for of and in itself it lacks any force that would be its own enforcement, outside the utopia of a justice whose force lay precisely in the absence of force. Such a utopia was realized *once* by someone:

> It would have been superfluous for Our Lord Jesus Christ to descend as a King in order to be revealed in the splendour of His kingdom of holiness; but He came in the splendour of His own order. It is ridiculous to be outraged by the lowliness of Jesus Christ, as if His lowliness were of the same order as the greatness which He had come to show forth.
>
> (793)

"Force without justice is tyrannical." Justice is devoid of force, in and of itself it is impotent—the degree zero of force. Tyranny is an excess of force; without justice, mere strength is *overstrong*. Here, more accurately, is the point at which the essence of all force emerges as a fantastical desire to be the greatest force of all or, what amounts to the same thing, as a desire for the destruction of all other forces.

> Tyranny consists in a desire for universal domination, unre-stricted to its rightful order. There are separate chambers for the strong, the handsome, the intelligent, or the God-fearing, each with a master in his own house. But occasionally they meet, whereupon the strong and the handsome contend for mastery over one another—foolishly, for their mastery is of different kinds. They cannot understand one another; the fault of each is that he seeks to reign over all. Nothing can do this, not even force, which is indeed as nothing in the kingdom of the learned, having mastery only over external action. . . . Tyranny is the desire to obtain by one means that which one may have only by another.
>
> (332)

Two definitions of tyranny, that is, of force without justice which is *pure* force; absolute violence. The boundless desire of the strong to be the absolute degree of force—a paradox itself as infinite as that desire—amounts to the desire for pure homogeneity, that is, the desire for destruction of all het-erogeneity. Thus all force is by its essence tyrannical, a movement towards universal entropy (or death). "Justice without force is contradicted, because there are always wicked men; force without justice is denounced." This is the key moment of the reversal of the apparent symmetries between force and justice—the negative moment of a leap into the domain of discourse. Justice, which is nonviolent and devoid of force, which is the degree zero of force, is contra-*dicted* (contre-*dite*). Discourse states the opposite of what the just prescription, which has no foundation to its prescriptive authority other than itself, prescribes. In a single phrase, it says that what is just is unjust. Fact, accident or event: the just prescription is reversed in and through the enunciation of this newly apparent discourse. And why? Because *there are always* wicked men. The accident or event of this singular discourse has always already occurred. It has always already happened, without explanation or justification. There have always been wicked men. A discourse of evil, a *de facto* presence of evil in its discourse is always already *there*. This is no speculative or theoretical fable, such as that of Descartes's Evil Spirit, which would permit of a foundation for justice and its prescriptions. The discourse of evil has always been in existence. But evil is merely a discourse, and powerless as such to damage the just prescription or its innate justice. Evil is that discourse which gainsays or contradicts justice.

Force without justice is denounced. Another, parallel, discourse exists to match that of the wicked who contradict: a discourse through which the strongest are charged with their crimes, a discourse of accusation of tyranny. Two discourses, then, which confront one another: that which contradicts justice and that which denounces force. But if we know who, from time immemorial, has contradicted justice without force—the wicked, we yet do not know who denounces force without justice. The just man who is crucified before a tyrant on his throne—could it be him? Or perhaps the only possible denunciation of tyranny is lodged in the silence of the accuser . . . perhaps this silence in the act of denunciation is actually the secret, inaudible sign of a just man?

> And Jesus stood before the governor: and the governor asked him, saying "Art thou the King of the Jews?" And Jesus said unto him "Thou sayest." And when he was accused of the chief priests and elders, he answered nothing. Then said Pilate unto him, "Hearest thou not how many things they witness against thee?" And he answered him to never a word; insomuch that the governor marvelled greatly.
>
> (Matt. 27:11–14)

"Justice and force must therefore be brought together, and to that end let us make it the case that that which is just be strong, and that which is strong be just." Conclusion. Up to this point, the two themes of strength and justice have been developed independently of one another out of the two original propositions that "It is just that what is just should be followed; it is necessary that what is the strongest should be followed," that is to say, out of the opposition between justice and necessity, the consequences of which were twice formulated in two propositions through the double exclusion of justice by force and force by justice. This double exclusion, however, which conforms to the general principles of Pascal's method of reasoning via the negation of what is not the truth to be demonstrated, has led us to the perception of a double displacement. In the first place, whilst as regards justice (lacking or exclusive of force) we came up against the fact that it is absolutely devoid of force, we found that force (which excludes justice) is a universal desire for domination in every respect. In other words, justice without force *cannot* make justice manifest—it is impotent—whereas force without justice manifests itself as force outside its own "proper" domain as constituted by external actions. In the second place, we have entered the realm of discourses, that which contradicts justice and that which denounces force, two discourses which work a remarkable reversal of each other's modalities. For the discourse of contradiction inverts the original prescriptive proposition "One must follow what is just, because it is just" into a descriptive one "The just is non-just," "The just is unjust," whose implicit consequence would be the negation of the original prescription: "That what is just should be followed, is unjust (since the just has been called not just)," or "The just must not be followed, for it is unjust (or non-just)." Likewise and conversely, the discourse of denunciation performs a reversal in the opposite direction, implicitly transforming the original statement of the necessity of following the strongest into a negative prescription: "That the strongest should be followed, is unjust."

Hence Pascal's conclusion (in the form of a pragmatic principle and consequence) designed to dispel the confusion and disorder inherent in the discourses of contradiction and denunciation. For to contradict the just is in itself *contradictory* ("It is unjust that the just should be followed"), and the denunciation of the strongest is itself—*qua discourse*—a transgression of order, perfectly homologous to the tyrannical transgression committed by force. When it converts the statement of necessity into a negative prescription ("It is unjust that what is necessary should be followed"), the discourse of denunciation becomes, to borrow Pascal's word, *ridiculous*. "Justice and force must therefore be brought together," since reasoning along the lines of contraries has shown that justice without force and force without justice end up either in contradiction (in the case of the discourse of contradiction) or in the ridiculous (in the case of discourse of denunciation). Both necessary force and categorical justice are silent. Once they have been displaced into discourse in general—that of force without justice and that of justice without force—then this absurdity is revealed: in the contradiction of a discourse of force and in the ridiculousness of a discourse of justice. The bringing together of justice and force should thus make it possible to avoid both these absurdities.

It is noteworthy, however, that in the Pascalian discourse this conclusion is voiced as a prescription: "Justice and force must therefore be brought together . . . ," a prescription which is to be accomplished by means of an act, a "making": "and to that end let us make. . . ."

What is the nature of this prescription? It is both ambivalent in its presentation and weak in what is presented. Ambivalent, because it represents at once a rational, epistemic demand aimed at resolving the contradictoriness of the discourse of contradiction (whose subject is force without justice), and a moral or ethical obligation to seek to rescue from the ridiculous the negative prescription of the discourse of denunciation on the subject of tyrannical force. Weak in what it presents, for it does no more than to bring together force and justice, while leaving them, in their very conjunction, as terms external to one another.

Nevertheless, it is equally noteworthy that it is in the act of realization, the "making" which is at once the consequence of the principle that "justice and force must therefore be brought together" and the means of its accomplishment, that both the reason behind the ambivalence and the force behind the weakness become apparent. Let us reread the passage: "Justice and force must therefore be brought together, and to that end let us make it the case that that which is just be strong, and that which is strong be just." This is indeed a pure principle, which, thanks to the ellipse of the grammatical form of obligation in French (*il faut*), belongs both to the realm of ethics and to that of operational instruction; it is an imperative command which contains within itself the cognitive conditions for the success of the task, undertaking or action which it demands. And this task, undertaking or action aims at nothing less than an identification of the two terms which the principle had placed in juxtaposition to each other while yet maintaining them in their relations of mutual exteriority. It is at this point, however, that the original opposition between the categorical imperative of the just man and the mechanical necessity of the strongest reappears. It reappears in the shape of two propositions which are mutually and exclusively disjunctive of the process of identifying force and justice. The identity to be forged is not inert, the conjunction is not static; "$x = y$" is not equivalent to "$y = x$." The identification of force and justice is a dynamic process which can work from either of two mutually exclusive orientations, two contrary directions; either force becomes an attribute of justice, or justice becomes a determining quality of force. Yet even this may be misleading, for, in the operation called for both by an ethical command and by a technical instruction, we are no longer dealing with entities or essential notions such as "force" or "justice." The task to be undertaken is concerned with qualities, and the process of identification of "force" and "justice" is none other than one of reduction of qualities or attributes, the existence of whose substance-subjects are in suspense: ". . . make it the case that that which is just be strong, and that which is strong be just."

"Justice and truth are two points so fine that our instruments are too blunt to touch them exactly. . . ." ". . . could we love the substance of a man's soul, in the abstract, regardless of the qualities it possessed?" Would we have the justice to be force, or force justice? "It cannot be, and would be unjust. Therefore it is never a person we love, but only qualities" (323). Thus we operate never on essences or substances, but only on qualities and by exchange or substitution of qualities. Which of the two exchanges, between what is strong and what is just, is possible? Which substitution is realizable?

Demonstration: "Justice is open to dispute; force is easily recognizable and beyond dispute." Justice is interminably arguable. Justice, the idea of justice, is the object of polemical debate. Why is this? Justice is, no doubt, categorically imperative: "It is just that what is just should be followed"; but what *is* just? It seems that the very nature of the just description as deontic "tautology" must imply an inquiry into the ontological determination of justice. This inquiry leads in turn, necessarily so it seems, towards a deduction of the just prescription from a theoretical, speculative statement positing the Being of justice as the Good, as Nature, or as God:

> Why should I divide my ethics into four parts rather than six?
> Why should I ascribe four parts to virtue, rather than two, or
> one? Why is "desist" and "resist" rather than by "following nature"
> or by "discharging your private business without injustice," like
> Plato, or anything else?—But, you will say, here is everything
> encapsulated in a phrase.—Yes, but that is of no use unless ex-
> plained, and no sooner does one uncover, to explain it, the precept
> that encloses all others, than they tumble out in the very confusion
> that one sought to avoid. And when they are all enclosed in one,
> they remain hidden and useless as though in a safe.
>
> (120)

Philosophical discourses, polemical discourses: discourses at war and in confusion, interminable dispute as to the ontological determination on which
the imperative of justice might depend for its full validity as imperative. Its
ought-to-be would find its "ought" in a Being. But how may this be determined without falling into dispute? "Justice and truth are two points so fine
that our instruments are too blunt to touch them exactly. . . ." Yes, indeed,
the just (by its very nature as a value), the just prescription, has no other
foundation than itself, granted. But fine and almost indiscernible point that
it is, it appears that a discourse will always seek to determine the just as a
"palpable quality," the ontological predicate of the Being of justice. Thus
justice can never be exempt from the fray, or avoid becoming the butt of
mutually opposed and belligerent philosophical discourses.

Force, on the other hand, is easily recognizable and beyond dispute. It
is impossible not to notice it, for it compels recognition by its very manifestation—such is the mechanical necessity of the strongest. By the same
token, and of necessity, force cannot be an object of discourse. Force is not
a topic of conversation; one either wields it or yields to it.—But, you may
object, surely we can denounce the tyranny of force?—No doubt, but such
a discourse is ridiculous because it is "literally" without object, that is,
without effect upon that of which it speaks. It is an impotent discourse,
forever open to the ultimate threat, the threat of death: "Silence, or I shall
kill you, because I am the strongest." The argument of the strongest invariably prevails, and the wolves will always carry off into the depths of the
forest, there to devour without trial, any lambs who have been too eloquent
in denunciation of the tyrant.

"Thus was force bestowed upon justice. . . ." A somewhat surprising
conclusion is here under way. Lo, rejoice! force has been given unto justice!
Men, mankind, societies, have had the power to subjugate force and to deliver
it into the hands of justice! Justice is henceforth strengthened; policy has
turned into morality and politics has become indistinguishable from ethics.
Alas, no . . . We have misread. Once more: "Justice is open to dispute; force
is easily recognizable and beyond dispute." We expect the conclusion, "Thus
was justice given, delivered unto force. . . ." But that would constitute a
transgression of order, as Pascal might say. The principal proposition that
stands at the beginning of the sentence is in reality only an effect of the
subordinate clause of causation that follows; the inversion of the true order
is thus reproduced in the syntax. For politics to be identical with ethics
implies, by an abrupt, instantaneous inversion, the contrary—a masterstroke
of force in a stroke of discourse.

"Thus was force bestowed upon justice, because force has contradicted justice, and has said that it was unjust, and that it was force itself which was just." Force could be given to justice, because force, which simply *is*, and cannot be an object of discourse, has accorded itself the right to speak. It has set itself up as a subject of discourse, producing language, passing into the world of signs. Here is the "true" degree zero of force: mute violence becomes, at a stroke, mutated into meaning without loss of its polemical character. Force takes possession of signs, language and discourse by way of that universal desire for infinite domination outside the bounds of the order (of external actions, external bodies) that constitutes its tyrannical essence. Seizing language, force becomes mirrored in discourse and represented in signs. It is converted into meaning. And we are left to wonder, with Pascal, whether discourse, all discourse in general, might not already and since time immemorial be force reflected and represented, reactive and reactivated within signs; whether signs themselves and the symbolic function in general might not be the retrodden tracks of force, its delegated representatives or authorized agents. As a subject of discourse, force speaks; and the force which is represented in signs is a force that sets itself up as autonomous and self-instituting—enacting the law (its law) in order to endow itself with legitimacy and authority. Its position is a self-positioning whereby the pure manifestation of force, in this movement of self-reflection, institutes itself as a legitimate and autonomous source of power; power of discourse/ discourse of power, identity and mutual appropriation.

This discourse of force—a discourse of self-institution and self-legitimation and which *is* power—comprises a twofold dimension, two facets, one negative and one positive. It is a two-stroke machine, but simultaneously as it were. Force has contradicted justice and decreed it to be unjust. Force does not quibble about what justice, or the just, may consist of—that is the business of the interminable philosophical and speculative discourses. Force contra-dicts and with all the more assurance because it is easily recognizable and beyond dispute; with all the more certitude, since behind its representation or reflection in discourse the absolute threat is always looming, the possibility of a return to silence or to the inarticulate cry of wordless violence: "Justice is unjust! I speak the truth and you shall acknowledge the immutability of my truth or else I shall kill you." Force contradicts justice in the enunciation of a pure contradiction: A is non-A, the just is non-just, justice is unjust. But the contradictoriness of the contradiction is resolved without mediation, *immediately*, and in the absence of any dialectic, for when force asserts that justice is unjust, it is *simultaneously* asserting its own justice. In the act of uttering the contradiction, force takes possession of justice, what is strong appropriates what is just; the strong becomes literally just. And by virtue of this very same move, this single stroke of force which is a stroke of discourse, the strong(est) who calls himself just, *is* just. A happy performative, to be so favoured by its situation of utterance as to be incapable of being contradicted; for to contradict the discourse of force (i.e., power) is not only injustice but also self-exposure to force, to the strongest whom it is necessary to follow. At the degree zero where mute violence or the silence of force cancels itself out, power, the discourse of force, is the force of the discourse which by saying, makes to be; by saying that it is just, makes itself to be just. By the same token we discover who the wicked are who had been contradicting justice (devoid of force); they are the strong who begin to speak, to hold forth in discourse, instead of striking and killing. Evil, the fact of evil, is the discourse of the strongest, or power. Far from policy being transformed into morality, it is rather ethics which, in one stroke, becomes politics. There is no morality: there is only the political.

"Thus being unable to make what is just to be strong, we have made what is strong to be just." The first conclusion is duplicated and displaced by a second. What the former had envisaged as a possibility (to endow justice with force), because force through its discourse, as ruling power, had become justice, is revealed by the latter as impossible, as a negative necessity. It is impossible to ensure that the just should be strong or to give force to justice other than in mere "words," other than in an unhappy discourse that says without doing, an impotent and ineffectual, in short a ridiculous discourse. It is impossible to endow justice with force: this negative necessity is simply the obverse of the positive necessity, easily recognizable and beyond dispute, that the strongest be followed. Within power, within the discourse of strength, this necessity has become the power of discourse—the powerful and happy discourse that is the justification of force.

Our original statement of the necessity of following the strongest has been transformed in and by the discourse of strength, in and by power (discourse of power, power of discourse) into a final prescription as follows: It is just that what is the strongest should be followed; for the strongest has called himself just, and it is just that the just should be followed. "We have made what is strong to be just": that final "made" is a performative of language, an act of discourse for which the conditions of success and pragmatic validity are being established throughout Pascal's entire thought. All politics is discourse (discourse of power) and it is very likely that all discourse is political (power of discourse).

SARA E. MELZER

Pascal's Theory of Figures:
Rhetoric as Fall and as Redemption

Pascal develops a theory of figures based on obscurity which was only implicit in Barcos. For Pascal, human language is obscure and therefore always figures itself; it figures its own obscurity and corruption. But language is not to be limited by its self-referentiality; it also has a figural reference beyond itself. This indirect or figural pointing to something beyond itself is complicated by its own figural nature. The signifier can never enclose a single signified or an indirect, figural signified; new, uncontrollable signifieds may always slip past its guard. Yet precisely because language is uncontrollably figurative, it opens up the possibility of slipping past human meaning and of turning toward Redemption.

THE JUDEO-CHRISTIAN HISTORY

Pascal develops his theory of figures most explicitly in his discussion of the Jews and their relation to Christianity. In Pascal's view, the Jewish religion laid the foundation for Christianity, and the latter ultimately superseded the former. In what follows, I show how the shift from Judaic law to the Christian vision is a shift from semiological to a figurative view of language. Like classical discourse, Jewish discourse adopts a semiological system that blinds itself to its fallen and figurative nature. As a result, the Jews fail to recognize the Messiah they predicted. Conversely, Christian

From *Discourses of the Fall: A Study of Pascal's* Pensées. © 1986 by the Regents of the University of California. University of California Press, 1986.

discourse accepts its fallen and figural nature which enables Christians to recognize Jesus as the Messiah.

Pascal portrays the Jews as "the forerunners and heralds" ("les avant-coureurs et les hérauts" [Pensée 694, Sellier edition]) who not only predicted the coming of the Messiah but also established the specific signs by which he would by recognized. As the "depository of the spiritual covenant," the Jews carry "for all to see the books foretelling the Messiah, assuring all nations that he must come in the manner foretold in the books they held open for all to read" ("à la vue de tout le monde ces livres qui prédisent leur Messie, assurant toutes les nations qu'il devait venir, et en la manière prédite dans les livres qu'ils tenaient ouverts à tout le monde" [738]). Their prophecies constitute semiological codes that enable one to interpret the signs of Christ as those of the true Messiah. One of these prophecies announces the downfall of Jewish law. The prophets said that "the law they had was only provisional, while they waited for the Messiah to give them his law" ("la loi qu'ils avaient n'était qu'en attendant celle du Messie" [9]). The Jewish prophets foresaw that Jewish law, a semiological system providing a literal, legalistic logic for coding and decoding of signs, was only temporary; it would change after the coming of the Messiah. The new law of the Messiah would be figurative; as such, it would put in question the literal, Jewish law.

Although the Jews prophesied the end of their own law, Pascal says, they failed to understand what the prophecy meant. Similarly, although they transmitted the texts upon which divine truths were based, their law, their semiological codes, were not sufficient to interpret the texts properly. Because their interpretive codes operated along literal and not figurative lines, the Jews misunderstood their own texts and were blinded to the reality they designated. Imprisoned in the letter of their semiological system, "this carnal people" (738) was attached only to "temporal goods" (693), for they could not see the spiritual, figurative message. Pascal explains their literal reading of the world by pointing out that the Old Testament presents God as bestowing material benefits upon the Jewish people. He saved them from the Flood, he helped them cross the Red Sea, he led them into the promised land. Accustomed to God's material gifts, the Jews saw the Messiah as a Being who would also bestow material goods upon them. They were thus unable to recognize the divine personage of Christ, who appeared, not in material splendor and wealth, but draped in rags. "The carnal Jews awaited a carnal Messiah" (318), the "carnal Jews understood neither the greatness nor the lowliness of the Messiah foretold in their prophecies. They failed to recognize him in his greatness, . . . they sought in him only a carnal greatness" ("Les Juifs charnels n'entendaient ni la grandeur ni l'abaissement du

Messie prédit dans leurs prophéties. Ils l'ont méconnu dans sa grandeur prédite, . . . ils ne cherchaient en lui qu'une grandeur charnelle" [288]). The letter of Jewish law trapped them in a hermeneutic circle. The law established the code for the recognition of a truth they prophesied as lying outside their law. Their understanding of this truth was, however, locked in by the literalness of their law, which did not allow them to recognize anything that lay outside its codes.

To escape this hermeneutic impasse and to prove that Jesus Christ is the Messiah, Pascal has to show that there is an alternative system, a figurative one, which transcends Jewish law. "For if we believe that [the prophecies] have only one meaning, it is certain that the Messiah has not come, but if they have two meanings, it is certain that he has come in Jesus Christ" ("Car si on croit que [les prophéties] n'ont qu'un sens, il est sûr que le Messie ne sera point venu, mais si elles ont deux sens il est sûr qu'il sera venu en J-C" [305]). Pascal seeks to demonstrate that the prophecies have two meanings by showing that a figurative meaning was already implied in the Jewish literal, semiological system, although the Jews did not realize it. The Jewish people "carry the books and love them and do not understand them" ("porte les livres et les aime et ne les entend point" [736]); they do not grasp the meaning of their own discourse, which is figurative. Their semiological system allows for only one literal meaning and is thus inadequate to decode its own signs. Pascal uses this obstacle, the insufficiency of their semiological system, to point to a new one.

Pascal transforms the Jews' misreading of their own texts into a figure of the rhetorical nature of all language which he hopes will ultimately point to God. In other words, he seeks to show that Jewish discourse is already figurative; however, the Jews are unaware of it: they misread their own discourse. The Jews mistakenly believe that their texts point directly and clearly to the conditions that will enable them and others to recognize the Messiah. According to Pascal, however, their texts point only indirectly and obscurely to the Messiah. Pascal observes that, according to the Jews' prophecies in the Old Testament, the Messiah "will be rejected and will be the cause of scandal" ("sera rejeté et en scandale" [738]), the prophets' law will be replaced by the Messiah's new law, and the obscurity of the prophets' discourse will prevent it from being properly understood. The prophets state that "their sayings are obscure and that their meaning will not be understood" (737). In enunciating these conditions, the Jews intended them to designate a referent outside their semiological system. They believed that other people, not they, would misunderstand and reject the Messiah. After all, they felt that they wanted the Messiah and thus that, when he and his superior law appeared, they would abandon their own law. The literalness of Jewish law, however, limits the Jews to what its codes will allow them to perceive. As long as they hold to their law, they can never recognize the conditions that should lead them to abandon it. As the Messiah and his new law lie in a figurative system outside their semiological codes, they fail to recognize them. The Jews themselves thus necessarily fulfill the very conditions that their prophets had predicted, for they are the ones to reject the Messiah, misunderstand their own texts, and show the insufficiency of their own law. The Jews unintentionally figure themselves as cut off from God and imprisoned in language. Jewish discourse, then, is figural in spite of itself. And in referring back to its figural nature, it becomes the primary historical figure of a fallen discourse which does not recognize that it is fallen.

By pointing to its own fallenness, Jewish discourse points indirectly to what it misunderstands: the Messiah:

> The Jews, by killing him in order not to accept him as the Messiah, conferred upon him the final sign that he was the Messiah.

> Les Juifs en le tuant pour ne le point recevoir pour Messie, lui ont donné la dernière marque du Messie.

> (734)

> Those who rejected and crucified Jesus Christ, who was for them a cause of scandal, are also those who carry the books that bear witness to him and say that he will be rejected and will be a cause of scandal. Thus they showed that he was the Messiah by refusing him.

> Ceux qui ont rejeté et crucifié Jésus-Christ qui leur a été en scandale sont ceux qui portent les livres qui témoignent de lui et qui disent qu'il sera rejeté et en scandale de sorte qu'ils ont marqué que c'était lui en le refusant.

> (738)

In their very inability to recognize the Messiah, the Jews indirectly point to him. Paradoxically, the fallen nature of Jewish discourse figures Christ, the Redeemer. The Jews, blind to the fallen and figural nature of their own discourse, blindly serve as figures of the Christian new order, which subverts the codes in which they believe.

The Jews' very inability to recognize that their codes are already figurative becomes a figure of their status as figure. Blindness or obscurity is an important part of the figurative structure. Figures are created by a strange mixture of clarity, which facilitates representation, and obscurity, which impedes direct representation but creates an indirect reference. "Nature has perfections to show that it is the image of God and has imperfections to show that it is no more than his image" ("La nature a des perfections pour montrer qu'elle est l'image de Dieu et des défauts pour montrer qu'elle n'en est que l'image" [762]). Nature, in this instance, functions as a figure of God because if fulfills two essential conditions: similarity and difference or, in other terms, clarity and obscurity. Because nature manifests some perfection, participating in a part of God's perfection, it is able to establish a link with God. If there were no basis for association, be it natural or conventional, nature would be powerless to evoke God. If, however, the similarities were to coincide, or overlap significantly, nature would be so powerful that it could replace God. Nature would cease to serve as a representation and would become an end in itself. To counteract the similarities, Pascal explains, God added important differences which can be created by obscurity. Differences point to the sign's impotence. Through the obscurity of difference, nature points to the defects that distance its signs from God by preventing any confusion between its signs and their objects. Difference and obscurity, then, are not defects that inhibit the signification process; rather, they enhance it. Because the sign does not fuse with the object, it creates a figure that brings out its fallen status as figure.

The Jews, in their capacity as figures, function in ways similar to that of nature viewed as figure.

Figurative.
Nothing is so much like charity as cupidity, and nothing is so unlike it. Thus the Jews, rich with possessions to flatter their greed, were very much like Christians and very much unlike them. And thus they had the two qualities they had to have: they were very much like the Messiah in order to figure him, and were very much unlike him so that they would not be suspect as witnesses.

Figuratif.
Rien n'est si semblable à la charité que la cupidité et rien n'est si contraire. Ainsi les juifs pleins de biens qui flattaient leur cupidité, étaient très conformes aux Chrétiens et très contraires. Et par ce moyen ils avaient les deux qualités qu'il fallait qu'ils eussent d'être très conformes au Messie, pour le figurer, et très contraires pour n'être point témoins suspects.

(508)

The Jews are made to function as figures and establish the conditions necessary for the functioning of all figures: similarity and difference. Like the
Messiah, the Jews possess many admirable qualities that evoke him and make
them worthy of him. They are a people of "diligence, faithfulness, extraordinary zeal and are known to all the world. . . . So here are the people of
the world the least susceptible to the suspicion of favoring us. They are the
most strict and zealous for their law and prophets, who carry their books
without corruption" ("une diligence et fidélité et d'un zèle extraordinaire et
connues de toute la terre. . . . De sorte que voilà le peuple du monde le
moins suspect de nous favoriser et le plus exact et zélé qui se puisse dire
pour sa loi et pour ses prophètes, qui porte [leurs livres] incorrompus" [738]).
Their dissimilarity lies in their blindness to their own figural nature, which
is a crucial part of their function as figure. "If the Jews had all been converted
by Christ we would have left only suspect witnesses" ("Si les Juifs eussent
été tous convertis par Jésus-Christ nous n'aurions plus que des témoins
suspects" [492]). By failing to penetrate the veil of obscurity or even to
perceive that there is a veil, the Jews lend credence to those who do penetrate
it. Their blindness gives credibility to those who properly interpreted
Christ's signs.

Figures function when obscurity puts clarity in question:

> A portrait conveys absence and presence, pleasantness and un-
> pleasantness. Reality excludes absence and unpleasantness.
> *Figures.* To know whether the law and the sacrifices are literal
> or figurative, we must see whether the prophets in speaking of
> these things thought and looked no further, so they saw only the
> old covenant, or whether they saw something else of which it
> was the representation, for in a portrait we see the thing figured.

> Un portrait porte absence et présence, plaisir et déplaisir. La
> réalité exclut absence et déplaisir.
> *Figures.* Pour savoir si la loi et les sacrifices sont réalité ou figure
> il faut voir si les prophètes en parlant de ces choses y arrêtaient
> leur vue et leur pensée, en sorte qu'ils n'y vissent que cette an-
> cienne alliance, ou s'ils y voient quelque autre chose dont elle fut
> la peinture. Car dans un portrait on voit la chose figurée.

> (291)

The portrait, cited as an example of a figure, has two dimensions, presence
and absence, whereas reality operates on only one dimension: presence. A
portrait contains presence for it can introduce "the thing figured" as if it

were present by acting as a substitute for the represented object. It is, however, only a substitute, and it must not be confused with the object itself. In this connection the image of the portrait is revealing, for it underlines the material aspect of the representative element as a figure of something else. By insisting on the figurative element of the representing sign, it is made distinct from the represented object. Were they to be confused, the portrait would lose its status as a figure capable of representing something outside itself. It is precisely its absence of reality which maintains the portrait in its role as figure. This absence is crucial: were it not perceived, one might be tempted to confuse the figure with reality, for reality has no absence at all. Absence is a necessary defect that permits the correct functioning of any representative system.

Because God, too, is partly present, partly absent, figures may be the only means of access to the divine. "*Figures.* . . . Because the things of God are inexpressible, they cannot be spoken of otherwise" ("*Figures.* . . . Car les choses de Dieu étant inexprimables, elles ne peuvent être dites autrement" [303]). God and figures share a similar structure: a play of presence and absence, clarity and obscurity. "It is . . . useful for us that God is partly hidden and partly revealed, as it is equally dangerous for man to know God without knowing his own wretchedness as to know his own wretchedness without knowing God" ("Il est . . . utile pour nous que Dieu soit caché en partie, et découvert en partie, puisqu'il est également dangereux à l'homme de connaître Dieu sans connaître sa misère, et de connaître sa misère sans connaître Dieu" [690]). "What is seen on earth indicates neither a total exclusion nor a manifest presence of divinity, but the presence of a God who hides himself. Everything bears this character" ("Ce qui y paraît ne marque ni une exclusion totale, ni une présence manifeste de divinité, mais la présence d'un Dieu qui se cache. Tout porte ce caractère" [690]).

Pascal's rhetorical system, viewed from the perspective of faith, tries to be all-inclusive. No matter which way the figures turn, if followed out to their end, they ultimately should figure the same truths: "There is nothing on earth which does not show either man's wretchedness or God's mercy, either man's helplessness without God or man's strength with God" ("Il n'y a rien sur la terre qui ne montre ou la misère de l'homme ou la miséricorde de Dieu, ou l'impuissance de l'homme sans Dieu ou la puissance de l'homme avec Dieu" [705]). Figures, even when they do not point directly to God, may do so indirectly in the Pascalian perspective of faith. The Jews' blindness establishes the centrality of obscurity which Pascal transforms into a figure of figural truth: "Recognize then the truth of religion in its very obscurity" ("Reconnaissez donc la vérité de la religion dans l'obscurité même de la religion" [690]). The ability of words to escape their denotative role and to create new, perhaps unintended, meanings points to their figurative function. And this slippery property of figures becomes a figure of figurative, fallen language. The obscurity of figures can point not only back to itself but also to the corruption of humankind: "What are we to conclude from all our obscurities if not our unworthiness?" ("Que conclurons-nous de toutes nos obscurités, sinon notre indignité?" [690]; "S'il n'y avait point d'obscurité, l'homme ne sentirait point sa corruption" [690]). And the corruption of fallen language can figure Jesus Christ, the ultimate figure of God. As both man and God, Jesus Christ, who is aware that he represents both absence and presence, Jewishness and non-Jewishness, satisfies the conditions necessary for discourse in a fallen world that is aware of having fallen into figures.

Many of Pascal's fragments suggest that he has already made the wager that there is a God who, by definition, transcends rhetoric. These fragments, written from a perspective of faith, reveal that, for Pascal, divine discourse is devoid of slippery figures and constitutes an unfallen linguistic model. The Cartesian and classical ideal of the total coincidence of language with thought is possible, according to Pascal, but only in God, a Being situated outside the fallen world: "In God, word and intention do not differ, for he is truthful; nor do word and effect differ, for he is powerful; nor do means and effect differ, for he is wise" ("En Dieu la parole ne diffère pas de l'intention car il est véritable, ni la parole de l'effet car il est puissant, ni les moyens de l'effet car il est sage" [416]). Jesus Christ, speaking from a state of grace, can also communicate with perfect clarity:

> *Proofs of Jesus Christ.*—Jesus Christ said great things so simply that he seems not have thought them, and yet so clearly that it is obvious that he thought them. This clarity coupled with this simplicity is admirable.

> *Preuves de Jésus-Christ.*—Jésus-Christ a dit les choses grandes si simplement qu'il semble qu'il ne les a pas pensées, et si nettement néanmoins qu'on voit bien ce qu'il en pensait. Cette clarté jointe à cette naïveté est admirable.

> (340)

This linguistic ideal was accessible to humans only through their connection with God in their prelapsarian state and can be realized only through Redemption.

In the *Pensées*, humankind's relationship to a nonfigural, divine discourse structures both the idyllic prefallen state and the postfallen world. Pascal characterizes the prelapsarian state as one in which humans and God shared a common sign system; they were in clear and direct communication with each other. In fact, in the only prosopopeia created by Pascal, God communicates directly with humankind: "But you are no longer in the state in which I formed you. I created man holy, innocent, perfect. I filled him with light and intelligence, I communicated to him my glory and my wonders. Man's eye then beheld the majesty of God. He was not then in the darkness that now blinds his sight, nor was he subject to mortality and the woes that afflict him" ("Mais vous n'êtes plus maintenant en l'état où je vous ai formés. J'ai créé l'homme saint, innocent, parfait, je l'ai rempli de lumière et d'intelligence, je lui ai communiqué ma gloire et mes merveilles. L'oeil de l'homme voyait alors la majesté de Dieu. Il n'était pas alors dans les ténèbres qui l'aveuglent, ni dans la mortalité et dans les misères qui l'affligent" [182]). In their prelapsarian state humans were bathed in light, removed from obscurity and blindness, and thus they had no need for figures, which in fact could not function in a world of direct intelligence.

After the Fall, God not only withdrew from the world but also removed most of his light and the signs of his existence: ". . . man is fallen from a state of glory and communication with God" (". . . l'homme est déchu d'un état de gloire et de communication avec Dieu" [313]). God no longer appears to speak to humans: "The eternal silence of these infinite spaces terrifies me" ("Le silence éternel de ces espaces infinis m'effraie" [233]). Whereas one had come to expect the indications of divine guidance, one now finds only a deafening silence: "the universe [is] mute" [229]. Pascal suggests that God does still speak to humans, but he does so in a language that is not immediately accessible to human sign systems. After the Fall, there can be no semiological code that can join humans to God. For Pascal, a semiological, classical discourse can exist only in an ideal state before the Fall. Adam had the power sought by Descartes; he was granted mastery over the earth within the order of creation by his God-given gift of naming the animals in Eden (Gen. 2:19). And God, who endorsed his choice, guaranteed the correspondence between word and thing named. The evocation of this ideal world serves to accentuate the fall into rhetoric. Rhetoric is the heritage of the Fall.

For Pascal, the attempt of classicists and Cartesians to transcend rhetoric, or at least to subordinate it to their semiological structures, is the ultimate act of pride. They and their discourses are fallen, yet, like the Jews, they are blinded to it. Their texts, like Jewish texts, are figures of an unintended meaning. Although the classical, Cartesian, and Jewish discourses believe themselves to be guided by a logic and law that can control the production and interpretation of meaning, Pascal shows that these discourses

produce unintended meanings and are inhabited by a rhetoric that puts their
semiological system in question. Their blindness to their fallen and figural
nature becomes a figure of all rational consciousness which will always be
blinded to its own texts. All logical systems may be unaware of the direction
in which they are headed. And, of course, Pascal's text is no exception.
Although rhetoric may wreak havoc with logic, it shows that language can
express meaning indirectly. In this way, rhetoric opens itself up to a Christian
discourse that, in this fallen world, can communicate only indirectly.

Although the Christians, unlike the Jews, know that their language is
fallen and figural, they are unable to interpret the figures with any certainty.
Pascal bemoans the fact that there are no new miracles to indicate that our
interpretations are right or wrong. In this fallen world, Christian discourse,
like Jewish discourse, may be blinded to the unpredictable turns of its own
figures. Indeed, it may be impossible to know with certainty whether figures
only turn understanding back toward their own linguistic structure, or
whether they figure something outside their structure, either God, or perhaps
something other. Pascal's theory of figures contains the seeds of its own
possible destruction. Lacking certainty, all one can do is wager that language's
figures of its own otherness will turn toward God's Otherness.

Chronology

1623 Blaise Pascal born June 19 in Clermont, son of Antoinette Begon and Etienne Pascal.

1640 The family moves to Rouen. Pascal publishes his *Essai sur les sections coniques*.

1643 Pascal invents the *machine arithmétique*, a mechanical calculator.

1646 The family is converted to Jansenism. Pascal begins his experiments on the vacuum.

1647 Pascal returns to Paris and publishes the *Expériences nouvelles touchant le vide*. Controversy with the Père Noël.

1653 Pascal at the height of his "période mondaine," becomes friends with the chevalier de Méré and the financier Damien Mitton and joins the entourage of the duc de Roannez.

1654 Pascal finishes the *Traité sur l'équilibre des liquides* and the *Traité sur la pesanteur de la masse de l'air*. On November 23, Pascal has the visionary experience known as the second conversion and recorded in the *Mémorial*.

1655 Pascal goes into retreat at Port-Royal-des-Champs, the occasion of the *Entretien avec M. de Saci*.

1656 Pascal writes the *Ecrits sur la grâce* and publishes the *Lettres provinciales*, defending Arnauld and attacking the Jesuits. Pascal's niece is cured by the "miracle of the holy thorn," and Pascal begins his notes toward an Apology.

1661 Pascal breaks with Arnauld and Nicole over the proper response to the signing of the Papal encyclical denouncing Jansenism.

1662   Pascal dies August 19.

1670   First publication of the *Pensées* by Arnauld and Nicole.

Contributors

HAROLD BLOOM, Sterling Professor of the Humanities at Yale University, is the author of *The Anxiety of Influence, Poetry and Repression*, and many other volumes of literary criticism. His forthcoming study, *Freud: Transference and Authority*, attempts a full-scale reading of all of Freud's major writings. A MacArthur Prize Fellow, he is general editor of five series of literary criticism published by Chelsea House. During 1987–88, he served as Charles Eliot Norton Professor of Poetry at Harvard University.

RONALD A. KNOX was Roman Catholic chaplain at Oxford University from 1926 to 1939 and an influential critic and writer until his death in 1957. Among his books are a translation of the Bible, *New Testament Commentaries, The Belief of Catholics, Let Dons Delight*, and detective novels.

ERICH AUERBACH, who died in 1957, was Sterling Professor of Comparative Literature at Yale University. He was one of the most influential critics of his generation. His best-known books are *Mimesis: The Representation of Reality in Western Literature* and *Dante als Dichter der irdischen Welt*.

JEAN-JACQUES DEMOREST has been a professor of French and Italian literatures at Cornell University, Harvard University, and the University of Arizona. His books include *Dans Pascal, Les Passiones ont vécu*, and *Pascal écrivain*.

LUCIEN GOLDMANN, born in Romania, taught and wrote in France for most of his career. In addition to *The Hidden God*, he is the author of studies on Kant, Lukács, and Heidegger, and works such as *Cultural Creation in Modern Society* and *Epistémologie et philosophie politique*.

MARTIN PRICE is Sterling Professor of English at Yale University. His books include *Swift's Rhetorical Art, To the Palace of Wisdom: Studies in Order and Energy from Dryden to Blake*, and a number of edited volumes on the literature of the seventeenth, eighteenth, and nineteenth centuries.

JEAN MESNARD is Professor in the Faculty of Letters of the University of Bordeaux. He is the editor of numerous editions of Pascal's writings and the author of *Pascal: His Life and Works* and *Pascal et les Roannez*.

JAN MIEL teaches at Wesleyan University.

PHILIP LEWIS is Professor of Romance Studies at Cornell University. He is the author of *La Rochefoucauld: The Art of Abstraction* and the editor of *Diacritics*.

PAUL DE MAN was, until his death in 1983, Sterling Professor of Comparative Literature at Yale University. He is the author of *Blindness and Insight: Essays in Contemporary Criticism*, *Allegories of Reading: Figural Language in Rousseau, Nietzsche, Rilke, and Proust*, and *The Rhetoric of Romanticism* and of the collections *The Resistance to Theory*, *Aesthetic Ideology*, and *Fugitive Essays*.

ROBERT J. NELSON is Professor of Comparative Literature at the University of Illinois at Urbana-Champaign.

LOUIS MARIN is a French philosopher teaching at the Ecole des hautes études en sciences sociales in Paris. He has written extensively on seventeenth-century literature and painting. His books include *La Critique du discours*, *Le Portrait du roi*, and *Le Récit est un piège*.

SARA E. MELZER is Professor of French at the University of California at Los Angeles.

Bibliography

Baird, A. W. S. "Pascal's Idea of Nature." *Isis* 61, part 3, no. 208 (Fall 1970): 297–320.

————. *Studies in Pascal's Ethics*. International Archives of the History of Ideas, no. 16. The Hague: Martinus Nijhoff, 1975.

Barker, John. *Strange Contrarieties: Pascal in England during the Age of Reason*. Montreal: McGill-Queen's University Press, 1975.

Barnett, Richard L. "*Maxim*-al Codes of Minimal Closure: Pascal's Sequestered Schema." *L'Esprit créateur* 22, no. 3 (Fall 1982): 28–38.

Beitzinger, A. J. "Pascal on Justice, Force, and Law." *Review of Politics* 46, no. 2 (April 1984): 212–43.

Birchall, Ian H. "The Appropriation of Pascal." In *1642: Literature and Power in the Seventeenth Century*, edited by Francis Barker et al., 101–13. Colchester, U.K.: Department of Literature, University of Essex, 1981.

Bishop, Morris. *Pascal: The Life of Genius*. New York: Reynal & Hitchcock, 1936.

Blaise Pascal, l'homme et l'oeuvre. Cahiers de Royaumont, Philosophie, no. 1. Paris: Editions de Minuit, 1956.

Broome, J. H. *Pascal*. New York: Barnes & Noble, 1965.

Brunet, Georges. *Le Pari de Pascal*. Paris: Desclée de Brouwer, 1956.

Brunschvicg, Leon. *Descartes et Pascal, lecteurs de Montaigne*. Neuchatel: La Baconnière, 1945.

————. *Le Génie de Pascal*. Paris: Hachette, 1924.

Chambers, Frank M. "Pascal's Montaigne." *PMLA* 65 (1950): 790–804.

Chevalier, Jacques. *Pascal*. Translated by Lilian A. Clare. London: Sheed & Ward, 1930.

Costabel, Pierre, "La Physique de Pascal et son analyse structurale." *Revue d'histoire des sciences et leurs applications* 29 (1976): 310–24.

Davidson, Hugh M. *The Origins of Certainty: Means and Meanings in Pascal's* Pensées. Chicago: University of Chicago Press, 1979.

————. "Pascal's Arts of Persuasion." In *Renaissance Eloquence: Studies in the Theory and Practice of Renaissance Rhetoric*, edited by James J. Murphy, 292–300. Berkeley and Los Angeles: University of California Press, 1983.

Demorest, Jean-Jacques. *Dans Pascal; essai en partant de son style*. Paris: Editions de Minuit, 1953.

Demorest, Jean-Jacques, and Lise Leibacher-Ouvrard, eds. *Pascal, Corneille: Désert, retraite, engagement*. Paris: Papers on French Seventeenth-Century Literature, 1984.

Dijksterhuis, E. J. "Pneumatics: Blaise Pascal." In *The Mechanization of the World Picture*, translated by C. Dikshoorn, 444–55. Oxford: Clarendon, 1961.

Eastwood, D. M. *The Revival of Pascal*. Oxford: Clarendon, 1936.

Eliot, T. S. "The *Pensées* of Pascal." In *Selected Essays*, 355–68. Rev. ed. New York: Harcourt, Brace & World, 1960.

L'Esprit créateur 2, no. 2 (Summer 1962). Special Pascal issue.

Europe 57, no. 597–98 (January–February 1979). Special Pascal issue.

Ferreyrolles, Gérard. *Pascal et la raison du politique*. Paris: Presses universitaires de France, 1984.

Fletcher, Frank Thomas Herbert. *Pascal and the Mystical Tradition*. New York: Philosophical Library, 1954.

Friedenthal, Richard. *Entdecker des Ich: Montaigne, Pascal, Diderot*. Munich: Piper, 1969.

Goldmann, Lucien. *The Hidden God: A Study of the Tragic Vision in the* Pensées *of Pascal and the Tragedies of Racine*. Translated by Philip Thody. London: Routledge & Kegan Paul; New York: Humanities Press, 1964.

Howe, Virginia K. "*Les Pensées:* Paradox and Signification." *Yale French Studies* 49 (1973): 120–31.

Hubert, Sister Marie-Louise. *Pascal's Unfinished Apology*. New Haven: Yale University Press, 1952.

Jaymes, David. "Conscience as a By-Product of Philosophy: Pascal on Epictetus and Montaigne." *French Literature Series* 6 (1979): 1–8.

La Charité, Raymond C. "Pascal's Ambivalence towards Montaigne." *Studies in Philology* 70 (1973): 187–98.

Lafuma, Louis. *Histoire des* Pensées *de Pascal*. Paris: Editions du Luxembourg, 1954.

———. *Recherches pascaliennes*. Paris: Delmas, 1949.

Le Guern, Michel. *L'Image dans l'oeuvre de Pascal*. Paris: A. Colin, 1969.

Lonning, Per. *Cet effrayant pari: Une "pensée" pascalienne et ses critiques*. Paris: J. Vrin, 1980.

MacKenzie, L. A. "To the Brink: The Dialectic of Anxiety in the *Pensées*." *Yale French Studies* 66 (1984): 57–66.

Marin, Louis. *La Critique de discours: sur la* Logique *de Port-Royal et les* Pensées *de Pascal*. Paris: Editions de Minuit, 1975.

———. "On the Interpretation of Ordinary Language: A Parable of Pascal." In *Textual Strategies: Perspectives in Post-Structuralist Criticism*, edited by Josue V. Harari, 239–59. Ithaca: Cornell University Press, 1979.

———. " 'Pascal': Text, Author, Discourse. . . ." *Yale French Studies* 52 (1975): 129–51.

Melzer, Sara E. *Discourses of the Fall: A Study of Pascal's* Pensées. Berkeley and Los Angeles: University of California Press, 1986.

Mesnard, Jean. *Pascal, His Life and Works*. Translated by Ronald A. Knox. New York: Philosophical Library, 1952.

———. *Pascal*. Translated by Claude and Marcia Abraham. University: University of Alabama Press, 1969.

———, ed. *Méthodes chez Pascal: Actes du colloque tenu à Clermont-Ferrand, 10–13 juin 1976*. Paris: Presses universitaires de France, 1979.

Miel, Jan. *Pascal and Theology*. Baltimore: Johns Hopkins University Press, 1969.

Moles, Elizabeth. "Pascal's Theory of the Heart." *MLN* 84 (1969): 548–64.

Mortimer, Ernest. *Blaise Pascal: The Life and Work of a Realist*. London: Methuen, 1959.

Mueller, Gustav E. "Pascal's Dialectical Philosophy and His Discovery of Liberalism." *Journal of the History of Ideas* 6, no. 1 (January 1945): 67–80.

Nelson, Robert James. *Pascal: Adversary and Advocate*. Cambridge: Harvard University Press, 1981.

Poulet, Georges. "Pascal." In *Studies in Human Time*, translated by Elliot Coleman, 74–96. Baltimore: Johns Hopkins University Press, 1956.

————. "Pascal." In *The Metamorphoses of the Circle*, translated by Carley Dawson and Elliot Coleman in collaboration with the author, 32–49. Baltimore: Johns Hopkins University Press, 1966.

Reisler, Marsha. " 'Persuasion through Antithesis': An Analysis of the Dominant Rhetorical Structure of Pascal's *Lettres provinciales*." *Romanic Review* 69 (1978): 172–85.

Russier, Jeanne. *La Foi selon Pascal*. Paris: Presses universitaires de France, 1949.

Sellier, Phillipe. *Pascal et Saint Augustin*. Paris: A. Colin, 1970.

Stanton, Domna C. "Pascal's Fragmentary Thoughts: Dis-Order and Its Over-Determination." *Semiotica* 51 (1984): 211–35.

Stewart, H. F. *The Holiness of Pascal*. Cambridge: Cambridge University Press, 1915.

————. *The Secret of Pascal*. Cambridge: Cambridge University Press, 1941.

Topliss, Patricia. *The Rhetoric of Pascal: A Study of His Art of Persuasion in the* Provinciales *and the* Pensées. Leicester: Leicester University Press, 1966.

Valéry, Paul. "Variations on a 'Pensée.' " In *Masters and Friends (Collected Works, volume 9)*, translated by Martin Turnell, 86–107. Princeton: Princeton University Press, 1968.

Webb, Clement C. J. *Pascal's Philosophy of Religion*. Oxford: Clarendon, 1929.

Wetsel, David. *L'Ecriture et le reste: The* Pensées *of Pascal in the Exegetical Tradition of Port-Royal*. Columbus: Ohio State University Press, 1981.

Wohinsky, Barbara R. "Biblical Discourse: Reading the Unreadable." *L'Esprit créateur* 21, no. 2 (Summer 1981): 13–24.

Acknowledgments

"Pascal and Jansenism" (originally entitled "Jansenism: The Setting") by Ronald A. Knox from *Enthusiasm: A Chapter in the History of Religion* by Ronald A. Knox, © 1950 by A. P. Watt Ltd. Reprinted by permission of A. P. Watt Ltd. on behalf of the Earl of Oxford and Asquith.

"On the Political Theory of Pascal" by Erich Auerbach from *Scenes from the Drama of European Literature* by Erich Auerbach, © 1959 by Meridian Books, Inc. Reprinted by permission of the Estate of Erich Auerbach.

"Pascal's Sophistry and the Sin of Poesy" by Jean-Jacques Demorest from *Studies in Seventeenth-Century French Literature Presented to Morris Bishop*, edited by Jean-Jacques Demorest, © 1962 by Cornell University. Reprinted by permission of Cornell University Press.

"The Wager: The Christian Religion" (originally entitled "The Wager" and "The Christian Religion") by Lucien Goldmann from *The Hidden God: A Study of the Tragic Vision in the* Pensées *of Pascal and the Tragedies of Racine*, translated from the French by Philip Thody, English translation © 1964 by Routledge & Kegan Paul Ltd. Reprinted by permission of Routledge & Kegan Paul Ltd. and Humanities Press International, Inc., Atlantic Highlands, New Jersey.

"The Three Orders: Flesh, Spirit, Charity" (originally entitled "Ideas of Order: Introduction") by Martin Price from *To the Palace of Wisdom: Studies in Order and Energy from Dryden to Blake* by Martin Price, © 1964 by Martin Price. Reprinted by permission.

"The Revelation of God" by Jean Mesnard from *Pascal*, translated by Claude and Marcia Abraham, © 1965 by Desclée de Brouwer, English translation © 1969 by Desclée de Brouwer. Reprinted by permission of Georges Borchardt Agency, Inc.

"Pascal and Theology" (originally entitled "The *Pensées*") by Jan Miel from *Pascal and Theology* by Jan Miel, © 1969 by the Johns Hopkins University Press, Baltimore/London. Reprinted by permission of the Johns Hopkins University Press.

"Dialogic Impasse in Pascal's *Provinciales*" by Philip Lewis from *Canadian Review of Comparative Literature* 3, no. 1 (Winter 1976), © 1976 by Philip Lewis. Reprinted by permission.

"Pascal's Allegory of Persuasion" by Paul de Man from *Allegory and Representation: Selected Papers from the English Institute, 1979–1980*, edited by Stephen J. Greenblatt, © 1981 by the English Institute. Reprinted by permission of the Johns Hopkins University Press, Baltimore/London.

"The Convert" by Robert J. Nelson from *Pascal: Adversary and Advocate* by Robert J. Nelson, © 1982 by the President and the Fellows of Harvard College. Reprinted by permission of Harvard University Press.

"Discourse of Power—Power of Discourse: Pascalian Notes" by Louis Marin, translated by Lorna Scott Fox, from *Philosophy in France Today*, edited by Alan Montefiore, © 1983 by Cambridge University Press. Reprinted by permission of Cambridge University Press.

"Pascal's Theory of Figures: Rhetoric as Fall and as Redemption" (originally entitled "Seventeenth-Century Discourse: Sin and Signs") by Sara E. Melzer from *Discourses of the Fall: A Study of Pascal's* Pensées by Sara E. Melzer, © 1986 by the Regents of the University of California. Reprinted by permission of the University of California Press.

Index

195